PERSPECTIVES ON EARLY CHILDHOOD PSYCHOLOGY AND EDUCATION

Volume 5, Issue 1
Spring 2020

ISBN: 978-1-935625-50-6
ISSN: 2471-1527

Member

CELJ

Council of Editors of Learned Journals

PERSPECTIVES on EARLY CHILDHOOD PSYCHOLOGY and EDUCATION

TABLE OF CONTENTS

Editor's Note

The special section focused on promoting health and wellness in preschoolers is timely. Initially, the focus of the special section was on the mind-body health of preschool-aged children with emphasis on assessment, intervention, and physical health practices. As Guest Editors, Dr. Melissa Bray, Dr. Cheryl Maykel, and Johanna deLeyer-Tiarks note, the COVID-19 pandemic resulted in some shifting of the special issue. Therefore, several authors discuss how the COVID-19 pandemic has and continues to be traumatic for many young children. Several of the manuscripts included in the special section offer psychologists, teachers, and parents useful information to assist young children as they prepare to attend school in the fall.

This issue also includes two general manuscripts reflecting an increasing number of general submissions resulting in the expansion of topics published. Looking forward, a special section is being developed focused on the psychological and educational needs of young children who are deaf and hard of hearing.

David E. McIntosh, Editor

GENERAL ARTICLES

Validity of the Emotional Attachment Zones Evaluation (EA-Z): Assessing Attachment Style Across a Developmental Spectrum

Hannah E. Wurster and Zeynep Biringen

Abstract

Sensitive, consistent caregiving and a secure attachment style are important to healthy child development. However, the lack of continuity in measures from infancy into adulthood limits conclusions regarding the stability of attachment styles across the lifespan. A new measure, the Emotional Attachment Zones Evaluation (EA-Z), derived from the Emotional Availability Scales (Biringen, 2008; Biringen, Robinson, & Emde, 1998), offers a tool to assess attachment style across a broad developmental spectrum. In order to validate this measure as an attachment style measure, we used three studies to compare the EA-Z to empirically validated attachment tools. In study 1, we compared the EA-Z to the Strange Situation Procedure. There was moderate concordance between these two measures for both mother and infant. In study 2, we compared the EA-Z to the Attachment Q-Sort in an infant/toddler childcare setting. Child EA-Z scores related to child attachment security, whereas teacher EA-Z scores did not relate to child attachment security. Finally, in study 3, we compared the EA-Z to the mother's Adult Attachment Interview. Results indicated moderate concordance between these measures, both for the adult mother and the preschool child. All three of these studies offer promising evidence for the validity of the EA-Z as an attachment tool, as well as future directions for research and practice using the EA System.

Keywords: *Attachment, Emotional Availability, Measurement, Validation, Child Development, Family Relationships*

Introduction

Attachment Theory

Attachment theory posits that the bond between a primary caregiver and child serves not only to ensure the survival of an otherwise vulnerable infant but also to offer the developing child an internal working model of herself and her social world (Bowlby, 1969; Bretherton, 1990). Further, this attachment bond grants infants a secure base from which to explore the world safely and a safe haven that offers comfort when distressed. However, the degree to which children explore comfortably versus seek out their caregiver varies based on the nature of the parent-child relationship (Ainsworth, 1967; Ainsworth, Blehar, Waters, & Wall, 1978). Caregivers who are consistently responsive to child cues, yet supportive of autonomy and exploration, promote a secure caregiver-child attachment, which is characterized by the child showing a balance of exploration and caregiver-seeking behaviors.

In contrast, caregivers who are inconsistently responsive and less supportive of autonomy-seeking behaviors promote an insecure-resistant/anxious attachment, in which children explore minimally and often use negative emotions to maintain a connection with the caregiver. Caregivers who reject a child's bids for connection, are consistently unresponsive, and emphasize autonomy without connection foster an insecure-avoidant attachment. Children with this attachment seek little connection with a caregiver and appear to explore, yet are less comfortable doing so (Ainsworth et al., 1978). Finally, in the context of abuse, chaotic family life, or parental unresolved trauma, children are at risk for a disorganized attachment. Caregivers may show frightening behaviors, fearful emotions, dissociation, or highly intrusive behaviors, and children display contradictory behaviors, approaching a caregiver for comfort while also avoiding him or her out of fear or uncertainty (Main & Solomon, 1986).

Child attachment style predicts later outcomes. A child's attachment style to her primary caregiver is reflective of the quality of that relationship, yet it also predicts the individual's sense of self and social-emotional development. In line with the concept of internal working models, an individual's attachment style influences the way he processes social information (Dykas & Cassidy, 2011). Across the lifespan, individuals with a secure attachment process social information with a positive bias, whereas those with an insecure attachment are more likely to process social information with a negative bias (Dykas & Cassidy, 2011).

A child's secure attachment predicts greater emotional regulation, self-esteem, and school engagement later in childhood (Drake, Belsky, & Fearon, 2014; Sroufe, 1983; 2000). It is also associated with greater social competence, fewer externalizing behaviors, and fewer internalizing symptoms (Groh, Fearon, van IJzendoorn, Bakermans-Kranenberg, Roisman, 2017). Moreover, the ability of a child's primary caregivers to be consistently and sensitively responsive predicts later child functioning. In other words, not only does a parent's sensitivity predict the child's attachment style, but it also directly relates to the child's later positive social-emotional and cognitive outcomes (Friedman & Boyle, 2007; NICHD Early Child Care Research Network, 2006; Roelofs, Meesters, ter Huurne, Bamelis, & Muris, 2006).

In contrast, children with an insecure attachment style during infancy are at a greater risk for relational challenges and social-emotional problems during later childhood (Groh et al., 2017; Sroufe, 1983; 2000). Specifically, insecure-avoidant children at a heightened risk for poorer social competence, greater externalizing problems, and more internalizing symptoms (Groh et al., 2017). Children with an insecure-resistant/anxious style are likely to have lower social competence (Groh, 2017). A disorganized attachment in infancy poses a unique risk for hostility, aggression, and other externalizing problems (Fearon, Bakermans-Kranenburg, van IJzendoorn, Lapsley, & Roisman, 2010; Groh et al., 2017).

The predictive value of early attachment relationships extends into adolescence and adulthood. A history of secure attachment is associated with greater social competence and more efficient emotional regulation during adolescence (Carlson, 1998; Sroufe,

1997; 2000; Warren, Huston, Egeland, & Sroufe, 1997). In contrast, adolescents with a history of insecure attachment continue to be at risk for negative social-emotional outcomes (Carlson, 1998; Groh et al., 2017; Ogawa, Sroufe, Weinfield, Carlson, & Egeland, 1997; Sroufe, 2000). Finally, a disorganized attachment during infancy predicts dissociative symptomatology during adolescence, and disorganization is a partial mediator between an individual's early trauma and later dissociative symptoms (Lyons-Ruth, 2015). Into adulthood, early insecure attachment contributes to a cognitive coping style that puts individuals at risk for depressive symptomatology following stressful situations (Morley & Moran, 2011). Further, a history of an insecure attachment style relates to anxiety, excessive reassurance seeking, and lower relationship quality with one's romantic partner during adulthood (Shaver, Shachner, & Mikulincer, 2005).

It is important to note that many of the effect sizes linking a child's attachment style to later outcomes are small or moderate in size (Friedman & Boyle, 2007; Groh et al., 2017). Further, it is difficult to determine whether long-term effects are due to early attachment relationships or to continuity in the caregiving experience or family-level variables (Groh et al., 2017). Therefore, many researchers have examined how attachment interacts with other child and family-level factors. Its effect on school engagement is mediated by improvements in self-regulation (Drake et al., 2014). Child temperament and family-level risk also play a role. For example, children who have both an uninhibited temperament and an avoidant attachment style are at a particularly elevated risk for externalizing behaviors in early childhood (Burgess, Marshall, Rubin, & Fox, 2003). Further, secure mother-child attachment can also serve as a protective factor against the development of anxiety in the context of stressful life events (Dallaire & Weinraub, 2007). Next, a secure attachment with one parent can serve as a protective factor against later negative outcomes, even when the child has insecure attachment with the other parent (Boldt, Kochanska, Yoon, & Nordling, 2014; Kochanska & Kim, 2013). In summary, although a child's attachment style is an

important predictor of later outcomes, it is not a sufficient or necessary cause. Rather, it interacts with many other risk and protective
factors in driving development (Friedman & Boyle, 2007; Groh, 2017).

Individual differences in attachment. In sum, the literature
on attachment theory supports the argument that a child's early
attachment style contributes to his or her later social and emotional
development, even into adolescence and adulthood. However, longitudinal studies tracing these specific pathways have been mixed,
with some studies supporting the stability and predictive value of
infant attachment style for later development (Hamilton, 2000; Main,
Hesse, & Kaplan, 2005), and others finding low stability in attachment
security (Fraley, 2002; Groh et al., 2014; Lewis, Feiring, & Rosenthal,
2000). What remains unclear from these mixed findings is whether
an individual's true attachment style actually changes across the
lifespan, due to relational changes or psychosocial stress, or whether
the measurement tools used in these studies lack continuity (Groh
et al., 2014).

Attachment assessment tools vary in whether they assess
attachment security in a categorical or continuous manner, and
the methods used vary from observational to questionnaires and
semi-structured interviews. Such changes are often necessary, for
methods used to measure an infant's experience of a caregiving relationship (i.e., brief separation and reunion) are often not the same as
those used for an older child. Additionally, as individuals grow older,
it becomes possible to learn about their internal representations of
attachment relationships, rather than their dyadic attachment style
in the context of one specific relationship (Bretherton & Oppenheim,
2003; Robinson, 2007). For these reasons, many studies examining
attachment longitudinally use a variety of different tools. However,
this can create challenges in determining the stability of an individual's dyadic attachment relationships or internal working model
over time (Groh et al., 2014).

The Strange Situation Procedure (SSP; Ainsworth et al., 1978)
is considered the gold standard tool for assessing an infant's (12 to

24 months) attachment style with one caregiver. The SSP consists of a series of separations and reunions between a primary caregiver and infant; these separations are designed to cause stress to the infant, activating the attachment system. With the system activated, an observer can note how effectively an infant uses his caregiver to soothe distress, which is indicative of the infant's attachment style (Ainsworth et al., 1978). This tool has been adapted for use among preschool aged children (Britner, Marvin, & Pianta, 2005) and 6-year-olds (Main & Cassidy, 1977), and the procedure is modified. The length of separation is increased; characteristics of the stranger are changed (e.g., a male instead of a female); or the reunion with the stranger is eliminated (Solomon & George, 1999). These modifications are implemented in order introduce sufficient stress and activate an older child's attachment system.

Although the SSP can be adapted for preschool aged children, the Attachment Q-Sort (AQS; Waters & Deane, 1985), a tool that can be used with children ranging from 12 months to 5 years, is often the assessment of choice for this age group. The AQS is also an observational method, but it takes place in a naturalistic setting, most often the home. A trained observer watches how the child behaves, expresses emotions, and interacts with a target caregiver. The observer then categorizes 90 statements about a child's behavior. For example, one statement reads, "When child finds something new to play with, he carries it to mother or shows it to her from across the room." The observer ranks the statements from "most descriptive of child" to "least descriptive of child." The resulting description of the child is then correlated with a behavioral profile of a stereotypical secure child, as described by attachment experts. Using the same process, observers also assign each child a dependency score. This tool does not discriminate among the insecure styles (Waters & Deane, 1985). In addition to the home, studies also have used the AQS successfully in child care settings (e.g., Biringen et al., 2012; Cassibba, van IJzendoorn, & D'Odorico, 2000).

As children grow older and internalize their relational experiences as internal working models, it becomes possible to measure these inner representations. This is done through a variety of story-stem methods that use fictional stories (e.g., Bretherton & Oppenheim, 2003; Robinson, 2007). Children are asked to complete an emotionally charged or attachment-related story through play or words. Their responses are coded based on content, coherence, and the child's behavior. Children's storytelling can offer insight into the ways in which they represent relationships and their social world. Children with secure attachment relationships tend to tell stories with pro-social content and positive resolutions (Laible et al., 2004).

During adolescence and adulthood, attachment represen-tations and behaviors are assessed through self-report measures (Bartholomew & Horowitz, 1991; Brennan et al., 1998; Fraley, Waller, & Brennan, 2000; Hazan & Shaver, 1987) or through the Adult Attachment Interview (AAI; George et al., 1984; 1985; 1986; Hesse, 2008). Self-report measures assess an individual's conscious thoughts and behaviors in current and past relationships. The AAI, in con-trast, assesses emotionally-charged implicit memories regarding early attachment relationships. Therefore, unsurprisingly, the overlap between these approaches is small (Roisman et al., 2007). Further, attachment styles gleaned from self-report measures predict different behaviors and psychosocial factors than do styles gleaned from the AAI (Roisman et al., 2007). Thus, it seems that self-report measures of attachment style and the AAI may measure different constructs. Finally, neither tool uses behavioral observation to determine attach-ment style.

Therefore, although attachment is relevant to an individual's well-being and mental health across the lifespan, there is not yet a single assessment tool that can provide a consistent measure over time. The concordance among various attachment measures tends to be moderate to high, yet not high enough to feel confident that they measure exactly the same construct. Security scores on the AQS are related to SSP-measured attachment security at $r = .31$

(van IJzendoorn et al., 2004). Attachment security assessed by the AQS is a strong predictor of children's security score on representational story-stem tasks, $r = .54$ (Waters, Rodrigues, & Ridgeway, 1998). As mentioned above, the overlap between self-report attachment measures and the AAI is very small, $r = .09$ (Roisman et al., 2007). The moderate and inconsistent concordance among these various measures may partially explain the limited stability in attachment style that is often found in longitudinal studies (e.g., Groh et al., 2014)

A New Approach: Attachment Measured with the Emotional Availability (EA) System

Given the lack of continuity in attachment measurement tools across the lifespan, as well as mixed conclusions about the stability of attachment styles, there is a need for a tool that can measure attachment across a broad developmental spectrum. The Emotional Attachment Zones Evaluation (EA-Z; previously called Clinical Screener; Baker, Biringen, Meyer-Parsons, & Schneider, 2015; Biringen, 2008; Espinet, Jeong, Motz, Racine, Major, & Pepler, 2013) is relatively new tool used in conjunction with the Emotional Availability Scales (EA Scales; Biringen, 2008; Biringen, Robinson, & Emde, 1998).

The EA Scales examine six dyadic qualities of relationships using semi-continuous/ dimensional observational scales: adult sensitivity, adult structuring, adult non-intrusiveness, adult non-hostility, child responsiveness, and child involvement. In doing so, the EA Scales move beyond attachment behaviors demonstrated by the adult and child in order to include qualities relating to affective expression and control-related aspects of the relationship. This includes the capacity of an adult to express a healthy range of mostly positive emotions (sensitivity), to support learning and autonomy (structuring and non-intrusiveness), and to regulate the expression of his or her own negative emotions (non-hostility). This is important, for the correlation between measures of sensitivity and attachment security is sometimes fairly small, $r(1,097) = .24$ (De Wolff & van IJzendoorn, 1997). Also, other aspects of parent-child relationship quality, such as structuring and autonomy support, are relevant to child development (Bernier, Carlson, & Whipple, 2010; Saunders, Sarche, Trucksess, Morse, & Biringen, under review).

Further, the EA System considers both the parent and child side of the same relationship. The system takes into account not only the child's ability to use the caregiver to manage distress, but also the child's range of emotional expression, autonomy-seeking behaviors, and proclivity to involve the adult in his or her world (Biringen, 2008; Biringen et al., 1998). Thus, the EA Scales can be considered a broad view of the adult-child relationship, one that considers not only attachment-related behaviors, but also emotional expression and behaviors that occur outside of stressful contexts (Biringen et al., 2014). In fact, the assessment of EA can be completed in a variety of observational settings, including play, center-based care, separation-reunion contexts, and with multiple caregivers or with multiple children in the same context (Biringen et al., 2014). Furthermore, the EA Scales were theoretically conceptualized as a life-span construct and for use in parent-child relationships across infancy, childhood, and adolescence (Biringen et al., 2014). The scales were developed some time ago and were designed and empirically validated for caregivers and children between 0 and 14 years old (Biringen et al., 2014; Biringen, Robinson, & Emde, 1993; 1998). They are currently the most commonly used measurement tool of caregiver-infant relationship quality (Lotzin et al., 2015) and have been used in over 20 varied cultural contexts including western as well as non-western societies (Biringen et al., 2014) and caregivers, including mothers, fathers, child care providers (Biringen et al., 2014), therapists (Söderberg et al. 2013), and adult caregivers of those with dementia (Cohen, Palgi, & Sher-Censor, 2019). Although they have mostly been examined for parents and infants and young children, the system has also been used with parents and older children (e.g., Easterbrooks, Bureau, & Lyons-Ruth, 2012), parents and adolescents (e.g. Benton, 2017; Biringen et al., 2010) adolescent mothers and young children (Easterbrooks, Chaudhuri, & Gestsdottir, 2005), and expectant mothers as they speak to and about their unborn fetus using specific prompts (Salo et al., 2019). They are also being further explored for use in relationships between a parent and his or her adult child (Flykt & Biringen, 2016). The wide use of the EA Scales suggests promise in the system's applicability across a wide developmental spectrum.

Emotional Attachment Zones Evaluation. Whereas the EA Scales have been described in close to 300 research publications and in approximately 25 cultures (Biringen et al., 2014), the Emotional Attachment Zones Evaluation (EA-Z) is fairly new. It relies heavily on two of the EA Scales, adult sensitivity and child responsiveness, to classify each member of the dyad into four continuous attachment-like zones: emotionally available (secure), complicated (insecure-resistant/ambivalent), detached (insecure-avoidant), and problematic/disturbed (insecure-disorganized). When the adult expresses mostly positive emotions, is consistently responsive to child cues, and is accepting of the child, he or she is rated as emotionally available. An adult who demonstrates inconsistencies in emotional expression and responsiveness to the child is categorized as complicated. An adult who is emotionally withdrawn or harsh and often unresponsive to child cues is classified as detached. Finally, an adult who appears traumatized, frightening, and/or blatantly unresponsive to child cues is categorized as problematic/disturbed.

Similarly, a child who shows positive emotions, responds appropriately to the adult, and pursues autonomy is classified as emotionally available. A child who is often distressed, overconnected, and/or dependent on the adult is classified as complicated. A child who is distant, emotionally shut down, and avoidant of the adult is classified as detached. Finally, a child who appears traumatized, dissociative, highly emotionally dysregulated, and/or exhibits contradictory approach/withdraw behaviors (e.g., approaching parent with hands held upward and face turned away) toward the adult is considered problematic (Biringen, 2008; Main & Solomon; 1986).

When directly scored, the EA-Z is coded using specific guidelines that describe each of the four zones of attachment, yet it is not coded in isolation (Biringen, 2008). Rather, an observer codes the EA Scales and the EA-Z in conjunction in order to incorporate all relevant information. In doing so, the coder relies heavily on the sensitivity and child responsiveness EA dimensions. However, the observer also incorporates a degree of judgment based on other aspects of the interaction. For example, a child who displays high levels of anxiety toward the caregiver yet responds in a secure manner to a separation-reunion paradigm may nonetheless be categorized in the "emotionally available" zone of the EA-Z, albeit on the lower end of that zone. Additionally, a caregiver who displays high levels of hostility and intrusiveness but appears competent in responding to basic child cues may still be categorized as "problematic." Thus, an observer uses the sensitivity and responsiveness EA scores as a starting point for determining EA-Z score, yet can flexibly consider other aspects of the interaction to most accurately assign a score.

Further, the EA-Z offers an advantage in that it provides both a categorical and continuous/dimensional score for attachment security. Interventions targeting the attachment relationship are often more successful at enhancing caregiver sensitivity than changing child attachment classification (Bakermans-Kranenberg, van IJzendoorn, Juffer, 2003). Using a more fine-tuned, continuous measure of child attachment security may offer more sensitivity to change following intervention (Bakermans-Kranenberg et al., 2003). For example, even if a child classified as "complicated" is not classified as "emotionally available" following an intervention, his EA-Z score may have improved within the "complicated" zone.

In summary, the EA-Z offers a tool to assess caregiver-child attachment style across a wide developmental spectrum, and in a variety of observational contexts. This tool has the potential to address the discontinuity in measurement tools that are used to assess attachment style longitudinally. Therefore, it is important to determine whether the EA-Z is indeed an empirically valid tool to measure attachment style. Espinet and colleagues (2013) compared EA-Z scores to dyadic scores on the Parent-Infant Relationship

Global Assessment Scales (PIR-GAS; ZERO TO THREE, 2005), a validated measurement of overall parent-child relationship quality, and their results indicated a moderate association between the two tools. However, studies have not yet examined the link between the EA-Z and observed attachment.

Further, numerous studies have demonstrated significant links between dimensions of the EA Scales and child or parent attachment security, with children ranging from 1 month to 8 years (e.g., Altenhofen, Clyman, Little, Baker, & Biringen, 2013; Biringen et al., 2012; Kim, Chow, Bray & Teti, 2017; Sagi, Koren-Karie, Gini, Ziv, & Joels, 2005). Although these studies did not directly use the EA-Z, this tool is derived from the sensitivity and responsiveness dimensions of the EA Scales (Biringen, 2008), and many of these studies found relations between attachment-based measures and those two dimensions.

Taken together, several characteristics of the EA System set it apart from other observational systems (Saunders, Krause, Barone, & Biringen, 2015). The EA Scales and the EA-Z can be coded in short time intervals, with any age group, and in any observational setting; this sets them apart from longer observations, such as the AQS and Maternal Behavioural Q-Sort (MBQS; Pederson, Moran, & Bento, 1999), as well as from more structured and age-limited assessments, such as the SSP. Next, the EA Scales and EA-Z code the adult and child simultaneously, yet separately (Biringen, 2008). This means that the parent and child are can (potentially) have differing perspectives of the same relationship. The separation of the parent and child side of the relationship is especially important as the child grows older and has outside experiences that differ markedly from the experiences the child has with a specific parent. It is also relevant when a child comes into a specific parent-child relationship with prior significant experiences (e.g., foster care, adoption). Such experiences may affect or "be brought into" the target parent-child relationship (Biringen, Harman, Saunders, & Emde, 2017).

Further, the EA Scales and EA-Z place a priority on affect, coding not only behavioral responsiveness, but also emotional responsiveness and regulation. This sets the system apart from more behavioral-ly-focused attachment measures, such as the MBQS, SSP, and AQS. Finally, EA considers multiple aspects of parent and child emotions and behaviors that extend beyond a sole focus on sensitivity or on general relationship quality (e.g., Parent-Infant Relationship Global Assessment; PIR-GAS; ZERO TO THREE, 2005). This is informative not only for obtaining a multidimensional view of the relationship, but also in determining attachment style (Saunders et al., 2015).

Hypotheses

Therefore, although many studies have found relevant relations among dimensions of EA and measures of attachment style, there has yet to be a study that explicitly examines the validity of the EA-Z in assessing child and parent attachment styles across a broad developmental spectrum. Here, we present a series of studies in which we aim to validate the EA-Z as an attachment tool by comparing it to a range of empirically-validated attachment tools, the Strange Situation Procedure (SSP; Ainsworth, 1978), the Attachment Q-Sort (AQS; Waters & Deane, 1985), and the Adult Attachment Interview (AAI; George et al., 1984; 1985; 1986). As such, we hypothesize that:

1. Child attachment security, as assessed through the SSP and the Attachment Q-Sort, will be associated with caregiver score on the EA-Z.

2. Child attachment security, as assessed through the SSP and the Attachment Q-Sort, will be associated with child score on the EA-Z.

3. Parent attachment security, as assessed through the AAI, will be associated with parent score on the EA-Z.

4. Parent attachment security, as assessed through the AAI, will be associated with child score on the EA-Z.

Study 1: EA-Z and The Strange Situation Procedure

Participants

Participants consisted of 36 mother-infant dyads living in the Western U.S., recruited via telephone through local newspaper birth announcements in 1998-1999. Over 90% of mothers contacted consented to participate in the study.

Table 1:

Basic descriptives for study 1

	Minimum	Maximum	Mean	Standard Deviation (SD)
Mother's age	23.00	42.00	32.56	5.00
Father's age	25.00	43.00	34.28	4.61
Child's age (months/ rouded up or rounded down as half months)	1.70	12.00	13.70	0.49
Family income	3.00	7.00	6.46	0.95
Mother's education	3.00	7.00	5.08	1.02

Note. Family income: (1= less than $5,000, 4=$15,000-$20,000, 7=greater than $50,000); Mother's education (1=less than 7 years, 4=up to 3 years of college, 7=beyond master's degree

As shown above in Table 1, both mothers and fathers on average were in their early thirties. Mothers were highly educated, with nearly all holding a bachelor's degree or beyond. Infants ranged from 12 to almost 14 months at the time of informed consent, and 15 (41.67%) were female. Infants were a combination of first- and later-born. Additionally, mothers reported on ethnicity, with all being non-Hispanic White (Caucasian), with the exception of nine who did not respond to this question.

Procedure

Prior to recruitment and data collection, this study was reviewed and approved by the university's institutional review board. Data collection was conducted over three years ago, so the protocol has been archived by the institutional review board. When infants were between 12 and 14 months old, mother-infant dyads were observed in their homes for a total of two hours, one hour on two separate days. Mothers were instructed to go about their regular routine, but to avoid having visitors or other family around and to avoid going outdoors. Home observations were videotaped and coded using the EA Scales (3rd ed., Biringen et al., 1998). The week after home observations, mother-infant dyads were invited into the laboratory to complete the Strange Situation Procedure (SSP; Ainsworth et al., 1978). The SSP was scored by different coders than the EA Scales, and both sets of coders were blind to other aspects of the data.

Measures

Emotional Availability Scales. The EA Scales (3rd ed., Biringen et al., 1998) consist of four adult scales (sensitivity, structuring, non-intrusiveness, and nonhostility) and two child scales (responsiveness and involvement). For the purposes of this study, only adult sensitivity and child responsiveness were included in analyses, for they offer the most salient information regarding attachment, especially when using secondary data analysis. Adult sensitivity encompasses the caregivers' positive emotional expression, ability to read child cues, timing and flexibility of responsiveness, and acceptance of the child. Highly sensitive adults demonstrate a wide range of mostly positive emotions, read cues effectively, and respond consistently and effectively. Sensitivity was scored on a 9-point semi-continuous scale, where 1 is least sensitive and 9 is most sensitive. It is important to note that, in the 4th edition of the EA Scales, sensitivity was revised to a 7-point scale. In the 3rd edition, scores between 5.5 and 9 were considered on the upper end of sensitive, and scores between 7 and 9 only indicated differences in positive emotional expression. Therefore, for the purposes of this study, scores between 7 and 9 will be considered "highly sensitive" and transformed to the highest score on the EA-Z.

Child responsiveness refers to the child's positive emotions, responsiveness to the adult's bids for connection, and tendency to seek age-appropriate autonomy. Highly responsive children express mostly positive emotions, use the adult to help regulate negative emotions, respond often to the adult, and seek autonomy. Child responsiveness was scored on a 7-point semi-continuous scale, where 1 is lowest and 7 is highest. The EA Scales have been used in a wide variety of settings, with many ages, and in many cultural contexts. Evidence of their validity can be found in Biringen et al. (2014). For this study and all other studies presented here, EA coders were centrally trained by the developer of the scales. Training consists of a 3 day (live or online) seminar, followed by a rigorous reliability training in which the trainees code seven parent-child interaction videos until they are reliable with the EA System (Biringen, 2008).

For this study, coders scored the EA Scales after every 15 minutes of observation, resulting in 8 sets of EA scores for each dyad (i.e., a set of scores after initial 15 minutes, a set after 30 minutes, a set after 45 minutes, and so forth). To check inter-rater reliability, the first 15 minutes of the initial 10 cases were coded by two coders and intraclass correlations for each scale were: sensitivity (.97, $p < .001$), structuring (.95, $p < .001$), nonintrusiveness (.37, $p = .25$), nonhostility (.96, $p < .001$), child responsiveness (.90, $p = .001$), and child involvement (.99, $p < .001$). The intraclass correlation for the nonintrusiveness scale is low partially due to low variability in scores (Coder 1: $M = 4.95$, $SD = .16$; Coder 2: $M = 4.6$, $SD = .52$). Percent agreement between the two coders was 70% within 0.5 point and 100% within 1 point. For this study, after an initial reliability check on the first 10 cases, the second author (blind to the outsourced SSP coding) scored all home observations. Please note that data analysis is based on the full two hour observations.

Emotional Attachment Zones Evaluation. The 3rd edition of the EA Scales did not include guidelines for scoring the EA-Z. Therefore, for the purposes of this study, EA-Z zones and scores were derived directly from the sensitivity and responsiveness EA Scale codes using a standardized algorithm (see Table 2). These two scales were used because they consider the most salient attachment-relevant information for the parent and for the child. Further, in the later development of the EA-Z for the 4th edition of the EA Scales, these two scales are considered the primary sources of information. In general, we recommend directly coding the EA-Z whenever possible so that coders can consider additional EA qualities besides sensitivity and responsiveness when assigning scores and zones. However, when the EA-Z has not been directly coded, it is appropriate to use sensitivity and responsiveness from previously coded EA Scales in order to derive EA-Z codes with the standard algorithm provided here.

In order to transform adult sensitivity and child responsiveness scores into EA-Z scores, a simple algorithm was applied (see Table 2), for the parent and then for the child. The algorithm matched the EA-Z continuous scores, which range from 1 to 100, with scores on the EA Scales. The algorithm also categorized EA scores into the four EA-Z zones, "emotionally available," "complicated," "detached," and "problematic/disturbed." On the EA Scales, a score between 5.5 and 9 on sensitivity and between 5.5 and 7 on responsiveness is "emotionally available." Scores between 3.5 and 5 on sensitivity/responsiveness are "complicated," scores between 2.5 and 3 are "detached," and scores 2 and below are "problematic/disturbed." Please note that the adult and the child each receive their own EA-Z score and zone. This permits large or small differences between parent and child, such as a child who is highly emotionally available, with a score of a 100, and a parent who is emotionally available but slightly less sensitive, with a score of 85. Further, a child and parent may even be scored in different attachment zones, such as a complicated parent and a detached child. However, it is challenging to conceptualize one member of the relationship as "emotionally available," while the other is not, given EA is a relationship construct. Yet, such disparate zones can happen in adoptive or foster families, or other contexts that are especially challenging.

Table 2.
EA Scale Direct Scores Converted to EA-Z Scores and Zones

Sensitivity	Responsiveness	EA-Z Score	EA-Z Zone
7-9[1]	7	100	
6.5	6.5	95	Emotionally Available
6	6	90	
5.5	5.5	81	
5	5	80	
4.5	4.5	75	Complicated
4	4	61	
3.5	3.5	60	
3	3	55	Detached
2.5	2.5	41	
2	2	40	
1.5	1.5	25	Problematic/ Disturbed
1	1	1	

[1] When using Version 4 of EA Scales (Biringen, 2008), 7 = 100. All other sensitivity conversions are the same.

Strange Situation Procedure. Mother-child attachment security was assessed using the Strange Situation Procedure (SSP; Ainsworth et al., 1978). The SSP is a standardized 20-minute procedure that includes two infant-mother separations and two infant-mother reunions. During the first separation, the infant is left in the room with a stranger, and during the second, the infant is left alone in the room. Trained independent observers classified infants into four attachment styles based on their responses to the mother upon reunion. Infants classified as secure happily greeted their mother and resumed connection; infants classified as insecure-ambivalent/resistant sought out the mother but were not soothed by her presence; infants classified as secure-avoidant did not seek out the mother upon reunion or even moved away; and, finally, infants classified as insecure-disorganized showed contradictory or fearful behaviors upon the mother's return.

The SSP is a widely used instrument for measuring attachment style, and evidence of its validity and of the resulting classifications can be found in Ainsworth et al. (1978) and in Main and Solomon (1986). The SSP was completed by a coder who was centrally trained and certified at the University of Minnesota and was experienced in coding the SSP. Previous study kappas were at or greater than .70.

Results

Descriptive statistics. After the two hours of home observation, five mothers were coded as "detached," seven as "complicated," and 24 (66.67%) as "emotionally available." Six children were scored as "detached," nine as "complicated," and 21 (58.33%) as "emotionally available." For the purposes of primary data analyses, scores from the two hour observations will be used.

Among 36 total infants in the study, 24 (66.67%) were classified in the SSP as secure (Group B), five (13.89%) as insecure-resistant/ambivalent (Group C), two (5.56%) as insecure-avoidant (Group A), and five (13.89%) as insecure-disorganized (Group D). Due to the limited sample size, all infants in groups A, C, and D were grouped into one category, "insecure," and compared to infants classified as secure. Independent-samples t-tests and correlations were used to examine whether SSP classification or EA-Z scores related to child gender, child age, or mothers' education. None were significant, indicating that attachment style, assessed through either the SSP or the EA-Z, was not related to these demographic variables.

Data analyses. Chi-square analyses and logistic regression were used to compare attachment classifications based on the SSP and EA-Z zones. Continuous EA-Z data were transformed so that the mothers and infants with a score of 85 or above were categorized as "emotionally available" (i.e., secure), and those with a score of 80 or below were categorized as "not emotionally available" (i.e., insecure). A chi-square test examining crosstabs of child EA-Z zones and SSP classifications was significant, $X^2(1, N = 36) = 18.51, p < .001$. Of 24 infants classified as secure based on the SSP, four were inaccurately scored as "not emotionally available" based on the EA-Z. Among the 12 infants classified as insecure on the SSP, one was inaccurately scored as "emotionally available" on the EA-Z.

A chi-square test examining crosstabs of mother EA-Z zones and SSP classifications was also significant, $X^2(1, N = 36) = 14.06$, $p < .001$. Of 24 infants classified as secure on the SSP, three were classified as "not emotionally available" based on the mother's EA-Z scores. Of 12 infants classified as insecure on the SSP, three were classified as "emotionally available" based on the mother's EA-Z scores.[1] Binary logistic regression with the child's continuous EA-Z score as the predictor variable and SSP classification as the dependent variable offered similar results. The overall model tested against a constant-only model was significant, $X^2(1, N = 36) = 13.89, p < .001$, indicating that EA-Z significantly distinguished between insecure and secure classifications. Further, as an independent predictor, EA-Z score was significant, *Wald* $= 8.78, p = .003$. Specifically, for every one unit increase in child EA-Z score, children had a 10.4% increased likelihood of being classified as secure on the SSP. The overall sensitivity was high, with 91.7% of children accurately classified as secure based on EA-Z score, yet the specificity was low, with only 50% of children accurately classified as insecure on the SSP based on EA-Z score.

A model testing binary logistic regression, with the mother's continuous EA-Z as the predictor and SSP classification as the dependent variable, was also significant. Compared to a constant-only model, the model with mother EA-Z scores was significant, $X^2(1, N = 36) = 7.62$, $p = .006$, and EA-Z was a significant predictor, *Wald* $= 6.32, p = .012$. Specifically, for every one unit increase in a mother's EA-Z score, children had a 6.5% increased likelihood of being classified as secure on the SSP. However, although sensitivity in classifying secure infants was high, at 87.5%, specificity in classifying insecure infants was low, at 41.7%.[2]

---

1. Chi-square analyses using the first 15 minutes and first 30 minutes of EA observation also revealed a significant, yet smaller, association between EA-Z and SSP for both the child and mother side.

Discussion

This study compared infants' and mothers' EA-Z scores to attachment style classifications derived from the Strange Situation Procedure. Results indicate partial support for the EA-Z as a tool for assessing attachment style. Chi-square analyses indicted that both infants' and mothers' scores on the EA-Z aligned well with SSP classifications, with only five and six infants incorrectly classified, respectively. Further, logistic regression using the EA-Z continuous scores as a predictor of SSP classification indicated that both infant and mother scores were effective in predicting attachment classification. These results support hypotheses 1 and 2, which predicted that EA-Z scores of the child and mother would be associated with attachment style.

It is interesting to note that EA-Z scores derived from the full 2-hour period of observation did not appear to be vastly more accurate in predicting attachment classification than scores derived from shorter observation periods. This suggests that relatively short observational periods can be informative regarding caregiver-child relationship quality and attachment style, and this conclusion is consistent with de Wolff and van IJzendoorn (1997) However, longer observational periods of at least 20 to 30 minutes are generally recommended when coding EA (Biringen, 2008). Further, other nuances of a caregiver-child relationship quality, such as the adults' ability to regulate negative emotions (nonhostility) and to remain accepting toward the child (sensitivity) often are missed during shorter observational periods. Although these may not seem as relevant as sensitivity and responsiveness when considering a child's attachment

2. Binary logistic regression using the first 15 minutes and 30 of EA observation also showed significant results with both mother and child EA-Z scores as predictor variables of SSP classification. Child EA-Z scores based on 15 and 30 minute observations were equally predictive of SSP classification when compared to EA-Z scores from the 2 hour observation. Compared to the 2 hour observational period, mother EA-Z scores from 15 minutes were most accurate in predicting SSP classificatior, and mother EA-Z scores from 30 minutes were least accurate. Zero-order correlations using the first 15 mins also indicated strong correlations with SSP (mother EA zone at 15 min -.54, p <.001 and child EA zone at 15 mins at -.61, p < .001).

style, caregiver hostility can be a precursor of disorganized attachment (Lyons-Ruth, Melnick, Bronfman, Sherry, & Llanas, 2004). Therefore, although shorter observational periods may be necessary and appropriate sometimes, it is generally recommended that EA and EA-Z scores be derived from periods no shorter than 20 minutes, and the longest possible observation is recommended.

Several limitations of this study exist. The small sample size did not permit a more detailed analysis of insecure styles, and all three styles were combined as "insecure." Ideally, future studies with larger sample sizes will aim to align EA-Z zones with their respective insecure attachment styles in order to more thoroughly validate the tool. Further, although five infants were classified using the SSP as insecure-disorganized, no infants or mothers were placed in the "problematic" zone of the EA-Z. This calls for a more detailed description of disorganized interactions from the perspective of the EA framework. Finally, not only was the sample small, but it also lacked socioeconomic and ethnic diversity. The sample consisted largely of Caucasian, highly educated mothers. In order to generalize these findings to a wider population, further research with a more diverse sample will be necessary.

Study 2: EA-Z and the Attachment Q-Sort

Participants

Participants were infant/toddler-child care professional dyads. Fifty-four children participated, and each was paired with one of 33 child care professionals. Professionals could be paired with between one and four children, and they were observed separately with each target child (51.5% of providers were paired with one child; 27.3% were paired with two children; 18.2% were paired with three, and 3% were paired with four). This resulted in a total of 57 dyads. Children were included in the study if they spent at least 20 hours per week at the child care center, had been attending the center for at least one month, and had been under the care of the target child care professional for at least one month.

Children ranged from 10 to 31 months at the start of the study ($M = 18.78$, $SD = 5.06$), and 37% ($n = 20$) were female. In terms of ethnicity, 89% of children were Caucasian. Approximately 70% of children came from two-parent households, and 54% were first-born. Family income of children ranged from less than $15,000 a year to over $75,000 a year. Approximately half of families reported the highest income bracket, and five families reported an annual income below $30,000. Further, a majority of parents had achieved at least a college degree. The age of child care professionals ranged from 19 to 54 ($M = 32$), and all were female. Child care providers were almost all Caucasian, with approximately 10% Hispanic/Latino. The majority of child care professionals had 1-3 years of college or beyond. Data were collected between 2005 and 2008.

Procedure

This study used data from an intervention study that tested the efficacy of a child care center-based emotional availability program. Prior to recruitment and data collection, this study was reviewed and approved by the university's institutional review board (protocol number 02-071H, renewal number 04-320H). Ten child care sites were contacted to participate in an intervention, and eleven were contacted to participate as a control group. All centers provided baseline data prior to the intervention implementation data, and, in order to maximize sample size, only baseline data were used for this study. Center directors from each site provided letters of support, and child care professionals and parents of participating children completed informed consent procedures. Over 70% of child care directors, professionals, and parents expressed interest in the study and consented to participate. When completing the informed consent procedure, parents and child care professionals also provided demographic information.

Child care professionals were paired with between one and four participating children in their classroom, meaning that some professionals were observed more than once with separate children. At baseline, professional-child dyads were observed for two hours in order to assess the Attachment Q-Sort (AQS; Waters, 1987; Waters & Deane, 1985) and the EA Scales (3rd ed., Biringen et al., 1998). Two observers were present for the full two hour observations in order to take notes and score the AQS. The first 30-minutes of this observational period were filmed in order to be coded using the EA Scales at a later time by an independent coder. Over 90% of observations occurred between 9:00 and 11:30 a.m., after the child was dropped off and before morning naptime. Child care professionals were instructed to go about their normal activities and to interact as they normally would with all children. Observers avoided interfering with activities or interacting with children and professionals, with the exception of a few brief interactions to be coded for the AQS protocol (Waters, 1987; Waters & Deane, 1985). Finally, the EA Scales (3rd ed., Biringen et al., 1998) were coded by certified EA coders (see training details on p. 13) using the initial 30-minute filmed portion of the 2-hour observation at child care sites.

Measures

Attachment Q-Sort. The AQS (Version 3.0, Waters, 1987), includes 90 items describing the child's attachment-related behaviors toward the adult. Most items describe aspects of secure based behavior, and some include other attachment-related behaviors. An example item reads, "If held in caregiver's arms, child stops crying and quickly recovers after being frightened or upset" (Waters, 1987, p. 21). The AQS was developed for use with a mother or parent, so although it has been used in child care contexts in previous studies (Cassibba et al., 2000), a detailed manual was not available. Thus, we developed a manual to guide observers in coding the child care context. Everett Waters and German Posada provided guidance during this process (personal communication, 2005); the child care manual developed for this project can be requested from Everett Waters.

All AQS observations were direct and did not involve videotaping, and they lasted at least two hours, for prior research indicates that this is the minimum time period to reliably code the AQS (Howes

& Smith, 1995). If an observation needed to end before the full two hours, a separate observation was scheduled in order to ensure all observations were two hours. After the two hours, coders ranked the child's behavior using the AQS items from "most descriptive of the child" to "least descriptive of that child." Items not seen that day were placed in the middle pile, as instructed by Waters and Posada (2005, personal communication).

In order to score the AQS, the resulting profile of the child was correlated with a behavioral profile of a stereotypical secure child, as described by attachment experts and provided by Waters and Deane (1985). This process results in a security score ranging from -1.0 to +1.0, where -1.0 is a perfect negative correlation with the prototypical secure child and +1.0 is a perfect positive correlation (van IJzendoorn, Veriejken, Bakermans-Kranenburg, & Riksen-Walraven, 2004; Waters & Deane, 1985). The AQS does not classify children into specific attachment styles, but instead offers a continuous measure of the child's attachment security. However, in typical samples of children, a score of 0.3 or above indicates the child is securely attached, and a score below 0.3 indicates the child has an insecure attachment (personal communication, E. Waters, 10 November 2016). More details on the AQS and its scoring process are available at Everett Waters' website: www.psychology.sunysb.edu/attachment.

Observers were trained in the AQS over several months, during which a trainee first watched videotapes coded by a master trainer and then later accompanied the master trainer to child care observations. Following each observation, both completed the AQS and checked agreement. There were two AQS observers at every single observation session in the child care sites, and after completion of the sorting, observers went to an off-site location near these sites so that they could quickly and independently finalize their AQS sorts, then check their agreement and discrepancies. Interrater reliability was above .70 for most visits. Whenever reliability (percent agreement) was lower than .80, the project coordinator contacted each of the observers to recommend supplemental training, as necessary, prior to the next site visit. In all cases, the conferenced code was entered into the data files for analysis purposes. AQS observers were blind to study condition, and EA scores. There were numerous AQS teams on the project so that observers could also be blind to time points of observation.

A meta-analysis of studies using the AQS supports the validity of the observer AQS, demonstrating its convergent validity with the SSP ($r = .31$), predictive validity with sensitivity ($r = .39$), and divergent validity with measures of temperament. Further, the AQS demonstrates stability over time ($r = .28$) (van IJzendoorn et al., 2004). The observer version of the AQS is superior to the self-report version in terms of validity and stability, both for parents and child care providers (Cassibba et al., 2000; van IJzendoorn et al., 2004).

EA Scores and EA-Z. The 3rd edition of the EA Scales (Biringen et al., 1998) was used to code the first videotaped 30-minutes of the 2-hour observations in child care sites (see Study 1). The first 8 cases were double coded by the second author and a trained graduate student. Intraclass correlations for each scale were: sensitivity (.93, $p = .001$), structuring (.89, $p = .005$), nonintrusiveness (.95, $p< .001$), nonhostility (.96, $p < .001$), child responsiveness (.78, $p = .03$), and child involvement (.74, $p = .049$). Once interrater reliability was established, the EA coding for baseline data was done by one research assistant who was blind to other information, including AQS scores, study condition, and time point. Additional reliability checks were done for post-intervention data. The same algorithm was used to transform scores on the sensitivity and responsiveness scales to EA-Z scores (see Study 1).

Results

Child AQS baseline security scores ranged from -0.05 to 0.66 ($M = 0.38$, $SD = .17$), and child EA-Z scores ranged from 30 to 100 ($M = 85.70$, $SD = 11.86$). One child was classified in the "problematic" zone of the EA-Z, one in the "detached zone," 20 in the "complicated zone," and 35 in the "emotionally available zone." Adult EA-Z scores ranged from 30 to 100 (M = 87.46, SD = 13.57). Of the 57 dyads (consisting of 33 professionals) one adult score was classified in the "problematic" zone, two scores were in the "detached zone," 20 in the "complicated" zone, and 34 in the "emotionally available" zone. Among providers who were observed with two or more children (n = 16), the mean standard deviation of providers' sensitivity scores was SD = 0.48. Correlations between AQS security score and EA-Z score are presented in Table 3. AQS security was significantly related to child EA-Z score, r = .32, p = .014, but AQS security and adult EA-Z scores were not significantly correlated.

Table 3
Correlations among AQS security and EA-Z scores.

	AQS Security	Child EA-Z
Child EA-Z	.32*	
Adult EA-Z	.21	.75**

*p< .05, **p< .001

In order to examine dichotomous secure vs. insecure classifications with both measures, a defined cutoff of 0.3 on the AQS security score was used. Using this cutoff, 30.4% of children were classified as insecure on the AQS, and 69.6% were classified as secure. On the EA-Z, 37% of children were classified as insecure, and 63% were classified as secure. Using adult EA-Z scores, 38.9% were classified as insecure, and 61.1% were classified as secure. Next, chi-square analysis examined the crosstabs of the AQS attachment security classification and the EA-Z attachment security classification. Neither child EA-Z classification nor adult EA-Z classification were significantly associated with AQS attachment security classification.

Discussion

The results of this study offer some preliminary evidence of the validity of the EA-Z in assessing child attachment style. Continuous/dimensional child EA-Z scores were significantly, albeit modestly, correlated with child security scores on the AQS. This supported hypothesis 2, which predicted that child EA-Z would be related to attachment security. However, adult EA-Z was not significantly correlated with child AQS security, contradicting hypothesis 1. Nevertheless, this makes sense, given the assessment tools and the context of observation. The AQS focuses solely on child behavior, both toward the target caregiver and toward other adults. Further, children in a child care setting likely interact with several caregivers, including their own parents and other child care professionals. Therefore, one particular child care professional's sensitivity toward a particular child may be less relevant for that child's attachment-relevant behaviors. For example, a child who is securely attached to a parent but paired with a less sensitive child care provider may still be observed as securely attached in the child care context, given the protective nature of a secure attachment with one primary caregiver (Boldt et al., 2014; Kochanska & Kim, 2013). This may also explain the modest size of the correlation between child EA-Z score and child AQS security score. Emotional Availability is inherently a dyadic context, so a child who is securely attached to one caregiver is not expected to be optimally responsive to other caregivers, particularly if other caregivers are less sensitive. Therefore, although the AQS observations were focused almost entirely on interactions between the target caregiver and target child, the children's attachment-relevant behaviors may still have been influenced by other relationships.

In addition, although the AQS and EA were both coded from the same observational period, the EA Scales were coded based on the first 30 minutes only. AQS observers had a longer observational period from which to derive scores. With the full 2 hours, AQS observers had a higher likelihood of witnessing caregiver-child separations, discipline situations, or other stressful contexts that may have been informative to the child's attachment security. If the EA Scales had been coded from the full observational context, the concordance between measures may have been higher. Finally, about half of caregivers were observed with more than one child, which likely led to nonindependence in the dyads' EA-Z scores and zones. Due to the small sample size and the small number of children paired with each provider (between 1 and 4), we were unable to address this possibility in analyses.

Future studies should examine the relations among EA-Z and AQS in other contexts, such as parent-child, in order to determine whether this enhances the validity of the EA-Z. Additionally, this sample was fairly small and homogenous, with a vast majority of parents and teachers being Caucasian and well-educated. In order to better validate the EA-Z and generalize it to a wider population, future studies should examine its validity in larger and more diverse samples. Finally, as with the other two studies, only one caregiver and one child were classified in the lowest, "problematic" zone of the EA-Z. This suggests that, either the sample was low-risk and did not exhibit problematic behaviors, or the coding using the EA Scales did not capture the lowest zone. Thus, future studies should both examine EA-Z and AQS in more at-risk samples and, potentially, clarify the EA-Z in order to better detect problematic interactions.

Study 3: EA-Z and The Adult Attachment Interview

Participants

Participants consisted of 35 mother-child dyads, recruited from the two most economically diverse elementary schools in a county in the Western U.S. between 1997 and 1999. Mothers ranged from age 25 to 48 ($M = 35.35$, $SD = 5.69$), and they were relatively diverse in terms of educational attainment; 27.8% of mothers had a high school degree or less; 16.67% had attended some college; and 52.8% had a bachelor's degree or higher. Mothers also reported on income; 5.6% reported an annual family income below $15,000; 66.7% reported an income between $15,000 and $50,000; and 25% reported an income above $50,000. Approximately 20% of mothers were single parents. Children ranged from 50 to 72 months old ($M = 62.31$, $SD = 4.55$), and 16 were female. The sample consisted both of first-born ($n = 16$) and later-born ($n = 19$) children.

Procedure

Prior to recruitment and data collection, this study was reviewed and approved by the university's institutional review board. Data collection was conducted over three years ago, between 1997 and 1999, so the protocol has been archived by the institutional review board. Parents were recruited during registration for kindergarten at two schools that served socioeconomically diverse populations in rural Colorado. All parents expressed interest in the project, and when contacted via telephone, 80% agreed to participate. Data were collected in the months prior to kindergarten entry.

Mothers and children came to a research lab at a large state university. A research assistant explained the study and obtained informed consent. Next, mother-child dyads played in a room together for a total of 20 minutes. For the first 5 minutes, dyads were instructed to work together with an Etch-A-Sketch to copy images of a house and a boat that were on the table. For the remaining 15 minutes, dyads were given a set of toys (princesses and knights) and instructed to "play as you normally would." Following the play inter-action, mothers were interviewed about their attachment history and family-of-origin using the Adult Attachment Interview (AAI; George et al., 1984; 1985; 1986). During the administration of the AAI, the child completed a developmental assessment in a separate room.

Measures

EA Scales and the EA-Z. EA Scales were coded using the 3rd edition (Biringen et al., 1998). The first 10 cases of this sample were double coded by the second author and a EA certified graduate student (see training details on p. 13), and intraclass correlations for each scale were: sensitivity ($.96, p < .001$), structuring ($.91, p = .001$), nonintrusiveness ($.95, p < .001$), nonhostility ($.86, p = .003$), child responsiveness ($.83, p < .001$), and child involvement ($.96, p < .001$). Following this, the remainder of the sample was coded by the graduate assistant. Sensitivity and responsiveness were transformed to EA-Z scores using the algorithm from Study 1 (see Table 2).

Adult Attachment Interview. The Adult Attachment Interview (AAI; George et al., 1984; 1985; 1986) assesses an adult's representations of his or her early attachment relationships. In order to assess the adult's state of mind regarding relational experiences in his or her family-of-origin, the AAI elicits a variety of information. The interviewer asks about general and specific experiences with each parent, separation and loss issues, perspectives on why attachment figures behaved in a certain way, and views on whether relationships have changed over time.

Based on the content and coherence of the AAI, participants are classified into one of four categories: Autonomous/Free to Evaluate/Secure, Preoccupied, Dismissing, or Unresolved. An Autonomous/Free to Evaluate/Secure individual expressed a balanced and integrated view of his or her attachment history. A Preoccupied adult expresses anger and resistance about his or her attachment figures, and he or she has not worked toward integration or resolution of such feelings. A Dismissing adult ignores attachment-related issues and experiences, or he or she may idealize a parent without specific experiences to support such positive ideals. Finally, an Unresolved individual may show confusion, seem disorganized, or express unresolved mourning (George et al., 1984; 1985; 1986). In addition to classifying adults into one of these four categories, the scoring of the AAI also offers continuous scores on many scales. For the purposes of this study, only the AAI coherence scale will be used.

Two coders were trained and certified by Mary Main and/or Deborah Jacobvitz. Approximately 10 cases were coded by the first coder and the remaining cases were coded by the second. No cases were double coded, since these coders were certified at an acceptable level of agreement in prior work. The AAI demonstrates stability over time and across interviewers, and its discriminant validity is evidenced by independence from non-attachment related memories, intelligence, and social desirability (Bakermans-Kranenburg & van IJzendoorn, 1993; Crowell et al., 1996).

Results

Descriptive statistics. Based on EA-Z scores, one mother was in the "Problematic" zone, one was in the "Detached" zone, five were in the "Complicated" zone, and 28 were in the "Emotionally Available" zone. Based on AAI scores, four mothers were "Unresolved", three were "Dismissing," two were "Preoccupied,", and 26 were "Autonomous/Free to Evaluate/Secure" (see Table 4). In regard to child EA-Z scores, three children were in the "Detached" zone, 11 were in the "Complicated" zone, and 21 were in the "Emotionally Available" zone. No children were categorized as "Problematic" with the EA-Z (see Table 5).

Table 4
Mother EA-Z Zone and Mother AAI Category

Mother AAI Category	Mother EA-Z Zone				
	Problematic	Detached	Complicated	Emot. Avail.	*Total*
Unresolved	**1**	0	1	2	4
Dismissing	0	**1**	0	2	3
Preoccupied	0	0	**1**	1	2
Secure	0	0	3	**23**	26
Total	1	1	5	28	35

Table 5
Child EA-Z Zone and Mother AAI Category

Mother AAI Category	Child EA-Z Zone				
	Problematic	Detached	Complicated	Emot. Avail.	*Total*
Unresolved	0	1	2	1	4
Dismissing	0	**1**	0	2	3
Preoccupied	0	0	**2**	0	2
Secure	0	1	7	**18**	26
Total	0	3	11	21	35

Data analysis. Chi square analyses were used to examine whether AAI classifications and EA-Z zones were related. Because cell sizes were too small to conduct a 4x4 chi-square based on attachment classifications, 2x2 chi-square analyses were conducted using binary secure-insecure classifications based on the EA-Z and the AAI. EA-Z scores were transformed so that a score of 85 or above was labeled "emotionally available" or "secure," and a score of 80 or below was labeled as "not emotionally available" or "insecure." The chi-square examining mother EA-Z security and AAI security was significant, $X^2(1, N = 35) = 4.53, p = .033$, yet when child EA-Z security was compared to AAI security, it was only marginally significant, $X^2(1, N = 35) = 3.57, p = .058$.

Binary logistic regression was also used to determine whether mother and child continuous EA-Z scores significantly predicted mothers' AAI classification. With mother EA-Z score as a predictor, the overall model tested against a constant-only model was significant, $X^2(1, N = 35) = 7.74, p = 005$, indicating that mother EA-Z score significantly distinguished between insecure and secure AAI classifications. Further, as an independent predictor, mother EA-Z score was significant, *Wald* $= 4.48 p = .034$. Specifically, for every one unit increase in mother EA-Z score, mothers had a 9.2% increased likelihood of being classified as secure on the AAI. The overall sensitivity was high, with 96.2% of mothers accurately classified as secure based on EA-Z score, yet the specificity was low, with only 22.2% of mothers accurately classified as insecure on the AAI based on their EA-Z score.

Binary logistic regression was run with child EA-Z score as the predictor and mother AAI classification as the dependent variable. Compared to a constant-only model, the model with child EA-Z scores was also significant, $X^2(1, N = 35) = 5.44, p = .02$, and child EA-Z score was a significant predictor of AAI classification, *Wald* $= 4.54, p = .033$. For every one unit increase in a child's EA-Z score, mothers had a 8.6% increased likelihood of being classified as secure on the AAI. However, as with the model using mother EA-Z, sensitivity in classifying secure infants was high, 96.2%, but specificity in classifying insecure infants was low, 22.2%.

Finally, bivariate correlations examined associations among AAI continuous coherence score, continuous mother EA-Z score, and continuous child EA-Z score. Mother EA-Z scores were significantly correlated with continuous AAI security, $r = .37$, $p = .03$, but child EA-Z scores were not, $r = .22$, $p = .21$ (see Table 6).

Table 6
Correlations amoung AAI coherence and EA-Z score

	AAI Coherence	Child EA-Z
Mother EA-Z	.37*	.84**
Child EA-Z	.22	

*$p< .05$, **$p < .001$

Discussion

This study compared mothers' AAI classifications to mother and child EA-Z scores in order to begin validating the EA-Z as an attachment style measurement tool across a broad developmental spectrum. The results of this study offer some evidence for the validity of the EA-Z in assessing attachment. Both chi-square analyses and logistic regression analyses demonstrated significant relations between mothers' attachment classification based on EA-Z zones and their attachment classification based on the AAI. Bivariate correlations between continuous AAI security and mothers' EA-Z scores were also significant. These results are particularly interesting, for the AAI assessed mothers' states of minds in regard to their family-of-origin attachment history, whereas the EA-Z derives from direct observation of maternal behaviors and emotional expression. Thus, these results not only offer a starting point for validating the EA-Z as an attachment measurement tool, but they also demonstrate links between mothers' internal working models and their concurrent interactional styles. Although cell sizes were too small to statistically examine EA-Z zones and specific AAI categories, Table 3 offers insight into the accuracy of the EA-Z in comparison to the AAI. Nine out of 35 mothers were classified into mismatched zones between the AAI and EA-Z.

Further, child EA-Z scores were also related to mothers AAI classification. Although the chi-square test was only marginally significant, the logistic regression significantly predicted maternal attachment security from child EA-Z scores. Although these results certainly need to be replicated with a larger sample size, they offer preliminary evidence that caregivers' internal working models impact their child's behavioral and emotional responsiveness to that caregiver. In terms of specific attachment classifications, 14 out of 35 children were classified into mismatched zones between maternal AAI and child EA-Z. However, it is to be expected that children are less accurately classified based on their mothers' AAI category. Therefore, these results can offer preliminary evidence of the validity of the EA-Z as an attachment assessment tool. Further, results support hypotheses 3 and 4, which predicted that maternal AAI would be related to both mother EA-Z and child EA-Z scores.

Several characteristics of this study limit its generalizability and conclusiveness. First, the sample size was small and relatively ethnically homogeneous. This meant that data analyses were restricted to examining secure and insecure, rather than a more rich examination of the various insecure subtypes, particularly because so few participants were in each category of insecure. Additionally, the sample limits the generalizability of results due to its size and homogeneity. Finally, in this sample, only one mother was placed in the "problematic" zone of the EA-Z, and no children were. Therefore, a closer look at this attachment zone will help inform whether the EA-Z can effectively capture it. Future studies and secondary data analyses should use larger samples, recruit more diverse participants, and include at-risk families in order to continue validating the EA-Z as a tool for assessing attachment style in both adults and children.

General Discussion

All three studies presented here offer promising evidence for the validity of the EA-Z as an attachment tool. We predicted that both caregiver and child EA-Z scores would relate to two empirically validated observational measures of child attachment security, the SSP and the AQS (hypotheses 1 and 2) These hypotheses were mostly supported. In studies 1 and 2, child EA-Z scores related as expected to child attachment security. Moreover, these studies were conducted in different contexts (home vs. child care) and with different caregivers (parent vs. child care provider). This suggests that the EA-Z can accurately assess child attachment security, even across caregiving contexts. Adult EA-Z score was also related to child attachment security, but only in study 1, which used the SSP in a sample of infants and their mothers. In contrast, the results of study 2 did not show a relation between the EA-Z scores of child care providers and the attachment security of children, as measured by the AQS. This may be due to the effects of multiple caregivers and a limited observational context to measure the EA-Z.

Next, we predicted that child and parent EA-Z scores would also relate to parent attachment security, as measured by the AAI (hypotheses 3 and 4). These hypotheses were supported in study 3. These findings were particularly promising, given the fact that the AAI is not an observational measure. Whereas the SSP, the AQS, and the EA-Z all utilize behavioral observation to measure attachment security, the AAI uses an interview format and assesses an individual's states of mind related to attachment. Thus, the results of Study 3, demonstrating links between AAI and EA-Z security, seem to further support the EA-Z as a theoretically-relevant tool. Finally, although the degree of concordance between the EA-Z and all three of these attachment measures was small to moderate, it was similar to the degree of concordance found among well-established attachment measures, such as between the SSP and the AQS (van IJzendoorn et al., 2004).

A consistent theme across the three studies was greater sensitivity and lower specificity in the logistic regression model. This suggests that there is relatively stronger concordance between the EA-Z and other attachment tools when children were securely attached than when they were insecure. The EA-Z, in its current form, may be most accurate in identifying secure children and less sensitive to indicators of insecure attachment. It is possible that the low-stress contexts used to assess the EA-Z in these studies made it more challenging to see the behaviors associated with insecure attachment and that studies using separation/reunion or other stress contexts may be useful in this regard. Additionally, there are many challenges in recognizing the subtler signs of disorganized attachment among low-risk dyads (Lyons & Spielman, 2004). Thus, it could be that the EA-Z failed to identify disorganized dyads due to the low-risk nature of our sample. Ongoing work in our lab is aiming to clarify the subtle signs of disorganization from the EA perspective.

Nevertheless, more studies and secondary data analyses are needed to further demonstrate the validity of the EA-Z as an attachment assessment. First, all three studies used Version 3 of the EA Scales (Biringen et al., 1998). Although the current version (Version 4, Biringen, 2008) can also be used to derive EA-Z scores, it is important to examine the validity of EA-Z scores derived from both versions. Next, all three studies used relatively small and homogenous samples. As discussed previously, it will be imperative to validate the EA-Z with large, ethnically diverse, and socioeconomically diverse samples in order to generalize its use. Larger and more diverse samples will likely also provide better variety in terms of EA-Z zones and specific attachment styles, allowing a more detailed analysis of these two constructs. Finally, although Study 3 examined adult attachment, all three studies used EA-Z data from young children between the ages of zero and five. In order to empirically validate the EA-Z as a tool to be used across the lifespan (as theorized by Biringen et al., 2014), research will need to utilize it with parents and a wider range of child, adolescent, and young adult ages.

Finally, the use of the arithmetic rubric in these studies, although necessary based on the use of secondary data analyses, limits the validity of the EA-Z classifications. A trained EA-Z coder, watching the same videos, may have assigned different EA-Z codes for some dyads, due to information from other scales or attachment-based observations. Thus, it will be important to continue validating the EA-Z using direct observation by trained EA-Z coders in order to replicate and expand upon the findings presented here.

As the EA-Z is validated as a tool for assessing attachment, its promise as a valuable lifespan measure will continue to be evaluated. To date, no other attachment measurement tool can be used beyond a limited age range. For example, the Strange Situation Procedure (Ainsworth et al., 1978) can only be used with children between the ages of 12 and 24 months, and the Attachment Q-Sort (Waters & Deane, 1985) can be used with children between one and five years old. Without a tool that can be used across a wide range of ages, it becomes difficult to examine the long-term stability and predictability of attachment style. Therefore, the EA-Z offers a measurement tool that can be used longitudinally to examine both the long-term stability of individuals' attachment styles, as well as the predictive value of attachment styles over time.

Suggestions for Research and Practice

From a conceptual standpoint, there is a benefit to using both the EA Scales and the EA-Z when assessing the quality of caregiver-child interactions. The EA Scales offer a multifaceted view of this quality, with dimensions that are often not utilized when using other attachment measurement tools. For example, using the EA Scales, a researcher or practitioner can also determine a caregiver's ability to guide learning, to resist interfering, and to effectively regulate negative emotions. These qualities add depth in understanding a parent-child relationship, yet they are also relevant in considering attachment style. For example, high levels of parent intrusiveness and hostility are often used indicators of disorganized attachment (Lyons-Ruth et al., 2004), and such qualities also provide information that is not specifically about attachment. Similarly, child involvement is rarely taken into account in any measure of attachment, and yet a child's ability and interest in taking initiative during interactions provides important information about the relational capacities of that child.

Also from a conceptual vantage point, the EA Scales and the EA-Z provide information about relationship qualities and about attachment from the perspective of the parent as well as the perspective of the child. In some samples, parents and children may not share the same views of their relationship. For example, Barone, Lionetti, Dellagiulia, Alagna, and Rigobello (2015) reported that in 22% of adoptive mother-child dyads, the child scored in a different EA-Z zone from his or her adoptive mother. In an interview-based study on parental alienation in the context of high-conflict divorce, investigators found that many parents (mothers as well as fathers) who described themselves as loving, caring, and sensitive in their interactions with their children described also that their children became alienated from them after divorce (Biringen et al., 2017; Harman & Biringen, 2016). Although observations may be more objective than interviews, and certainly only a subset of children become alienated from a parent after divorce, nonetheless such research paves the way for thinking about nonconcordance in the parental and child side of the same relationship.

The EA System, and the EA-Z specifically, provides a new conceptualization and method for addressing that a child and parent may have differing views of the same relationship. Although there may be limits to how far away these zones may be in a two-parent home with biological parents, the EA framework may help us to better understand and measure a wider range of families and relationships, children of different ages in the same family, as well as real-world conditions that may contribute to such complexities (e.g., immigrant or refugee families).

Furthermore, when using the EA Scales and the EA-Z to directly code interactions, we recommend starting with the algorithm (shown in Table 2) to convert sensitivity and responsiveness scores to EA-Z scores. This can offer consistency both within research or practice settings and across these settings. However, it is far better for coders to make a judgment call based on other EA qualities. An observer might rate sensitivity or responsiveness near the "border" of two zones but feel confident that the EA-Z zone is different, or the coder may observe that an individual's attachment security is slightly lower or higher than the score granted by his or her EA Scales score. For example, in some cases, a child rated in the middle range of the responsiveness scale may nonetheless appear to belong in the "emotionally available" zone of the EA-Z due to his or her response to a stressful situation. Also, a caregiver may display qualities inherent in both the detached and complicated zones. In this case, a coder will need to decide which zone best characterizes this caregiver based on his or her overall demeanor and behavior. However, when conducting secondary data analysis on previously coded EA interactions, we recommend using the more strict algorithm (Table 2) in order to ensure consistency and to reduce error.

Next, in order to best categorize dyads into EA-Z zones, it is important to ensure that the length and context of observation are sufficient. In general, contexts that elicit stress, such as separation-reunion contexts or challenging situations, are better than those that are entirely play. For young infants, this may consist of a still-face paradigm (Weinberg & Tronick, 1996). However, we caution researchers and practitioners when conceptualizing and/or scoring the EA-Z with very young infants. Although the EA Scales can certainly be used with very young infants, the EA-Z may not yet be valid in assessing attachment style per se with this age group. Instead, the EA Scales could be used in early infancy, or even during pregnancy (Salo et al., 2016), to predict an infant's later EA-Z score or zone or the EA-Z scores for young infants may be referred to as "attachment in the making" (Bowlby, 1969). For older infants, toddlers, and young children, a separation-reunion may be best to elicit stress. Among young or middle age children, the caregiver and child could be instructed to clean up toys or to follow a specific rule (e.g. not playing with toys on a certain shelf). Finally, with older children, adolescents, and couples, a challenging situation could consist of discussing a recent or ongoing conflict (Gottman, Coan, Carrere, & Swanson, 1988).

Additionally, longer observational periods are generally most adequate in assessing EA and attachment style, particularly if the context is low-stress. The attachment system is activated by stress (Ainsworth & Bell, 1970), so either stressful situations or long periods of time seem to be necessary to accurately assess a child's attachment style. Further, other important indicators, both of EA and of attachment-related constructs, are often more observable in stressful or long-lasting interactions. Caregiver nonhostility, which can be important in identifying disorganized attachment, can often be masked in shorter observational periods by a self-conscious caregiver. Additionally, certain behaviors, such as clinging, whining, and fussing are signs of an insecure-resistant/ambivalent attachment style or the middle zone of the responsiveness scale (Biringen, 2008), and an observer is more likely to witness these behaviors in longer or stressful situations.

However, having some portion of the observational context still contain play or another form of "everyday" interaction will also be beneficial, especially when coding the EA Scales. Dimensions, such as structuring and nonintrusiveness, may not be evident during a Strange Situation context, for caregivers tend to guide learning and grant autonomy in low-stress contexts (Biringen, 2008). Therefore, EA and EA-Z observations would ideally assess interactions no shorter than 20 minutes and that contain both a play or "everyday" inter-action and some sort of stressful situation, such as a separation and reunion.

In closing, the EA-Z offers potential as a valid tool to assess attachment security across the lifespan. Further, its source, the EA Scales, can assess other characteristics of dyadic relationships that are relevant for child development and adult well-being that are "larger" than attachment (see Biringen et al., 2014). Therefore, con-tinuing to validate the EA Scales and EA-Z can establish them as effective measures of both attachment security and the overall qual-ity of dyadic relationships. We hope that these three studies, which examine caregiver-child relationships from infancy to kindergarten, as well as adult mothers' attachment states of mind, will be a starting point for further inquiry across a broader age range.

Compliance with Ethical Standards

The studies presented here were funded by First Bohemian Foundation ("Project Secure Child in Child Care Grant") and the Temple Buell Foundation ("Project Secure Child in Child Care Grant," #535470 and #535230).

The procedures and methods for all three studies were reviewed by the Institutional Review Board at the authors' university. All procedures performed in studies involving human participants were in accordance with the ethical standards of the institutional review board and with the 1964 Helsinki declaration and its later amendments or comparable ethical standards. Participants for each study were thoroughly briefed on the study procedures. Informed consent was obtained from all individual participants included in the studies.

Finally, the second author discloses a potential conflict of interest in that she developed the Emotional Availability Scales and the Emotional Attachment Zones Evaluation. However, she reports no financial conflict of interest with the participants of these three studies.

References

Ainsworth, M.D.S., (1967). *Infancy in Uganda: Infant Care and the Growth of Love.* Johns Hopkins University Press.

Ainsworth, M.D.S., & Bell, S.M. (1970). Attachment, exploration, and separation: Illustrated by the behavior of one-year-olds in a strange situation. *Child Development,* 41(1), 49–67.

Ainsworth, M.D.S., Blehar, M. Waters, E., & Wall, S. (1978). *Patterns of attachment: A psychological study of the strange situation.* Erlbaum.

Altenhofen, S., Clyman, R., Little, C., Baker, M., & Biringen, Z. (2013). Attachment security in three-year-olds who entered substitute care in infancy. *Infant Mental Health Journal,* 34, 435–445. doi: 10.1002/imhj.21401

Altenhofen, S., Sutherland, K., & Biringen, Z. (2010). Families experiencing divorce: Age at onset of overnight stays, conflict, and emotional availability predictors of child attachment. *Journal of Divorce & Remarriage,* 51, 141-156. doi: 10.1080/10502551003597782

Bakermans-Kranenburg, M.J., & van IJzendoorn, M.H. (1993). A psychometric study of the Adult Attachment Interview: Reliability and discriminant validity. *Developmental Psychology*, 29(5), 870. doi: 10.1037/0012-1649.29.5.870

Bakermans-Kranenberg, M.J., van IJzendoorn, M.H., & Juffer, F (2003). Less is more: Meta-analyses of sensitivity and attachment interventions in early childhood. *Psychological Bulletin*, 129(2), 195–215.

Barone, L., Lionetti, F., Dellagiulia, A., Alagna, C., Rigobello, L. (2015, August 6). *Promoting emotional availability in mothers of late adopted children: A randomized controlled trial using the VIPP-SD*. 7th International Attachment Conference, New York.

Bartholomew, K., & Horowitz, L.M. (1991). Attachment styles among young adults: A test of a four-category model. *Journal of Personality and Social Psychology*, 61(2), 226–244. doi: 10.1037/0022-3514.61.2.226

Benton, J. (2017). *Examining the association between emotional availability and mindful parenting* [Unpublished master's thesis]. Colorado State University.

Bernier, A., Carlson, S.M., & Whipple, N. (2010). From external regulation to self-regulation: Early parenting precursors of young children's executive functioning. *Child Development*, 81(1), 326–339.

Biringen, Z. (2008). *The Emotional Availability (EA) Scales and the Emotional Attachment & Emotional Availability (EA2) Clinical Screener (4th ed.): Infancy/Early Childhood Version; Middle Childhood/Youth Versions; Therapist/ Interventionist Manual; Couple Relationship Manual*. International Center for Excellence in Emotional Availability. http://www.emotionalavailability.com/

Biringen, Z., Altenhofen, S., Aberle, J., Baker, M., Brosal, A., Bennett, S., . . . Swaim, R. (2012). Emotional availability, attachment, and intervention in center-based child care for infants and toddlers, *Developmental Psychopathology*, 24, 23–34. doi: 10.1017/S0954579411000630

Biringen, Z., Batten, R., Neelan, P., Altenhofen, S., Swaim, R., Bruce, A., Fetsch, R., Voitel, C., & Zachary, V. (2010). Emotional availability (EA): The assessment of and intervention for global parent-child relational quality. *Journal of Experiential Psychotherapy*, 49, 3–9.

Biringen, Z., Derscheid, D., Vliegen, N., Closson, L., & Easterbrooks, A.E. (2014). Emotional availability (EA): Theoretical background, empirical research using the EA Scales, and clinical applications. *Developmental Review*, 34, 114–167.

Biringen, Z., Harman, J., Saunders, H., & Emde, R. (2017). Attachment security and emotional availability: The broadening of two prominent concepts. In N.R. Silton (Ed.) *Family Dynamics and Romantic Relationships in a Changing Society* (pp. 246–265). IGI Global.

Biringen, Z., Moorlag, A., Meyer, B., Wood, J., Aberle, J., Altenhofen, S., Bennett, S. (2008). The emotional availability (EA) intervention with child care professionals. *Journal of Early Childhood and Infant Psychology*, 4, 39–52.

Biringen, Z., Robinson, J., & Emde, R. (1993). *Emotional Availability Scales, 2nd Edition*. [Unpublished Manual for the EAS-training]. www.emotionalavailability. com

Biringen, Z., Robinson, J., & Emde, R. (1998). *Emotional Availability Scales, 3rd ed.* [Unpublished Manual for the EAS-training]. www.emotionalavailability.com

Biringen, Z., Skillern, S., Mone, J., & Pianta, R. (2005). Emotional availability is predictive of the emotional aspects of childrens' "school readiness." *Journal of Early Childhood and Infant Psychology*, 1, 81–97.

Boldt, L.J., Kochanska, G., Yoon, J.E., Nordling, J.K. (2014). Children's attachment to both parents from toddler age to middle childhood: Links to adaptive and maladaptive outcomes. *Attachment & Human Development*, 16(3), 211–229. doi: 10.1080/14616734.2014.889181.

Bowlby, J. (1969). *Attachment and loss: Vol 1. Attachment.* Basic Books.

Brennan, K. A., Clark, C. L., & Shaver, P. R. (1998). Self-report measurement of adult romantic attachment: An integrative overview. In J. A. Simpson & W. S. Rholes (Eds.), *Attachment theory and close relationships* (46-76). Guilford Press.

Bretherton, I. (1990). Communication patterns, internal working models, and the intergenerational transmission of attachment relationships. *Infant Mental Health Journal*, 11(3). 237–252.

Bretherton, I., & Oppenheim, D. (2003). The MacArthur Story Stem Battery: Development, administration, reliability, validity, and reflections about meaning. In R.N. Emde, D.P. Wolf, & D. Oppenheim (Eds.) *Revealing the inner worlds of young children: The MacArthur Story Stem Battery and parent-child narratives* (pp. 55–80). Oxford University Press.

Britner, P.A., Marvin, R.S., & Pianta, R.C. (2005). Development and preliminary validation of the caregiving behavior system: Association with child attachment classification in the preschool strange situation. *Attachment and Human Development*, 7(1), 83–102. doi: 10.1080/14616730500039861

Burgess, K.B., Marshall, P.J., Rubin, K.H., & Fox, N.A. (2003). Infant attachment and temperament as predictors of subsequent externalizing problems and cardiac physiology. *Journal of Child Psychology and Psychiatry*, 44, 819–831. doi: 10.1111/1469-7610.00167

Carlson, E. (1998). A prospective longitudinal study of attachment disorganization/ disorientation. *Child Development*, 69(4), 1107–1128.

Cassibba, R., van IJzendoorn, M. H., & D'Odorico, L. (2000). Attachment and play in child care centres: Reliability and validity of the attachment Q-sort for mothers and professional caregivers in Italy. *International Journal of Behavioral Development*, 24(2), 241–255.

Crowell, J.A., Waters, E., Treboux, D., O'Connor, E., Colon-Downs, C., Feider, O., ... & Posada, G. (1996). Discriminant validity of the adult attachment interview. *Child Development*, 2584–2599.

Dallaire, D. H., & Weinraub, M. (2007). Infant–mother attachment security and children's anxiety and aggression at first grade. *Journal of Applied Developmental Psychology*, 28(5-6), 477–492.

De Wolff, M.S., & van IJzendoorn, M.H. (1997). Sensitivity and attachment: A meta-analysis on parental antecedents of infant attachment. *Child Development*, 68(4), 571–591.

Drake, K., Belsky, J., & Fearon, R. M. (2014). From early attachment to engagement with learning in school: The role of self-regulation and persistence. *Developmental Psychology*, 50(5), 1350–1361. doi: 10.1037/a0032779.

Dykas, M. J., & Cassidy, J. (2011). Attachment and the processing of social information across the life span: Theory and evidence. *Psychological Bulletin*, 137(1), 19–46. doi: 10.1037/a0021367

Easterbrooks, M. A., Chaudhuri, J. H., & Gestsdottir, S. (2005). Patterns of emotional availability among young mothers and their infants: A dyadic, contextual analysis. *Infant Mental Health Journal*, 26(4), 309–326.

Easterbrooks, M. A., Bureau, J.-F., & Lyons-Ruth, K. (2012). Developmental correlates and predictors of emotional availability in mother–child interaction: A longitudinal study from infancy to middle childhood. *Development and Psychopathology*, 24(1), 65–78.

Espinet, S.D., Jeong, J.J., Motz, M., Racine, N., Major, D., & Pepler, D. (2013). Multimodal assessment of the mother-child relationship in a substance-exposed sample: Divergent associations with the Emotional Availability Scales. *Infant Mental Health Journal*, 34, 496–507. doi: 10.1002/imhj.21409

Fearon, R.P., Bakermans-Kranenburg, M.J., van IJzendoorn, M.H., Lapsley, A.M., & Roisman, G.I. (2010). The significance of insecure attachment and disorganization in the development of children's externalizing behavior: A meta-analytic study. *Child Development*, 81(2), 435–456. doi: 10.1111/j.1467-8624.2009.01405.x

Flykt & Biringen, Z. (2016). *Explanation of the use of the EA Scales for use with parents and their adult children* [Unpublished manuscript]. Colorado State University.

Fraley, R. C., Waller, N. G., & Brennan, K. A. (2000). An item response theory analysis of self-report measures of adult attachment. *Journal of Personality and Social Psychology, 78*(2), 350–365.

Fraley, R.C. (2002). Attachment stability from infancy to adulthood: Meta-analysis and dynamic modeling of developmental mechanisms. *Personality and Social Psychology Review, 6*(2), 123–151. doi: 10.1207/S15327957PSPR0602_03

Friedman, S.L. & Boyle, D.E. (2008). Attachment in US children experiencing non-maternal care in the early 1990s. *Attachment and Human Development, 10*(3), 225–261. doi: 10.1080/14616730802113570.

George, C., Kaplan, N., & Main, M. (1984, 1985, 1986). *The Adult Attachment Interview* [Unpublished protocol]. University of California at Berkeley.

Gottman, J.M., Coan, J., Carrere, S., & Swanson, C. (1998). Predicting marital happiness and stability from newlywed interactions. *Journal of Marriage and the Family, 60*(1), 5–22.

Groh, A.M., Fearon, R.M.P, van IJzendoorn, M.H., Bakermans-Kranenberg, M.J., & Roisman, G.I. (2017). Attachment in the early life course: Meta-analytic evidence for its role in socioemotional development. *Child Development Perspectives, 11*(1), 70–76. doi: 10.1111/cdep.12213.

Groh, A.M., Roisman, G.I., Booth-LaForce, C., Fraley, R.C., Owen, M.T., Cox, M.J., & Burchinal, M.R. (2014). IV. Stability of attachment security from infancy to late adolescence. *Monographs of the Society for Research in Child Development, 79*(3), 51–66. doi: 10.1111/mono.12113

Hamilton, C. E. (2000). Continuity and discontinuity of attachment from infancy through adolescence. *Child Development, 71*(3), 690–694. doi:10.1111/1467-8624.00177

Harman, J.J., & Biringen, Z. (2016). *Parents acting badly: How institutions and societies promote the alienation of children from their loving families.* Colorado Parental Alienation Project.

Hazan, C., & Shaver, P. (1987). Romantic love conceptualized as an attachment process. *Journal of Personality and Social Psychology, 52,* 511. doi: 10.1037/0022-3514.52.3.511

Hesse, E. (2008). The Adult Attachment Interview: Protocol, method of analysis, and empirical studies. In J. Cassidy & P.R. Shaver (Eds.) *Handbook of attachment: Theory, research, and clinical applications*, 2nd ed. (pp. 552–598). Guilford Press.

Howes, C., & Smith, E. W. (1995). Relations among child care quality, teacher behavior, children's play activities, emotional security, and cognitive activity in child care. *Early Childhood Research Quarterly, 10*(4), 381–404.

Kim, B., Chow, S., Bray, B., & Teti, D.M. (2017). Trajectories of mothers' emotional availability: Relations with infant temperament in predicting attachment security. *Attachment & Human Development*, 19(1), 38–57. doi: 10.1080/14616734.2016.1252780

Kochanska, G., & Kim, S. (2013). Early attachment organization with both parents and futurebehavior problems: From infancy to middle childhood. *Child Development*, 84(1), 283–296.

Laible, D. (2004). Mother-child discourse in two contexts: Links with child temperament, attachment security, and socioemotional competence. *Developmental Psychology*, 40(6), 979–992. doi: 10.1037/0012-1649.40.6.979

Lewis, M., Feiring, C., & Rosenthal, S. (2000). Attachment over time. *Child Development*, 71, 707–720. doi: 10.1111/1467-8624.00180

Lotzin, A., Lu, X., Kriston, L., Schiborr, J., Musal, T., Romer, G., & Ramsauer, B. (2015). Observational tools for measuring parent–infant interaction: A systematic review. *Clinical Child and Family Psychology Review*, 18(2), 99–132. doi:10.1007/s10567-015-0180-z

Lyons-Ruth, K. (2015). Dissociation and the parent–infant dialogue: A longitudinal perspective from attachment research. *Attachment*, 9(3), 253–276.

Lyons-Ruth, K., Alpern, L., & Repacholi, B. (1993). Disorganized infant attachment classification and maternal psychosocial problems as predictors of hostile-aggressive behavior in the preschool classroom. *Child Development*, 64, 572–585. doi: 10.1111/j.1467-8624.1993.tb02929.x

Lyons-Ruth, K., Melnick, S., Bronfman, E., Sherry, S., & Llanas, L. (2004). Hostile-helpless relational models and disorganized attachment patterns between parents and their young children: Review of research and implications for clinical work. *Attachment Issues in Psychopathology and Intervention*, 65–94. doi: 10.1002/imhj.20008

Lyons-Ruth, K. & Spielman, E. (2004). Disorganized infant attachment strategies and helpless-fearful profiles of parenting: Integrating attachment research with clinical intervention. *Infant Mental Health Journal*, 25(4), 318–335.

Main, M., Hesse, E., & Kaplan, N. (2005). *Predictability of attachment behavior and representational processes at 1, 6, and 19 years of age: The Berkeley Longitudinal Study.* In K.E. Grossmann, K. Grosmann, & E. Waters (Eds.), *Attachment from infancy to adulthood: The major longitudinal studies* (pp. 245–304). Guilford Press.

Main, M. & Solomon, J. (1986). Discovery of an insecure disorganized/disoriented attachment pattern: procedures, findings and implications for the classification of behavior. In T. B. Brazelton & M.W. Yogman (Eds.), *Affective development in infancy*. Ablex Publishing.

Main, M. & Cassidy, J. (1988) Categories of response to reunion with the parent at age 6: Predictable from infant attachment classifications and stable over a 1-month period. *Developmental Psychology* 24(3), 415–426.

Morley, T.E., & Moran, G. (2011). The origins of cognitive vulnerability in early childhood: Mechanisms linking early attachment to later depression. Clinical Psychology Review, 31(7), 1071–1082. doi: 10.1016/j.cpr.2011.06.006

NICHD Early Child Care Research Network (1997). The effects of infant child care on infant-mother attachment security: Results of the NICHD study of early child care. *Child Development,* 68(5), 860-879.

NICHD Early Child Care Research Network (2006). Infant–mother attachment: Risk and protection in relation to changing maternal caregiving quality over time. *Developmental Psychology,* 42(1), 38–58.

Ogawa, J.R., Sroufe, L.A., Weinfield, N.S., Carlson, E., & Egeland, B. (1997). Development and the fragmented self: Longitudinal study of dissociative symptomatology in a non-clinical sample. *Development and Psychopathology,* 9(4), 855–1164.

Pederson, D.R., Moran, G., & Bento, S. (1999). Maternal Behaviour Q-sort. *Psychology Publications.* Paper 1. http://ir.lib.uwo.ca/psychologypub/1

Robinson, J. (2007). Story stem narratives with young children: Moving to clinical research and practice. *Attachment & Human Development,* 9(3), 179–185.

Roelofs, J., Meesters, C., ter Huurne, M., Bamelis, L., & Muris, P. (2006). On the links between attachment style, parental rearing behaviors, and internalizing and externalizing problems in non-clinical children. *Journal of Child and Family Studies,* 15(3), 319–332. doi: 10.1007/s10826-006-9025-1

Roisman, G.I., Holland, A., Fortuna, K., Fraley, R.C., Clausell, E., & Clarke, A. (2007). The Adult Attachment Interview and self-reports of attachment style: An empirical rapprochement. *Journal of Personality and social Psychology,* 92(4), 678–697. doi: 10.1037/0022-3514.92.4.678

Sagi, A., Koren-Karie, N., Gini, M., Ziv, Y., & Joels, T. (2002). Shedding further light on the effects of various types and quality of early child care on infant–mother attachment relationships: The Haifa study of early child care. *Child Development,* 73(4), 1166–1186.

Salo, S., Flykt, M., Isosävi, S., Punamäki, R-J., Kalland, M., Biringen, Z., & Pajulo, M. (2019).Validating an observational measure of prenatal emotional availability among mothers with depressive symptoms. *Journal of Prenatal and Perinatal Psychology and Health,* 34, 55–73.

Saunders, H., Krause, A., Barone, L., & Biringen, Z. (2015). Emotional availability: Theory, research, and intervention. *Frontiers in Psychology*, 6. 1069. Special Issue on "Parenthood from biology to relation: Prevention, assessment, and interventions for developmental and clinical issues." Hosted by Dr(s) Allesandra Simonelli and Silvia Silcuni. doi: 10.3389/fpsyg.2015.01069

Saunders, H., Sarche, M., Trucksess, C., Morse, B., & Biringen, Z. (under review). Parents' adverse childhood experiences and parent-child emotional availability in an American Indian community: Relations with young children's social-emotional development. [Submitted for publication].

Shaver, P.R., Schachner, D.A., & Mikulincer, M. (2005). Attachment style, excessive reassurance seeking, relationship processes, and depression. *Personality and Social Psychology Bulletin*, 31(3), 343–359. doi: 10.1177/0146167204271709

Söderberg A. K., Elfors, C., Holmqvist Larsson, M., Falkenstr.m, F., & Holmqvist, R. (2013). Emotional availability in psychotherapy: The usefulness and validity of the emotional availability scales for analyzing the psychotherapeutic relationship. *Psychotherapy Research*, 24(1), 91–102.

Solomon, J. & George, C. (1999). The measurement of attachment security in infancy and childhood. In J. Cassidy & P.R. Shaver (Eds.), *Handbook of attachment: Theory, research, and clinical applications*. Guilford Press.

Sroufe, L.A. (1983). Infant-caregiver attachment and patterns of adaptation in preschool: The roots of competence and maladaptation. In M. Perlmutter (Ed.), *Minnesota Symposium in Child Psychology* (Vol. 16, pp. 41–83). Erlbaum Associates.

Sroufe, L.A. (1997). Psychopathology as an outcome of development. *Development and Psychopathology*, 9(2), 251–268

Sroufe, L.A. (2000). Early relationships and the development of children. *Infant Mental Health Journal*, 21(1-2), 67–74.

Sutherland, K., Altenhofen, S., & Biringen, Z. (2012). Emotional availability during mother–child interactions in divorcing and intact married families. *Journal of Divorce & Remarriage*, 53(2), 126–141.doi: 10.1080/10502556.2011.651974

van IJzendoorn, M.H., Vereijken, C.M.J.L., Bakermans-Kranenburg, M.J., & Riksen-Walraven, J.M. (2004). Assessing attachment security with the Attachment Q-Sort: Meta-analytic evidence for the validity of the observer AQS. *Child Development*, 75(4), 1188–1213. doi: 10.1111/j.1467-8624.2004.00733.x

Warren, S., Huston, L., Egeland, B., & Sroufe, L.A. (1997). Child and adolescent anxiety disorders and early attachment. *Journal of the American Academy of Child and Adolescent Psychiatry*, 36(5), 637– 644.

Waters, E. (1987). Appendix A: The Attachment Q-Set (Version 3.0). *Monographs of the Society for Research in Child Development, 60,* 234-246. doi: 10.2307/1166181

Waters, E. & Deane, K. (1985). Defining and assessing individual differences in attachment relationships: Q-methodology and the organization of behavior in infancy and early childhood. In I. Bretherton and E. Waters (Eds.), Growing pains of attachment theory and research: *Monographs of the Society for Research in Child Development, 50,* Serial No. 209 (1-2), 41–65.

Waters, H.S., Rodrigues, L.M., & Ridgeway, D. (1998). Cognitive underpinnings of narrative attachment assessment. *Journal of Experimental Child Psychology, 71*(3), 211–234.

Weinberg, M.K., & Tronick, E.Z. (1996). Infant affective reactions to the resumption of maternal interaction after the still-face. *Child Development, 67*(3), 905–914.

ZERO TO THREE. (2005). Diagnostic classification of mental health and developmental disorders of infancy and early childhood (rev. ed.). Washington, DC: Author.

Using Filling Stations for Mathematics Skill Building in Kindergarten: Harnessing Technology Tools to Remediate Skill Deficits

Melissa Stormont and Mary Decker

Abstract

Education professionals and researchers have underscored the importance of mathematics education for young children and the awareness that young children can learn early mathematics concepts that serve as a foundation for later years. The need for teachers to support individual needs for some children to build their conceptual understanding is clear as many children show deficits during kindergarten while others are ready to advance to the next areas of instruction. One way to meet the needs of children who need more work in foundational areas of mathematics is to utilize technology within filling stations in the classroom. To this end, this article discusses ways to expose children to more work in basic concepts and skills in mathematics through the use of a filling station with technology supports for children to work on foundational skills.

Keywords: Kindergarten Readiness, Early Math Concepts, Technology

Allison Hernandez looks around her kindergarten classroom buzzing with learning. She has just finished a whole group math lesson and is waiting on a small group of students to join her at a table for some more individualized practice. Ms. Hernandez wondered how she was going to meet the needs of all 20 students? At times meeting the learning needs of all the students in her classroom seemed overwhelming. The school bought the class some iPads to use, but Allison didn't know where to begin with incorporating them into daily instruction. Shannon, a bubbly child, came bounding to the table eager to start work with her group. Shannon loves math, science and technology but struggles to illustrate or talk about her thinking. Ms. Hernandez wondered how if she could use the two class iPads to help Allison practice math in an engaging way when she was meeting with other students. This problem is one that many teachers face, meeting the needs of all of the learners, especially in mathematics, and leveraging technological resources that teachers already have access to in ways that aid student learning.

For many years, experts in the areas of teaching, young children, and mathematics education have stressed the importance of mathematics for young children, emphasizing that 3- to 6-year-olds can learn early mathematics concepts that can be built upon in later years (National Association for the Education of Young Children, 2002; National Council of Teachers of Mathematics [NCTM], 2007; National Mathematics Advisory Panel, 2008). In addition, research has found that early math concepts such as knowledge of numbers and quantity were the most powerful predictors of later learning. Research indicates that mathematical teaching is under emphasized when compared to reading. This is unfortunate when considering that most young children are developmentally ready to build on their math knowledge. Therefore, the purpose of this article is to address the need to provide instruction in early mathematics and to outline some simple ways to support children with skill deficits. The following sections will review literature on children's early mathematics abilities and foundational skill deficits.

In most cases, children learn to discriminate between and among quantities of numbers as early as age 4 (Griffin, 2002, 2004). For example, given two piles of objects, they can tell which pile has more or less. By 6 years of age, most children use this knowledge combined with their counting knowledge to form a mental number line (Siegler & Booth, 2004). In time, they understand that numbers later in the count list have larger quantities than earlier quantities (LeCorre & Carey, 2006); for example, one is smaller than two. Many different factors influence children's early mathematics knowledge (Bodovski & Farkas, 2007; Crosnoe et al., 2010; Magnuson, Ruhm, & Waldfogel, 2007; Palardy & Rumberger, 2008) including whether teachers provide instruction in math. In many classrooms around the country kindergarten teachers report teaching mathematic far less than reading (Bargaglioti et al., 2009; Morton & Dalton, 2007).

In addition to mathematics content receiving less time than reading, the curriculum used for instruction may be misaligned with many students' abilities. Research using nationally representative data found that children received instruction in topics in which the majority of students entering kindergarten have already mastered (Engel et al., 2013). Skills such as counting and knowledge of basic shapes were highly emphasized, yet 95% of students were seen as proficient on these skills based on their kindergarten entry screening assessments. While most students do not need instruction on these core skills, it is imperative to quickly and efficiently remediate these skills with children who are lacking them. This remediation may place them on a math trajectory that is far more favorable than if the skills are not remediated. Accordingly, teachers should consider conducting more targeted mathematics skill assessments in kindergarten to determine children's conceptual levels and then make decisions regarding instructional needs.

Among the skills and concepts important to assess, children with early math difficulties, including children with and at risk for learning disabilities, often have weak number sense. Weak number sense is displayed by weak counting procedures, slow fact retrieval, and inaccurate computation (Geary, Hamson, & Hoard, 2000; Jordan, Hanich, & Kaplan, 2003a, 2003b). It can be challenging for teachers to determine how to remediate skill differences in some children when the vast majority of peers have mastered skills and need to move forward in the curriculum. Teachers can use criterion referenced assessments or teacher made skill assessments to determine children's current mathematics knowledge and skills in order to target skills for instruction.

Importantly, teachers can provide experiences that meet the needs of children with early math difficulties by using technological tools to provide learning experiences and meaningful feedback to children and teachers. To this end, in this article we provide two strategies for incorporating technology into early math skills instruction including video self-modeling and exit slips with technology. Creative ways to utilize existing technology features are also discussed. According to the Division of Early Childhood's (DEC) 2014 recommended practices, the supports outlined in this article can be matched to the assessment and instructional practice guidelines. For example, DEC recommended Instruction Practices include practices that: Identify skills for instruction and promote the development of skills in natural, inclusive environments (INS2); Use data for decision making and inclusion (INS3); provide appropriate level of support for learning (INS4); and Embed such instruction within environments to support authentic learning opportunities within a meaningful context (INS 5). These recommended practices could begin as an extension of daily instruction by using filling stations as a place children and go and build foundational skills.

Filling Stations

One way to structure classroom environments is to create "filling stations" for remediating prior knowledge needs. Filling stations are a metaphor for a place (e.g., centers) where children can be exposed to knowledge they currently lack. These centers provide support to students who may be lacking in understanding a place to practice a skill while still other students in the class work on other tasks. The remainder of the article will give educators examples of filling stations infused with technology to remediate skills essential to future success. For example, a teacher like Ms. Hernandez (case example from beginning) would likely find the idea of filling stations valuable.

Video self-modeling. Video modeling is an evidence based practice often used to help teach behaviors to students with disabilities, particularly individuals with autism (Franzone & Collet-Klingenberg, 2008). However, video modeling could easily be adapted to demonstrate academic skills for students who may need a little extra practice. Modeling with guided and independent practice opportunities are evidence based practices that are effective for children at risk for failure in school (Stormont, Reinke, Herman, & Lembke, 2012). Types of video modeling include basic video modeling, video self-modeling, and point-of-view video modeling. Basic video modeling involves recording someone besides the learner engaging in the target behavior or skill (i.e., models). The video is then viewed by the learner at a later time. Video self-modeling is used to record the learner displaying the target skill or behavior and is reviewed later. Point- of-view video modeling is when the target behavior or skill is recorded from the perspective of the learner. Any of these types of modeling would be an effective way to teach or record a student performing a mathematical task.

To implement this strategy in the classroom teachers could use a device of their choosing. IPads, Chromebooks, laptops, and many cell phones all come equipped with a program to record. Teachers would decide which type of video modeling they would want to record. The teacher would then record either themselves, or their students modeling the expected task and save the recording. Students needing extra practice could later access the recording and perform the task with the model or watch the model and then independently practice the task.

Another option would be to have the student record themselves performing the mathematical task. The would allow the teachers to have a copy to assess the student and check for growth. Students could go back and watch themselves. This can be an engaging task for many students and it allows teachers to go back at a time of their choosing to assess and make educational decisions.

Ms. Hernandez determined that in group work Shannon needed more practice with counting and one to one correspondence. At a quiet time of the day she set up an iPad to record herself with the built-in camera on the iPad. Using the counters that she used with her groups, she laid out a group and clearly touched each one and counted it. She did this each time, slowly counting the group 2 times so that the student had time to count along with the video later. She saved this video in the photos and taught Shannon how to get to it. With little instruction, Shannon navigated to the video with ease and had a little much needed practice on this essential skill.

Snap a Picture: Exit slips. Snap a picture is a flexible way to help students, especially those with limited verbal ability, show their understanding. In this filling station, students use technology to take a picture of their knowledge to explain what they know. Teachers could collect outdated technology such as older digital cameras or older cell phones, that still functionally take a digital picture, but may not be in use. The student is then given a task such as find or make groups of 4. The student would then find things related to the task and photograph them. In addition to allowing students to practice mathematical concepts, this allows teachers to have a record of performance. Many tasks or concepts could be addressed using this technology including size (snap a picture of something bigger than a counter or smaller than you), shapes (snap a picture of things that look like circles), or visual numbers (snap a picture of the number 4). This task allows documentation of student growth while assessing for understanding. It would be important that the teacher reviews the photographs and confers with the student about their pictures to give essential feedback.

Ms. Hernandez decided to have Allison and Shannon try snapping a picture with different groups of numbers. Ms. Hernandez made note cards with numbers on them. She then taught them both how to use the built in camera, and gave them a box of manipulatives. They were excited to use this filling station; they worked with the manipulatives to represent number groupings, carefully counting and recounting before they snapped a picture.

Utilizing existing technology applications for skill building. Every device comes with built in features that could reinforce ideas children are learning in the classroom. Students could use the calendar and weather feature to create their own physical calendar. Writing down the expected temperature to determine patterns, such as recording cloudy days in the form of graphs, are all ways to possibly encourage students to utilize their resources as well and build on routines that exist in many classrooms.

One feature that is on many devices is the calculator. Groves and Stacey (1998) found that when given the opportunity to use a calculator many students used it as a "scratch pad." When given a question (How many feet do you have? How many legs does a spider have?) students would record their answer with the numbers on the calculator. This encouraged students to connect words with numbers and quantities while taking the barrier of physically writing the numerals away. This is important because counting is fundamental to mathematical growth (NCTM, 2009). Teachers could use the automatic-constant feature that is programed to most devices to practice counting, skip counting and counting backwards. The calculator can help a student learn counting as they practice counting out loud with it. If this task is too difficult for students, talking calculator, and talking calculator apps are available for free. When the buttons are pushed, the calculator "speaks" the number, which is helpful language support for young children as well.

Finally, on iPads, old cell phones or iPods students could use a texting feature that is already built in. Using the building Wi-Fi, where available, students could text the teacher mathematical representations. For example, students may want to show the quantity 8. They could type the number 8 and represent that number with the appropriate amount of emojis. This engaging activity allows students to creatively engage in mathematics, while again allowing the teacher to collect student work samples and provide necessary feedback. This representation is more challenging for most children and should come after demonstrated fluency with manipulatives. These products can also be used as exit slips to document student performance.

Conclusion

Math education is an important but often under emphasized subject in kindergarten classrooms; many teachers struggle to meet the needs of all learners. Technology is one way to allow students to explore math related ideas in structured ways such as through filling stations. This article outlined in detail how teachers can both utilize filling stations in meaningful ways and take advantage of technology to support meeting more children's needs for support in kindergarten classrooms.

References

Bargagliotti, A. E., Guarino, C. M., & Mason, W.M. (2009). Mathematics Instruction in Kindergarten and First Grade in the United States at the Start of the 21st century. *UCLA: California Center for Population Research*. Retrieved from https://escholarship.org/uc/item/41d5q1c5

Bodovski, K., & Farkas, G. (2007). Do instructional practices contribute to inequality in achievement? The case of mathematics instruction in kindergarten. *Journal of Early Childhood Research*, 5(3), 301-322.

Crosnoe, R., Morrison, F., Burchinal, M., Pianta, R., Keating, D., Friedman, S. L., & Clarke-Stewart, K. A. (2010). Instruction, teacher–student relations, and math achievement trajectories in elementary school. *Journal of Educational Psychology*, 102(2), 407.

Division for Early Childhood. (2014). DEC recommended practices in early intervention/early childhood special education 2014. Retrieved from http://www.dec-sped.org/recommendedpractices

Engel, M., Claessens, A., & Finch, M. A. (2013). Teaching students what they already know? The (mis) alignment between mathematics instructional content and student knowledge in kindergarten. *Educational Evaluation and Policy Analysis*, 35(2), 157-178.

Franzone, E., & Collet-Klingenberg, L. (2008). Overview of video modeling. *Madison, WI: The National Professional Development Center on Autism Spectrum Disorders, Waisman Center. University of Wisconsin*, 1-2.

Geary, D. C., Hamson, C. O., & Hoard, M. K. (2000). Numerical and arithmetical cognition: A longitudinal study of process and concept deficits in children with learning disability. *Journal of Experimental Child Psychology*, 77(3), 236-263.

Griffin, S. (2004). Building number sense with Number Worlds: A mathematics program for young children. *Early Childhood Research Quarterly*, 19(1), 173-180.

Griffin, S. (2002). The development of math competence in the preschool and early school years: Cognitive foundations and instructional strategies. *Mathematical Cognition*, 1-32.

Groves, S., & Stacey, K. (1998). Calculators in primary mathematics: Exploring number before teaching algorithms. *The teaching and learning of algorithms in school mathematics*, 120-129.

Jordan, N. C., Hanich, L. B., & Kaplan, D. (2003). A longitudinal study of mathematical competencies in children with specific mathematics difficulties versus children with comorbid mathematics and reading difficulties. *Child Development*, 74(3), 834-850.

Jordan, N. C., Hanich, L. B., & Kaplan, D. (2003). Arithmetic fact mastery in young children: A longitudinal investigation. *Journal of Experimental Child Psychology*, 85(2), 103-119.

Le Corre, M., Van de Walle, G., Brannon, E. M., & Carey, S. (2006). Re-visiting the competence/performance debate in the acquisition of the counting principles. *Cognitive psychology*, 52(2), 130-169

Morton, B. A., & Dalton, B. (2007). Changes in Instructional Hours in Four Subjects by Public School Teachers of Grades 1 through 4. Stats in Brief. NCES 2007-305. *National Center for Education Statistics*.

Magnuson, K. A., Ruhm, C., & Waldfogel, J. (2007). Does prekindergarten improve school preparation and performance? *Economics of Education Review, 26*(1), 33-51.

National Association for the Education of Young Children and National Council of Teachers of Mathematics. (2002). *Early childhood mathematics: Promoting good beginnings.* [Position statement].

National Research Council. (2009). *Mathematics learning in early childhood: Paths toward excellence and equity.* National Academies Press.

National Mathematics Advisory Panel. (2008). *Foundations for success: The final report of the National Mathematics Advisory Panel.* US Department of Education.

Palardy, G. J., & Rumberger, R. W. (2008). Teacher effectiveness in first grade: The importance of background qualifications, attitudes, and instructional practices for student learning. *Educational Evaluation and Policy Analysis, 30*(2), 111-140.

Siegler, R. S., & Booth, J. L. (2004). Development of numerical estimation in young children. *Child Development, 75*(2), 428-444.

Stormont, M., Reinke, W., Herman, K., & Lembke, E. (2012). *Tier two interventions: Academic and behavior supports for children at risk for failure.* Guilford.

SPECIAL FOCUS

Promoting Health and Wellness
in Preschoolers

Positive Development for Preschooler Well-Being

Melissa Bray and Cheryl Maykel

Abstract

The intent of this special section on promoting mind-body health in preschoolers is to review the related areas of assessment, intervention, and physical health care practices. The preschool years are a time of critical development, growth, and vulnerability. Growth trajectories put in place and supported across settings can lead to positive outcomes. However, these can be interrupted during periods of trauma. It is at these times that the overall wellness of these youth requires careful support. This introduction reviews preschool mind-body health development, assessment, and intervention within a cultural context, both as part of typical development and in the case of traumatic events such as the COVID-19 pandemic.

Keywords: *Mind Body Health, Physical Health and Wellness*

The initial reason for this special section was to highlight what is known in the area of mind-body health in the preschool-aged child across the areas of assessment, intervention, and physical health practices that in their totality promote overall well-being. This introduction serves first to describe how a preschooler comes to be in relation to the topics covered by the articles in this issue. However, this introduction now also pays particular consideration to the effects of trauma and the current COVID-19 pandemic. The final summary piece of this special section reflects on the issue as a whole through the lens of broader considerations, while identifying areas that are in need of further consideration in future research.

There are a number of various perspectives from which we could consider the early years of a child's mind and body development and the foundation for an individual's overall well-being. Evidence shows that even before a child is conceived, there are a multitude of environmental and genetic influences at play in shaping the child's development. The importance of a mother's physical health and environment is often the focus during pregnancy, yet we know that beyond these basic needs, social supports and psychological health are also key to a healthy pregnancy and the caring of an infant. During the early years, children typically develop resilience against various stressors through access to protective factors, including (1) trusting nurturing relationships; (2) safety; and (3) experiences to thrive (Srivastav et al., 2020). Warm and responsive caregiving, the development of strong positive attachments and a sense of trust, as well as an enriching early learning environment that promotes growth are all important factors, in addition to proper nutrition, adequate sleep, and other physical essentials.

For some children, exposure to particular adverse childhood experiences (ACEs) will have a significant impact on their develop-ment in the early years. The CDC classifies ACEs in three categories: abuse, neglect, and household dysfunction. Greater exposure to trauma as a youth increases risk for behavioral, physical, and mental health issues throughout the lifespan. As we write this article, we are in the early stages of the disruption caused by the COVID-19 pandemic. At this point, one can only surmise how far and wide the ripples of the events caused by this virus will reach; we cannot fully understand the extent of the fear, closures, food shortages, social distancing, financial loss, increased time at home, distance learning/teaching/working and so forth, or how it will impact life as we know it when society transitions to reopening. Our thinking has been affected in light of our current adjustment to a so-called "new normal," and we would be remiss if we did not consider the impact that these events will undoubtedly have on young children and their development in particular. The COVID-19 pandemic and all that it entails has been traumatic for many young children, though exposure and experiences of disruption and stress likely differ widely among youth and their families.

An important consideration is the stark differences in the experiences of children from varied socioeconomic levels, cultural backgrounds, and family dynamics. With preschools and other child-care centers closed, access to a variety of resources is restricted for many young children. Some young children will benefit from having an abundance of essential resources at home, as well as stimulating learning materials, quality time with family members, and other comforts. Others will experience comparatively increased levels of stress, domestic abuse, food scarcity, illness, isolation, and a lack of education and connection with others. Most will likely have some combination of both positive and negative experiences, but all young children are likely experiencing significant disruptions to daily life as it once was and may be fearful of what the future holds. After COVID-19, the return to school is not likely to be smooth academically, socially, or emotionally. Children may or may not be eager to return, but they will surely find that they are returning to a drastically altered school environment with new protocols in place.

James Redford has described childhood trauma and the bio-logical underpinnings that lead to changes in behavior as a result of these types of negative experiences that interrupt development

(Edwards, 2018). Redford has projected that similar outcomes related to trauma from COVID-19 will occur and that children will require support. Trauma-informed care practices include such mental health and learning strategies as those that promote engagement, empowerment, safety, and trust (Simpson & Green, 2014). These techniques, such as universal social and emotional learning curricula for students, are beginning to be adapted and successfully used for social emotional well-being and academic success in the preschool population. School mental health professionals, namely school psychologists, have been working to move trauma-informed care practices to the front lines within child development curricula (Conners-Burrow, 2013). These psychoeducational practices are imperative during the COVID-19 pandemic crisis and these professionals are needed more than ever. There is and will continue to be an increased need for assessment of academic and social emotional concerns, counseling, and physical health supports.

The protective factors that have been identified as relating most to treating ACEs and promoting trauma-informed healing need to be included when assessing and treating all students, especially the preschool population, who are developing these resiliencies (Srivastav et al., 2020). The ACE indices have shown to be effective in identifying critical intervention points during traumatic periods (Stork et al., 2020) and should be promoted for use by educational, psychological, and health care professionals. It will be even more important in the coming months for educators and physicians as well as mental health providers to carefully consider the impact of trauma when working with young children and their families, and more providers should be encouraged to use this measure. Further, these areas are being highlighted for consideration in upcoming policy design options that promote both school- and community-based efforts aimed at the improvement of family and educational systems that have been interrupted and disrupted for many young children during the pandemic.

In summary, as each child begins school, they enter the class-room with varying familial, social, and educational experiences. Further, it has been stated that the first three years of life are the most important to development and that personalities are well-formed by the age of five (Cipriano & Stifter, 2010). Therefore, by the time most children enter preschool at three or four years of age, they have already begun to develop a sense of self, certain beliefs about others, and notions about how they fit into an evolving narrative of the world around them. In this special section, we decided to focus on promoting health and wellness among preschoolers. To this end, there are articles on physical health, including nutrition and physical activity, school-based relationships between students and teachers, mind-body health interventions, and three articles focusing on the assessment of preschoolers: in general; within the socioemotional domain; and cognitive/academic readiness. A final conclusion piece seeks to provide some perspective on these topics through the lens of mind-body health and raises implications for work with preschoolers into the future. Health and well-being are not granted universally to all and can be disrupted during times of trauma, but fortunately can also be promoted, repaired, and main-tained with effort and intention over time.

References

Cipriano, E., & Stifter, C. (2010). PREDICTING Preschool Effortful Control from Toddler Temperament and Parenting Behavior. *Journal of Applied Developmental Psychology, 31*(3), 221–230.

Conners-Burrow, N., Kramer, T., Sigel, B., Helpenstill, K., Sievers, C., & Mckelvey, L. (2013). Trauma-informed care training in a child welfare system: Moving it to the front line. *Children and Youth Services Review, 35*(11), 1830–1835.

Edwards, C. (2018). Film Review Resilience: The Biology of Stress & The Science of Hope (2016) by James Redford (Director). *Child and Adolescent Social Work Journal, 35*(4), 435–437.

Simpson, R. & Green, S.A. (2014). Is your organization trauma-informed? [Infographic] Adapted from: Fallot, R.D & Harris, M. (2001). *Using trauma theory to design service systems: New directions for mental health services.* Jossey-Bass.

Srivastav, A., Spencer, M., Strompolis, M., Thrasher, J., Crouch, E., Palamaro-Munsell, E., & Davis, R. (2020). Exploring practitioner and policymaker perspectives on public health approaches to address Adverse Childhood Experiences (ACEs) in South Carolina. *Child Abuse & Neglect, 102.* doi: 10.1016/j.chiabu.2020.104391.

Stork, B.R., Akselberg, N.J., Qin, Y., & MIller, D.C. (2020). Adverse Childhood Experiences (ACEs) and community physicians: What we've learned. *The Permanente Journal, 24*(2), 43–49.

Nutritional Wellness in Preschoolers with Autism Spectrum Disorder

*Jayanthi Kandiah, Constance McIntosh,
and Naomi R. Boucher*

Abstract

Preschool age is a time when children experience erratic appetite and fluctuations in growth and development. Typically developing preschoolers have picky eating habits leading to varied nutrient deficiencies. Dietary inadequacies are further compromised in preschoolers with autism spectrum disorder (ASD) due to abnormal sensory sensitivity, social deficits, and repetitive behaviors of interests. To promote health and wellness in this population, school psychologists and educators in collaboration with registered dietitian nutritionists who are the food and nutrition experts need to identify avenues to promote healthy eating for this pediatric population. This article focuses on nutritional needs and considerations of preschoolers with emphasis on those with ASD, the role of school-based interventions, and practical tips for school psychologists and educators in the promotion of nutritional wellness in preschoolers with ASD.

Keywords: Preschoolers, Autism Spectrum Disorder, Nutrition, Health Care Professionals

Nutritional Wellness in Preschoolers with Autism Spectrum Disorder

Wellness, as defined by the Oxford Dictionary (2018), is the "state of being in good health." According to the World Health Organization (2018), health is "a state of complete physical, mental and social well-being and not merely the absence of disease or infirmity." By definition, wellness is holistic. Wellness encompasses not just physical but emotional and mental health as well. When attempting to create positive changes to improve health and wellness, starting in childhood is essential (American Academy of Pediatrics, 2020). School systems often focus on creating wellness initiatives or teams to better promote wellness within their student body (Profili et al., 2017).

School psychologists can take a lead role in creating these initiatives. For school psychologists to be successful in promoting wellness in preschools, they must be able to conceptualize their preschoolers holistically. This means they must consider the mental, emotional, and physical aspects of students' health while also addressing cultural and financial backgrounds that may impact access to health care. Children with special needs, such as those with autism spectrum disorder (ASD), must be given careful consideration. An effective way to promote wellness in a school setting for all children is by working with a factor that impacts various components of health (i.e., the physical, mental, and emotional constituents).

Nutrition is an excellent avenue for this goal, which is why under the Obama Administration many initiatives for creating healthier school lunches and removing unhealthy options from vending machines went into effect (US Department of Agriculture, 2013). There is supporting evidence that nutrition impacts physical health (Szucs & Stoffel, 2016). Current literature is finding stronger ties on the influence of nutrition with mental and emotional health than what was once theorized (Clay, 2017). Due to the impact nutrition has on multiple areas of health, working from a nutrition-based foundation is necessary when promoting wellness in children. This is especially true for those on the autism spectrum. The intent of this article is to discuss key nutritional considerations for school psychologists and other school professionals (e.g , teachers) working with preschoolers with ASD. The paper will cover the nutritional needs of preschoolers and considerations to support their healthy development. Further, this provides a brief framework of the importance of integrating interprofessional collaborative care into nutrition care for preschoolers.

Nutritional Needs and Considerations for Typically Developing Preschoolers

Formative years during early childhood is a critical time to establish healthy eating habits (AAP, 2016). For this reason, addressing nutrition in preschoolers is imperative. Adherence of healthy eating habits learned at this time could prevent the onset of chronic diseases (e.g. obesity, heart disease, high blood pressure, and type 2 diabetes). Since nutrition impacts all aspects of health and wellness, food selection and consumption have significant implications on the overall health status of children (AAP, 2016).

Nutrients including macronutrients (i.e. carbohydrate, fat, and protein), micronutrients (i.e. vitamins and minerals), and water are essential. Healthy development of preschoolers is dependent on eating a varied, balanced diet (AAP, 2016). These diets must also be nutrient dense and follow the dietary recommendations appropriate for the child's age. For example, macronutrients such as carbohydrates should provide 45%-65% of the total calorie intake each day (AAP, 2016; Academy of Nutrition and Dietetics, 2014). Carbohydrates should come from foods such as bread, potatoes, pasta, and rice. When balancing the diet of preschoolers, a larger portion of recommended amount of carbohydrates should be met through consumption of complex carbohydrates (i.e., fiber, and starch) while simple carbohydrates (i.e., disaccharides and monosaccharides) should be given in moderation. Examples of complex carbohydrates are whole grain breads, whole wheat products, beans, and peas. Simple carbohydrates are fruit juices, white bread, and sugary cereals. Lipids (fats) should contribute 25%-35% of the total calories of the preschoolers' diet each day (AAP, 2016; Academy of Nutrition and Dietetics, 2014). Examples of foods with healthy fats for preschoolers to incorporate include consumption of avocados, assortment of nuts, and use of oils such as canola or olive oil.

It is important to remember that limited amounts of foods with trans-fatty acids should be given to preschoolers. Trans-fatty acids are known to elevate total cholesterol and low-density lipo-protein cholesterol (Koletzko, 2015, pp. 51). Too much of trans-fatty acids predisposes preschoolers at risk for developing cardiovascular disease. Examples of foods high in trans-fatty acids are snack foods such as potato chips and/or processed baked goods. Healthy fats that preschoolers should be ingesting come from monounsaturated and polyunsaturated foods such plants oils, flax seeds, sunflower seeds, chia seeds and vegetable oils. Lastly, preschoolers should have 5%-20% of their calorie intake coming from proteins such as nuts, lean meats, fish, cheese, yogurt, legumes, or tofu (AAP, 2016; Academy of Nutrition and Dietetics, 2014).

In addition to meeting recommended levels of macro- and micro-nutrients, calorie requirements must also be attained. For preschool girls and boys, 1,200 calories/day and 1,400 calories/day are recommended, respectively (Academy of Nutrition and Dietetics, 2014). However, for macronutrients, per gram of carbohydrate and protein provides 4 calories while fat provides 9 calories/gram. Selection of nutrient dense, low-calorie foods should be consumed to prevent the onset of obesity and/or other chronic diseases during young age. Obesity may lead to health problems later in life such as heart disease. According to the CDC (2019), around 18.5% of children in the US are overweight, and children with autism are at an even higher risk (Voulgarakis et al., 2017).

Due to the potentially detrimental impact of a poor diet, pro-moting wellness through nutrition is a preventative care measure. Sometimes when a child's nutrient needs or calorie intake are unbalanced, it is not as easy to notice signs of nutrient deficiencies. Schools and parents must consider the nutritional value of types of foods served to all preschoolers, not just with preschoolers who are overweight. A child having insufficient amounts of dietary vitamin C may be of a healthy weight, but this is still a nutrient deficiency which needs to be addressed. Additionally, rarely do professionals consider mental health concerns such as depression, Attention Deficit Hyper-Activity Disorder (ADHD), and anxiety as being related to food. However, current research is revealing this as a fallacy (Clay, 2017). Evidence is supporting that nutritional interventions for mental health issues like depression or anxiety, show a beneficial effect (Clay, 2017). One intervention is increasing omega 3 (e.g. mackerel, salmon, flaxseeds, chia seeds, and walnuts) intake for depression and anxiety. When paired with psychological counseling, the positive impact is especially powerful (Clay, 2017). This is because nutrient deficiencies appear to impact dopamine and serotonin production, which is linked to issues in mental and emotional well-being (Clay, 2017). Deficiencies can also have physical consequences which could lead to improper growth or development of infections and diseases.

During the preschool developmental age. children begin to experience changes in their food preferences based on the preferences of those around them (Koletzko et al., 2015 pp. 118). The social influences (e.g. peer pressure, role modeling) preschoolers develop around food choice and eating behaviors may cause families to struggle with ensuring children are eating a balanced diet (Academy of Nutrition and Dietetics, 2014). Often preschoolers will reject fresh fruits and vegetables in preference of sweet or salty snacks like chips. When children eat alternatives to fresh produce, they may meet recommended calorie intake but may lack vital nutrients. Fruits and vegetables are excellent sources of vitamins and minerals that are less prevalent in other foods. Crucial nutrients during preschool years are fiber, calcium, vitamin C, and protein (AAP, 2016; Capone & Sentongo, 2019). Fiber and vitamin C are plant-based nutrients, so avoidance or rejection of these foods can be concerning (Capone

& Sentongo, 2019). Other nutrients of concern are vitamins E, K, folate, and magnesium (Capone & Sentongo, 2019). Frequently eaten foods such as dairy products which are excellent sources of calcium and meats high in protein are generally eaten by preschoolers in larger inappropriate portion sizes. The types of meat (e.g. processed high fat meats versus lean) and additives (e.g. added sugars in milk and yogurt) within these food groups could also lead to nutrient deficiencies.

Nutritional Needs and Considerations for Preschoolers with Autism Spectrum Disorder

Although nutrient deficiencies may be common in all pre-schoolers, those with autism are at an even greater risk (Johnson et al., 2014). Autism spectrum disorder (ASD) is a developmental disorder which is characterized by social deficits, abnormal sensory sensitivity, and restricted or repetitive behaviors of interests (APA, 2013). According to the CDC, the prevalence of ASD is 1 in 59, with males have greater incidence than females (CDC, 2018). For this reason, schools have given greater emphasis to learn and understand more about supporting their students with ASD. Symptoms of ASD impact many areas of a preschooler's life including nutrient intake. Preschoolers with ASD require the same nutrient and caloric intake as their typically developing peers, but the presence of their symp-toms causes meeting these nutrient requirements to be a challenge. ASD causes sensory sensitivity which has a drastic impact on the types of foods preschoolers are willing to ingest (Johnson et al., 2014). These sensitivities lead to what is known as "food selectivity." Food selectivity is when preschoolers with ASD will only accept foods based on their color, texture, or flavor (McIntosh, Kandiah, & Boucher, 2019). For example, a preschooler with autism may only want to eat foods that are white in color like potatoes, tofu, or bread. While typically developing preschoolers may not want to try foods for social reasons, preschoolers with ASD may be unable to even tolerate these food based on sensory and tactile characteristics. For autistic preschoolers, the texture, smell, color, or taste of food may be intolerable to their senses (McIntosh, Kandiah, & Boucher, 2019). Therefore, forcing preschoolers with ASD to try a food can lead to an outburst and behavioral problems if handled improperly.

In conjunction with sensory issues, children with ASD also have a higher likelihood of having food-related allergies or intolerances (Brasher, 2016). Allergies and intolerances to food cause children with ASD to be placed on special diets (e.g., elimination diets). Elimination diets exclude troublesome foods such as dairy, casein, gluten, and red food dyes. These foods have been linked to not only issues with digestion, but also externalizing behavior problems such as hyperactivity or tantrums (Brasher, 2016). When following these elimination diets, children will avoid staple food items like bread, pasta, milk, and cereals. Exclusion of these foods may lead to deficiency of nutrients such as vitamins A, D, K, phosphorus, potassium, folate, iron, and manganese (Capone & Sentongo, 2019; Malhi et al., 2017). Although refraining from gluten, casein, and lactose may be beneficial, the deficiencies caused by elimination diets could impair overall growth, development, and health. For example, if children with ASD are lactose intolerant, depending on their severity of their intolerance, they may be unable to drink milk, or eat yogurt and cheese. These three products are excellent sources of calcium and vitamin D. The major mineral calcium and vitamin D are critical to ensure bone development and prevent the occurrence of fractures. Parents and caregivers with children with ASD must be educated in alternative foods rich in these nutrients when fo lowing elimination diets (Capone & Sentongo, 2019).

Another nutrition-related risk factor for preschoolers' occurs when they are taking medications for comorbid physical or mental health concerns. While some preschoolers may have these concerns, special consideration must be given to those with ASD. This is because children with ASD are more likely to take medications than their typically developing counterparts (Madden et al., 2017). Many medications deplete the body of nutrients or impact the body's ability to absorb certain nutrients adequately (Mohn et al., 2018). For example, long term use of cardiovascular medications like warfarin cause an increased need for vitamin D and calcium (Mohn et al., 2018). Without supplementing or increasing foods high in vitamin D, children on this type of medication will see decreases in bone density, poor skin health, and inadequate insulin production (Capone & Sentongo, 2019). If unaddressed, preschoolers may develop early onset of osteoporosis or diabetes. Concurrently, medications may also inhibit the child's ability to consume certain foods. This can also limit the availability of nutrients they absorb. For example, Selective Serotonin Reuptake Inhibitors (SSRI), are antidepressants used to treat depression or anxiety. This serotonin-based medication may be impacted by eating citrus fruits (e.g. grapefruit or Seville oranges). The interaction of SSRIs and citrus fruits can interfere with the metabolism of the medication and affect its efficacy. Citrus fruits are very high in vitamin C, which is vital for vision and connective tissue development of preschoolers (Capone & Sentongo, 2019). Therefore, considerations must be made for preschoolers taking SSRIs to receive recommended levels of vitamin C in a way which does not precipitate further health complications. Medications may also contribute to changes in appetite (Madden et al., 2017), causing increased food refusal. The impact of this refusal may exacerbate concerns for further nutritional deficiencies in children with ASD.

School-based Intervention

Due to the multifaceted impact of nutrition on overall wellness, addressing nutrition concerns in preschools may be an excellent intervention. Nutrition is an accessible tool to use to promote wellness in young children because preschools provide significant opportunities for an assortment of balanced meals (e.g., breakfast, lunch, and snacks) for many children in the US. Using options like nutrition is paramount because it facilitates early intervention to occur. Appropriate nutrition intervention is imperative for addressing wellness because it will refrain the prevalence and development of further health disorders. If deficiencies go unaddressed for long duration, reversal of health problems through dietary interventions could become a challenge. The connectedness to the school communities and availability of resources could make implementation of nutrition interventions an easy process in the promotion of better health to preschoolers. For example, a preschool may be able to invite a Registered Dietitian Nutritionist (RDN) to learn about incorporation of creative well-balanced meals and snacks in school menus. An RDN could even host cooking demonstrations catered for parents/caregivers of preschoolers. Another idea is working with the parents of students who have Individualized Education Programs (IEPs) to investigate about a preschoolers eating habits. Through the IEP meetings, school professionals and parents can discuss how the school could best support preschoolers in achieving better nutrition. For children with ASD, another route would be creating Individualized Education Plans (IEPs) which include realistic and attainable nutrition-related goals and objectives. IEPs are best administered when interprofessional collaboration is integrated into the preschool's policies and procedures. To promote wellness, school staff may need to provide parents or collaborate with multiple external referrals like counselors, nurses, or RDNs. An example wou d be a team effort between school psychologists and teachers knowledgeable on developmental concerns of preschoolers in partnership with RDNs, the food and nutrition experts.

While these suggestions may vary on a school-by-school basis, the following tips provide a guideline for how to integrate collaborative efforts in promoting nutritional wellness in preschools. These tips should be generalized to the local resources available in school communities and be adapted to multicultural needs of the preschoolers and their families. It is also at the discretion of each preschool and their personnel to discuss and disseminate these tips to their groups (e.g. resources, communities, parents/caregivers).

Tips for School Psychologists and Educators

1. Meet with other faculty and health care professionals (e.g. Registered Dietitian Nutritionist, Nurse, Special Education Teacher, etc.) in the school environment about physical, mental, or emotional concerns of preschoolers.

2. Talk to parents, families and caregivers of preschoolers about observations made and concerns for their eating behaviors and nutritional wellness.

3. Recommend parents of preschoolers to identify their food preferences and to complete a 3-day food diary to be assessed and counseled by an RDN.

4. Identify creative ways to engage the preschooler in eating while at school. Generally, children with ASD are visual learners so share pictures and talk about the foods that they would be offered and served at mealtime.

5. Recommend specific routines, when it comes to mealtimes, snacks, and education as preschoolers with ASD respond to structure well.

6. Use language that is clear, simple, and unambiguous when educating and interacting with preschoolers.

7. Reference MyPlate.gov for nutritional information which meets the needs of preschool-aged children.

8. Become familiar with local RDNs for parental/caregiver referrals.

9. Educate parents on healthy eating and its importance to physical, emotional and mental health.

10. Adopt strategies to reduce preschoolers anxiety especially when it comes to tasting or trying new foods. This maybe a visual or verbal cue that the school psychologist or educator have established in advance to not draw attention to the preschooler with ASD when compared to neurotypical peers.

11. Plan outdoor activities that involve preschoolers with ASD moving and embed this into the nutrition or education lesson plans. Exercise has been shown to alleviate symptoms of autism.

12. Teach social emotional learning skills to preschoolers with ASD using picture books as a class or reading. Educators and psychologists can also demonstrate through role play or by watching videos.

13. Become familiar with local counseling services to refer families for help with stress or behavioral issues related to eating.

14. Be proactive in having multiple school professionals involved in interprofessional education meetings such as IEPs.

15. Collaborate with other preschool professionals in setting individualized realistic goals and objectives for developing and implementing IEP plans for preschoolers with ASD.

References

American Academy of Pediatrics. (2016). *Childhood Nutrition*. https://www.healthychildren.org/English/healthy-living/nutrition/Pages/Childhood-Nutrition.aspx

Brasher, S.N. (2016) Characterizing children with autism spectrum disorders (ASD) who respond to a gluten-free casein-free (GFCF) diet [Doctoral dissertation, University of Florida]. Institutional Repository at the University of Florida. https://ufdc.ufl.edu/UFE0050261/00001

Centers for Disease Control and Prevention. (2019). Overweight & obesity: Childhood obesity facts. https://www.cdc.gov/obesity/data/childhocd.html

Centers for Disease Control and Prevention. (2018). Autism spectrum disorder: Data & statistics. https://www.cdc.gov/ncbddd/autism/data.html

Capone, K., & Sentongo, T. (2019). The ABCs of nutrient deficiencies and toxicities. *Pediatric Annals, 48*(11), e434-e440. https://doi.org/10.3928/19382359-20191015-01

Clay, R.A. (2017). *The link between food and mental health.* Monitor on Psychology, 48(8), 26. https://www.apa.org/monitor/2017/09/food-mental-health

Johnson, C. R., Turner, K., Stewart, P. A., Schmidt, B., Shui, A., Macklin, E., ... & Hyman, S.M. (2014). Relationships between feeding problems, behavioral characteristics and nutritional quality in children with ASD. *Journal of Autism and Developmental Disorders, 44*(9), 2175-2184. https://doi.org/10.1007/s10803-014-2095-9

Madden, J.M., Lakoma, M.D., Lynch, F.L., Rusinak, D., Owen-Smith, A.A., Coleman, K.J., ...& Croen, L.A. (2017). Psychotropic medication use among insured children with autism spectrum disorder. *Journal of Autism and Developmental Disorders, 47*(1), 144-154. https://doi.org/10.1007/s10803-016-2946-7

Malhi, P., Venkatesh, L., Bharti, B., & Singhi, P. (2017). Feeding problems and nutrient intake in children with and without autism: A comparative study. *Indian Journal of Pediatrics, 84*(4), 283-288. https://doi.org./10.1007/s12098-016-2285-x

McIntosh, C. E., Kandiah, J., & Boucher, N. (2019). Practical considerations for school nurses in improving the nutrition of children with autism spectrum disorder. *NASN School Nurse, 34*(5), 296–302. https://doi.org/10.1177/1942602X18822775

Mohn, E. S., Kern, H. J., Saltzman, E., Mitmesser, S. H., & McKay, D. L. (2018). Evidence of drug-nutrient interactions with chronic use of commonly prescribed medications: An update. *Pharmaceutics, 10*(1), 36. doi:10.3390/pharmaceutics10010036

Oxford University Press (2018). Oxford English Dictionary (n.d.). https://en.oxforddictionaries.com/

Profili, E., Rubio, D. S., Lane, H. G., Jaspers, L. H., Lopes, M. S., Black, M. M., & Hager, E. R. (2017). School wellness team best practices to promote wellness policy implementation. *Preventive Medicine, 101*, 34–37. https://dx.doi.org/10.1016/j.ypmed.2017.05.016

Szucs, T. D., & Stoffel, A. W. (2016). Nutrition and health—why payors should get involved. *Nutrition, 32*(5), 615-616. http://dx.doi.org/10.1016/j.nut.2015.11.009

Voulgarakis, H., Bendell-Estroff, D., & Field, T. (2017). Prevalence of obesity and autism spectrum disorder. *Behavioral Development Bulletin, 22*(1), 209–214. https://dx.doi.org/10.1037/bdb0000054

U.S. Department of Agriculture (2013). Nutrition standards for CACFP meals and snacks. https://www.fns.usda.gov/cacfp/meals-and-snacks

World Health Organization. (2018). Constitution. http://www.who.int.udel.idm.oclc. org/governance/eb/who_constitution_en.pdf

Understanding Factors Related to the Development of Obesity Among Preschoolers and the Importance of Promoting Physical Activity Early in Life

Cheryl Maykel and Jessica S. Reinhardt

Abstract

It is known that most children do not engage in the recommended amount of physical activity on a daily basis and that physical activity is inversely related to overweight status. Various physical and mental health concerns have been associated with overweight status. Conversely, various physical, mental, and cognitive health benefits have been associated with increased physical activity. While there is some evidence to suggest that the trend in overweight status may be leveling off, the rate of occurrence is still high (Hales et al., 2017). In addition, young children continue to fail to meet the recommendations for daily physical activity as well as for sedentary behavior (Colley et al., 2013). It is known that overweight status and physical activity habits both tend to persist from childhood and adolescence into adulthood. Therefore, the importance of intervening to increase physical activity among young children remains of great importance to overall well-being.

Keywords: *Physical Activity, Childhood Obesity, Preschool*

Understanding Factors Related to the Development of Obesity Among Preschoolers and the Importance of Promoting Physical Activity Early in Life

Physical Activity (PA) is important at every stage of life. Human beings are designed to be active throughout the day, every day, in pursuit and maintenance of resources (Eaton & Eaton, 2003). Though our society has evolved into one in which both vocational and recreational activities are often sedentary in nature, our bodies continue to require daily activity for healthy functioning. The term "physical activity" represents all types of gross motor movement, regardless of where it occurs, what type of activity it is or even the purpose of that movement; PA is no longer defined as a distinct, purpose-driven exercise session (Physical Activity Guidelines Advisory Committee [PAGAC], 2018). It is key to recognize that there are many opportunities for increasing PA throughout the day that do not require scheduling a substantial block of time.

The rates of obesity in the U.S. have climbed from the 1999-2000 to the 2015-2016 child and adult data reported by the National Center for Health Statistics, yet there was no significant increase from the 2013-2014 to 2015-2016 data (Hales et al., 2017). This suggests that while rates remain high, the trend in overweight status may be leveling off. There appears to be no significant difference between boys and girls overall or in any age group. It is also of interest to note that the prevalence of obesity among preschool-aged children from two to five years was reported as 13.9%, among school-aged children from six to eleven years as 18.4%, and among adolescents from twelve to nineteen years as 20.6% (Hales et al., 2017). The rates show a slight increase as children age, meaning that more children and adolescents become obese than those who are obese when they are younger improving their weight status, despite the many efforts that are made to intervene on behalf of children and adolescents. Though, these numbers reflect only children who meet the threshold for obesity, and not those who would be considered overweight or at-risk for becoming overweight. There are also racial disparities in rates of obesity among youth aged two to nineteen years, with rates among Hispanic youth reported at 25.8%, Black at 22%, White at 14.1%, and Asian at 11% (Hales et al., 2017). It is also well-known that children from families of lower socioeconomic status have a greater risk of being overweight as well (Wang & Beydoun, 2007).

There are many physical health risks for children that are associated with simply having low levels of regular PA, including an increased risk for cardiovascular disease (Tanha et al., 2011). There are also physical health concerns associated with obesity. In a nationally representative sample of youth aged 10-17, higher rates of bone, joint, and muscle problems, asthma, allergies, headaches, and ear infections were found among those who were obese (Halfon et al., 2013). Overweight status is also often comorbid with various mental health concerns (Reeves et al., 2008). Halfon and colleagues (2013) also found that rates of attention deficit/hyperactivity disorder, conduct disorder, depression, learning disability, and developmental delay were higher among children who were considered obese.

While it is difficult to accept, young children may be more susceptible to the negative self-concept, or body esteem issues related to overweight status than once believed. Body esteem has been defined as the attitudes, evaluations, and feelings that an individual has about their own body (Williams et al., 2012). Previous work indicated that body esteem was not impacted until later childhood or adolescence, however it has been found that even among five to seven-year-old boys and girls with a higher BMI (Body Mass Index), children of both sexes had lower body esteem girls experienced more bullying, while boys perceived having more physical health problems as a result of their overweight status (Williams et al., 2012). In addition, earlier work suggested that there were racial differences in body esteem, such that overall, Black or Hispanic children were not as negatively impacted by overweight status, yet those differences in perception appear to have diminished over time (Shaw et al., 2004). It is not yet known whether obesity is a cause of mental health problems or if it results from these issues, but it seems likely that there is a shared and complicated etiology, providing support for the needs of these youth to be addressed holistically (Kalarchian & Marcus, 2012).

Research has shown that patterns of PA (Telama et al., 2005) and weight status (Eaton et al., 2012) that are in place in the early years of life tend to continue throughout adolescence and adulthood. Further, health concerns associated with a lack of adequate PA are likely to be more detrimental to overall health if they persist for longer periods of time. In addition, it is known that children, despite often enjoying PA and experiencing spontaneous bouts of energy that might indicate they would naturally engage in PA as needed, are consistently not engaging in the amount of PA that experts recommend on a daily basis (Eaton et al., 2012; Colley et al., 2013). Young children also continue to exceed the recommendations for sedentary behavior (Colley et al., 2013). Therefore, intentional efforts must be made to increase the amount of physical activity that young children engage in as part of typical daily habits in order to promote overall wellness.

Diet as a Factor in the Development of Overweight

The simplest explanation for the overweight phenomenon is that of an interplay between calories consumed and calories burned, yet we know that the problem is not as simple as increasing PA in response to a high calorie diet. There are many genetic and environmental factors related to obesity status (Thaker, 2017). Research supports that parents who are overweight or obese are more likely to have children with higher BMIs (Burke et al., 2001). Children are presumed to share the same genetic material as well as the same home environment with their parents, within which they are likely to access most of what they eat and to adopt the eating behaviors (e.g., portion, regularity of second helpings, eating times, whether or not meals are taken in front of the television, speed of eating) that have been established by the family. For many families who have two working parents, are single parent families, or are otherwise often "on the go", everything that goes into mealtime preparation and execution can often be superseded by the amount of time and energy available in a given day to those responsible for providing meals, as well as to the food preferences of the family.

A careful review of the foods that families of lower socioeconomic means, who are at a greater risk for becoming overweight, choose to eat on a regular basis indicates that they are choosing less healthy, calorie dense foods more often (Pechey et al., 2013). One explanation is that these foods are perceived as being less expensive (Dammann & Smith, 2009), but it is also likely because they are satisfying and easy to procure. One study showed a higher preference for fatty foods, lower preference for vegetables, and a greater likelihood of overeating on a regular basis among children from families considered to be overweight (Wardle et al., 2001). In addition, general family eating behaviors, as well as parental pressure to eat or restrictions on eating have been shown to impact both risk for underweight and risk for overweight status among children (Jansen et al., 2012).

There is some evidence to suggest that the foundation for obesity during early childhood may be set in infancy (Andersen et al., 2012). Factors such as breastfeeding and delaying the introduction of solid foods until at least four months are associated with a higher likelihood of healthy weight status among two-and four-year-old children (Moss & Yeaton, 2014). Also of interest, is that while mothers tend to perceive heavier infants as healthier, this trend might increase rates of childhood obesity, as mothers may be less likely to intervene to curb weight gain as the child grows (Byrne et al., 2016). In particular, older mothers of normal weight children were more likely to perceive of their children as being underweight and mothers who were overweight themselves were more likely to describe children classified as overweight or at-risk for overweight as being of normal weight (Byrne et al., 2016).

Physical Activity as a Factor in the Development of Overweight

Physical activity behaviors are influenced by social, cultural, and environmental factors (PAGAC, 2018). For instance, PA habits and the encouragement of either a more active or a more sedentary lifestyle also tends to begin at home (Xu et al., 2018). Families who limit screen time and are more often active together tend to promote a more active lifestyle. Conversely, families that are considered to be overweight impart a preference for sedentary activities on to their children (Wardle et al., 2001). Children tend to prefer to have their parents involved in PA with them to being alone or to having parents watch them from the sideline (Rebold et al., 2016). Further, parental engagement in PA with the child has been found to increase the amount of PA for the child (Rebold et al., 2016).

For children who live in the inner cities, there are a host of barriers related to engaging in adequate levels of PA, chief among these is having access to a safe space to play (Ginsburg, 2007). Many urban homes are limited in space for indoor gross motor activities, while leaving the home may necessitate having supervision, traveling to a park or playground, owning sporting equipment, or other logistical concerns that many suburban and rural children who are able to walk out their back door and run around are not impacted by to the same extent.

Overweight status might result in compound effects that cause it to become a barrier to engaging in more PA. For example, reduced movement in the early years may impede the child's motor development, which could then impact physical abilities and fitness, or at least preference for PAs later in childhood. One study demonstrated that children who were considered overweight at five years old were at increased risk for deficient total and gross motor abilities at age 10 when compared to their peers (Cheng et al., 2016).

Benefits of Physical Activity

Various health benefits of physical activity have been identified in the literature, including direct benefits to physical health, cognitive ability, including executive functioning and classroom engagement, as well as mental well-being. Most of the documented benefits from PA are from moderate-vigorous PA (MVPA; PAGAC, 2018). The 2008 PAGAC indicated there was insufficient evidence on the amount of PA that would be appropriate to recommend. The current guidelines, however, recommend a minimum of three hours per day, though this would include light, moderate and vigorous intensity activities for children aged three to five (PAGAC, 2018). If children within this age range sleep between ten and fifteen hours per day, this recommendation would mean that children should spend a significant proportion of their day in motion.

Physical Benefits

There are many benefits of PA to physical health. MVPA has been associated with reductions in several health-related conditions including: excessive weight gain, a reduced risk of developing various types of cancers and reduced mortality from some types of cancers (PAGAC, 2018). Those engaging in more MVPA have also been reported to have improved sleep quality. This was found among the general population, as well as those with insomnia or sleep apnea (PAGAC, 2018). Improved sleep quality is determined by less time falling asleep, more time in bed sleeping, more time in deep sleep, less fatigue while performing daily tasks and a reduced frequency of using medications to aid in sleep (PAGAC, 2018). Each of these physical health benefits is linked to a variety of other aspects of functioning and overall well-being.

Specifically, among children, substantial evidence for the physical health benefits of PA for six to seventeen-year-olds includes improved weight status, bone health, and cardiovascular risk status (PAGAC, 2018). Preschool-aged children who are more physically active have been shown to have a healthier weight status and greater bone strength (PAGAC, 2018). Both of these characteristics have been shown to persist into later life (PAGAC, 2018).

Some school-based programs involving students in PA have been developed to target physical health outcomes, including the promotion of overall health among students (Hollar et al., 2010). The Happy 10 program was developed to combat obesity and has been shown to have a positive impact on student BMI (Liu et al., 2007). Other programs were designed to target both weight status and academic achievement and have found success in both domains. The Physical Activity Across the Curriculum program (PAAC; Donnelly et al., 2009) promoted the integration of multiple 10-minute breaks for PA throughout each school day. The Healthier Options for Public Schoolchildren (HOPS; Hollar et al., 2010), in addition to other components, increased the structure of PAs during recess, integrated PAs into the curriculum, and involved teacher encouragement to increase the amount of PA students engaged in.

Cognitive Benefits

In addition to the physical health benefits of physical activity, MPVA has been linked with improved cognition in children (PAGAC, 2018). The cognitive benefits of MVPA are mainly related to executive functioning, including attention, but also to memory, processing speed and overall academic performance (PAGAC, 2018). PA has also been shown to reduce ADHD symptoms, including oppositional behavior (Chang, 2012). A meta-analysis by Sibley and Etnier (2003) provides strong support for a relationship between PA and cognition in general populations of children. The research, which included 44 studies, provides insight into the general benefits of physical activity, as well as key outcome moderators (i.e., experimental design, age, activity, and types of cognition). Results demonstrated a significant and positive impact on cognition in children in general with an overall effect size of 0.32, with solid effects among elementary-aged children and middle schoolers (0.40 and 0.48 respectively).

Knowledge of the benefits of PA on executive functioning has become widespread in recent years, though research support for this relationship has been amassing for decades. For instance, Allen (1980) demonstrated the success of a six-week jogging program among 12 boys with behavioral disorders, showing a 50%

reduction in disruptive behaviors. In an early meta-analysis, Allison and colleagues (1995) explored the effects of chronic PA on disruptive behavior and provided support for its use as a method of changing behavior in children.

Since these early studies, there have been a number of others conducted in recent years that have also provided support for the use of PA specifically to improve time-on-task among elementary school children. Increased engagement, often measured by time-on-task, is also logically linked to academic achievement (Shapiro, 2011), which could partially explain the relationship between improved cognition resulting from PA and the improved academic achievement that has been associated with increased levels of PA; it may be the case that improvements in cognition result in increased engagement which then positively impacts achievement. Further research is needed in order to understand the processes involved in this group of findings.

Several studies involving elementary students have demon-strated a positive effect of PA on engagement in the classroom. One study showing improvements in this area among third graders involved MVPA as part of physically active classroom lessons (the Texas I-CAN! program; Grieco et al., 2009). While the students of higher BMI categories had lower rates of time-on-task following inactive lessons, there were no significant differences in rates between groups after the active lessons (Grieco et al., 2009). In another study among four classes of third and fourth grade students, higher time-on-task rates were found overall following PA, with the greatest benefits derived by students who had the lowest rates before the interven-tion (Mahar et al., 2006). Nicholson and colleagues (2011) found that with four third-grade boys with autism spectrum diagnoses who participated in a brief jogging intervention, each showed a significantly higher academic engaged time within an hour of PA (Nicholson et al., 2011). Yet another study demonstrated that the effects of one 10-minute break for PA resulted in improved time-on-task among third graders for at least 45 minutes following the active break (Maykel et al., 2018). This research supports the use of brief breaks for PA in the classroom to improve engagement for all students, particularly those who might typically have the most difficulty in this area, and that the benefits are likely to far outweigh the time taken away from class lessons. More research is needed in this area, however, and particularly in order to determine potential effects on very young children.

Mental Health Benefits

The mental health benefits of PA are compelling. There is substantial evidence to support that regularly engaging in MVPA reduces trait anxiety, or persistent characteristic anxiety among those with and without a diagnosed anxiety disorder (PAGAC, 2018). Further, immediate feelings of anxiety, also referred to as state anxiety, are reduced following individual episodes of MVPA (PAGAC, 2018). MVPA has also been shown to reduce the risk for developing major depression, and to reduce the symptoms of depression among individuals both with and without clinical levels of depression (PAGAC, 2018). In addition to these reductions in negative symptoms, individuals who engage in more MVPA have reported improved overall quality of life (PAGAC, 2018).

Research that pertains specifically to children indicates that six- to seventeen-year-olds who engaged in higher levels of PA were also found to have fewer symptoms of depression (PAGAC, 2018). A meta-analysis conducted by Ahn and Fedewa (2011) also found increased PA to be associated with reductions in symptoms of depression, anxiety and other forms of emotional distress in children and adolescents. Similar outcomes were noted for children of typical weight, as well as those classified as overweight or obese, and the results were consistent with prior research indicating that more vigorous PA yielded greater results (Ahn & Fedewa, 2011).

Discussion & Implications for Future Research

Research questions related to the role that PA plays on physical, cognitive, and mental health functioning in preschoolers remain largely unanswered due to a lack of quality research with children in this age group. A 2019 meta-analysis of PA interventions across childhood found no intervention nor observational studies that were completed with preschool-aged children (Rodriguez-Allyon et al., 2019.) Therefore, we are forced to extrapolate from research conducted with adults, adolescents and older children, while suspecting that there are unique differences between groups that should be taken into consideration. Further, given that movement related behaviors begin in early childhood and track into later childhood and adulthood (Biddle et al., 2010), it will be important to conduct research specifically with young children to learn how best to intervene early in life.

Intentional, adult-led physical activities have proven to be an important component in the overall amount of MVPA that young children engage in at childcare centers (Bower et al., 2008). Childcare providers should be educated on the guidelines for preschooler physical activity, as well as on the importance of making an intentional effort to meet these guidelines (Lanigan, 2014). There is also considerable evidence to support that sedentary behaviors, eating habits and food choices, and habits related to PA begin at home. Best practice puts forth that a child's stakeholders (school, family, community) should partner across settings (Lines et al., 2011), as programs that include both educators and families are likely to see the greatest results among young children.

School-based PA programs have shown an increase in popularity with the number of studies used in systematic reviews more than doubling from the 1980s to the 1990s, and from there, four times as many articles in the 2000s (Demetriou & Höner, 2012). Programs and practices that involve integrating PA into regular classroom routines can be beneficial to cognition, engagement and achievement, while also simply increasing the amount of PA that children are involved in each day. It is prudent to review the existing literature on physical activity in preschool to inform future research, practice and policy.

References

Allen, J. (1980). Jogging can modify disruptive behaviors. *Teaching Exceptional Children, 12*(2), 66–70.

Allison, D.B., Faith, M.S. & Franklin, R.D. (1995). Antecedent exercise in the treatment of disruptive behavior: A meta-analytic review. *Clinical Psychology: Science and Practice, 2*(3), 279–304.

Andersen, L.G., Holst, C., Michealsen, K.F., Baker, J.L., & Sorensen, T.I.A. (2012). Weight and weight gain during early infancy predict childhood obesity: A case-cohort study. *International Journal of Obesity, 36*(10), 1306–1311.

Biddle, S.J., & Asare, M. (2011). Physical activity and mental health in children and adolescents: A review of reviews. *British Journal of Sports Medicine 45*(11), 886–895.

Bower, J. K., Hales, D. P., Tate, D. F., Rubin, D. A., Benjamin, S. E., & Ward, D. S. (2008). The childcare environment and children's physical activity. *American Journal of Preventive Medicine, 34*(1), 23–29.

Burke, V., Beilin, L.J., & Dunbar, D. (2001). Family lifestyle and parental body mass index as predictors of body mass index in Australian children: A longitudinal study. *International Journal of Obesity, 25*(2), 147–157.

Byrne, R., Magarey, A. & Daniels, L. (2016). Maternal perception of weight status in first-born Australian toddlers aged 12–16 months—the NOURISH and SAIDI cohorts. *Child: Care, Health and Development, 42*(3), 375–381.

Chang, Y., Liu, S., Yu, H., & Lee, Y. (2012). Effect of acute exercise on executive function in children with attention deficit hyperactivity disorder. Archives of Clinical Neuropsychology: *The Official Journal of the National Academy of Neuropsychologists, 27*(2), 225–237.

Cheng, J., East, P., Blanco, E., Sim, E.K., Castillo, M., Lozoff, B., & Gahagan, S. (2016). Obesity leads to declines in motor skills across childhood. *Child: Care, Health and Development, 42*(3), 343–350.

Colley, R.C., Garriguet, D., Adamo, K.B., Carson, V., Janssen, I., Timmons, B.W., & Tremblay, M.S. (2013). Physical activity and sedentary behavior during the early years in Canada: A cross-sectional study. *International Journal of Behavioral Nutrition and Physical Activity, 10*(1), 54.

Dammann, K.W. & Smith, C. (2009). Factors affecting low-income women's food choices and the perceived impact of dietary intake and socioeconomic status on their health and weight. *Journal of Nutrition Education & Behavior, 41*(4), 242–253.

Demetriou, Y. & Höner, O. (2012). Physical activity interventions in the school setting: systematic review. *Psychology of Sport & Exercise 13*(2), 186–196.

Donnelly J.E., Greene, J.L., Gibson, C.A., Smith, B.K., Washburn, R.A. Sullivan, D.K., ... & Jacobsen D.J., (2009). Physical Activity Across the Curriculum (PAAC): A randomized controlled trial to promote physical activity and diminish overweight and obesity in elementary school children. *Preventative Medicine 49*(4), 336–341.

Eaton, D. K., Kann, L., Kinchen, S., Shanklin, S., Flint, K. H., Hawkins, J., ... & Whittle, L., (2012). Youth risk behavior surveillance—United States, 2011. *Morbidity and Mortality Weekly Report: Surveillance summaries, 61*(4), 1–162.

Eaton, S.B. & Eaton, S.B. (2003). An evolutionary perspective on human physical activity: Implications for health. *Comparative Biochemistry and Physiology. Part A, Molecular & Integrative Physiology, 136*(1), 153–159.

Ginsburg, K.R., American Academy of Pediatrics Committee on Communications, & American Academy of Pediatrics Committee on Psychosocial Aspects of Child and Family Health. (2007). The importance of play in promoting healthy child development and maintaining strong parent-child bonds. *Pediatrics, 119*(1), 182–191.

Grieco, L., Jowers, E., & Bartholomew, J. (2009). Physically active academic lessons and time on task: The moderating effect of body mass index. *Medicine & Science in Sports and Exercise, 41*(10), 1921–1926.

Hales, C.M., Carroll, M.D., Fryar, C.D., & Ogden, C.L. (2017). *Prevalence of obesity among adults and youth: United States, 2015-2016. NCHS data brief,* (288), 1–8.

Halfon, N., Larson, K., & Slusser, W. (2013). Associations between obesity and comorbid mental health, developmental, and physical health conditions in a nationally representative sample of US children aged 10 to 17. *Academic Pediatrics, 13*(1), 6–13.

Hollar, D., Messiah, S., Lopez-Mitnik, G., Hollar, T., Almon, M., & Agatston, A. (2010). Healthier Options for Public Schoolchildren program improves weight and blood pressure in 6- to 13-year-olds. *Journal of the American Dietetic Association, 110*(2), 261–267.

Jansen, P.W., Roza, S.J., Jaddoe, V.W., Mackenbach, J.D., Raat, H., Hofman, A., Verhulst, F.C., & Tiemeier, H. (2012). Children's eating behavior, feeding practices of parents and weight problems in early childhood: Results from the population-based Generation R Study. *The International Journal of Behavioral Nutrition and Physical Activity, 9,* 130.

Kalarchian, M.A. & Marcus, M.D. (2012). Psychiatric comorbidity of childhood obesity. *International Review of Psychiatry (Abingdon, England), 24*(3), 241–246.

Lanigan, J. (2014). Physical activity for young children: A quantitative study of child care providers' knowledge, attitudes, and health promotion practices. *Early Childhood Education Journal, 42,* 11–18.

Lines, C., Miller, G. B., & Arthur-Stanley, A. (2011). *The power of family-school partnering (FSP): A practical guide for school mental health professionals and educators.* Routledge.

Liu, A., Hu, X., Ma, G., Cui, Z., Pan, Y., Chang, S., ... & Chen, C. (2007). Report on childhood obesity in China (6) Evaluation of a classroom-based physical activity promoting program. *Biomedical and Environmental Sciences, 20*(1), 19–23.

Mahar, M., Murphy, S., Rowe, D., Golden, J., Shields, A., & Raedeke, T. (2006). Effects of a classroom-based program on physical activity and on-task behavior. *Medicine & Science in Sports & Exercise, 38*(12), 2086–2094.

Maykel, C., Bray, M.A., & Rogers, H.J. (2018). A classroom-based physical activity intervention for elementary student on-task behavior. *Journal of Applied School Psychology, 34*(3), 259–274.

Moss, B.G., & Yeaton, W.H. (2014). Early childhood healthy and obese weight status: Potentially protective benefits of breastfeeding and delaying solid foods. *Maternal & Child Health Journal, 18*(5), 1224–1232.

Nicholson, H., Kehle, T., Bray, M., & Heest, J.V. (2011). The effects of antecedent physical activity on the academic engagement of children with autism spectrum disorder. *Psychology in the Schools, 48*(2), 198–213.

Pechey, R., Jebb, S.A., Kelly, M.P., Almiron-Roig, E., Conde, S., Nakamura, R., ... & Marteau, T.M. (2013). Socioeconomic differences in purchases of more vs. less healthy foods and beverages: Analysis of over 25,000 British households in 2010. *Social Sciences & Medicine, 92*, 22–26.

Physical Activity Guidelines Advisory Committee. (2018). *2018 Physical Activity Guidelines Advisory Committee Scientific Report.* https://health.gov/sites/default/files/2019-09/PAG_Advisory_Committee_Report.pdf

Rebold, M.J., Lepp, A., Kobak, M.S., McDaniel, J., & Barkley, J.E. (2016). The effect of parental involvement on children's physical activity. *The Journal of Pediatrics, 170*, 206–210.

Reeves, G.M., Postolache, T.T., & Snitker, S. (2008). Childhood obesity and depression: Connections between these growing problems in growing children. *International Journal of Child Health and Human Development: IJCHD 1*(2), 103–114.

Rodriguez-Ayllon, M., Cadenas-Sánchez, C., Estévez-López, F., Muñoz, N.E., Mora-Gonzalez, J., Migueles, J.H., ... & Cantena, A. (2019). Role of physical activity and sedentary behavior in the mental health of preschoolers, children and adolescents: A systematic review and meta-analysis. *Sports Medicine 49*, 1383–1410.

Shapiro, E. (2011). *Academic skills problems: Direct assessment and intervention.* Guilford Press.

Shaw, H., Ramirez, L., Trost, A., Randall, P. & Stice, E. (2004). Body image and eating disturbances across ethnic groups: More similarities than differences. *Psychology of Addictive Behaviors, 18*(1), 12–18.

Sibley, B. A., & Etnier, J. L. (2003). The relationship between physical activity and cognition in   children: A meta-analysis. *Pediatric Exercise Science,15*(3), 243–256.

Ahn, S. & Fedewa, A.L. (2011). A Meta-analysis of the relationship between children's physical activity and mental health. *Journal of Pediatric Psychology, 36*(4), 385–397.

Tanha, T., Wollmer, P., Thorsson, O., Karlsson, M.K., Linden, C., Andersen, L.B., & Dencker, M. (2011). Lack of physical activity in young children is related to higher composite risk factor score for cardiovascular disease. *Acta Paediatrica, 100*(5), 717–721.

Telama, R., Yang, X., Viikari, J., Valimaki, I., Wanne, O., & Raitakari, O. (2005). Physical   activity from childhood to adulthood: A 21-year tracking study. *American Journal of Preventive Medicine, 28*(3), 267–273.

Thaker, V.V. (2017). Genetic and epigenetic causes of obesity. *Adolescent Medicine: State of the Art Reviews, 28*(2), 379–405.

Wang, Y. & Beydoun, M.A. (2007). The obesity epidemic in the United States—gender, age, socioeconomic, racial/ethnic, and geographic characteristics: A systematic review and meta-regression analysis. *Epidemiologic Reviews, 29*(1), 6–28.

Wardle, J., Guthrie, C., Sanderson, S., Birch, L., & Plomin, R. (2001). Food and activity preferences in children of lean and obese parents. *International Journal of Obesity, 25*(7), 971–977.

Williams, N.A., Fournier, J., Coday, M., Richey, P.A., Tylavsky, F.A., & Hare, M.E. (2013).

Body esteem, peer difficulties and perceptions of physical health in overweight and obese urban children aged 5 to 7 years. Child: Care, *Health and Development, 39*(6), 825–834.

Xu, C., Quan, M., Zhang, H., Zhou, C., & Chen, P. (2018). Impact of parents' physical activity   on preschool children's physical activity: A cross-sectional study. *PeerJ, 6*, e4405.

Cumulative Experience of Educational Assets from Preschool through First Grade and the Social-emotional Well-being of English- and Spanish-Speaking Children

Tutrang Nguyen, Tara Hofkens, Robert C. Pianta, Jessica V. Whittaker, Virginia E. Vitiello, and Erik A. Ruzek

Abstract

Children's social and emotional experiences influence brain development and are therefore central to outcomes of behavior, learning, and health. The current study examined associations between children's cumulative educational assets in the early grades and end of first grade social-emotional outcomes for children from English- and Spanish-speaking families. Data were drawn from a sample of preschool-aged children ($N = 1{,}132$) from low-income families in a large, culturally, and linguistically diverse sample followed annually from pre-kindergarten through first grade. A multi-method, multi-informant approach was used to assess predictor and outcome variables. Results indicate overall that cumulative experiences of educational assets (teacher-student interaction and relationships, parent-teacher communication) were associated with indicators of children's social-emotional well-being and matter in similar ways for children from English- and Spanish-speaking families. However, we did find some evidence of significant interactions of Spanish as a home language with cumulative educational assets on children's conduct problems and feelings about peers.

Keywords: English-Language Learners, Socioemotional development, Preschool and Primary Grades, Educational Experience

In the past few decades, researchers and policymakers have primarily focused on children's academic performance in efforts to narrow achievement gaps (Barnett, 2011; Coburn, Hill, & Spillane, 2016). However, less attention has been paid to children's social-emotional development, which has been recognized as essential for their well-being (Copple & Bredekamp 2009; Raver & Knitzer, 2002). In the early years of schooling, aspects of social functioning and well-being are important for activating educational resources in classrooms and as key outcomes in their own right (Wilson, Pianta, & Stuhlman, 2007). Children who are socially and emotionally well-adjusted perform better at school, have increased confidence, have good relationships with their teachers and peers, take on and persist at challenging tasks, and communicate well (Birch & Ladd, 1997; Burchinal, Vandergrift, Pianta, & Mashburn, 2010; Pakarinen et al., 2011; Pianta, Steinberg, & Rollins, 1995). Given the importance of social and emotional competence, it is important to understand how to deliver and mobilize appropriate educational resources to students, particularly for those who are linguistically and culturally diverse.

The present study draws from a multi-year study of a linguistically diverse sample of children enrolled in a large pre-kindergarten (pre-K) program and followed annually through first grade. It focuses on the manner in which students' cumulative experiences of three educational assets supporting their development—interactions and relationships with teachers and teacher-parent communications—across pre-K, kindergarten, and first grade are associated with social-emotional functioning and well-being by the end of first grade. Of particular interest is the extent to which students' experiences of these assets, and their associations with social-emotional outcomes, may differ for Spanish- and English-speaking children. Hereafter, we use the term "educational assets" to describe these socially salient interaction processes that children experience.

Social-Emotional Health and Well-Being of Young Children

Advances in neuroscience and child development research in recent years have helped us understand how children's earliest experiences shape their overall development and ability to learn. Developmental systems theory suggests that children's early experiences influence their biological development—early experiences lay the foundation for lifelong behavior, cognition, learning, and physical and mental health (Bronfenbrenner & Morris, 1998; Hertzman, 2012; McEwen, 2012; Shonkoff, 2012). And research suggests that the first few years of life are especially dramatic in terms of developmental neural changes (Shonkoff & Phillips, 2000). An environment rich in social interactions with caregivers prepares children's developing brain to function in a range of everyday contexts, whereas an adverse environment in which children are deprived of social experiences can have detrimental effects on further brain development (Center on the Developing Child, 2016; Nelson & Bloom, 1997). These "serve and return" interactions between children and their caregivers have an important influence on children's brain structure and function, and therefore function as resources for their health and well-being (Center on the Developing Child, 2016; Dong et al., 2004).

Promoting children's social-emotional health and well-being is an important outcome in and of itself for nurturing children's early brain development and contributing to their success in school and in life. The development of social and emotional competencies is the process whereby children are able to acknowledge and manage their emotions, recognize the emotions of others, develop empathy, make good decisions, establish positive relationships, and handle challenges effectively (Collaborative for Academic, Social, and Emotional Learning [CASEL], 2003). Social-emotional competence is especially important in the early years in that it supports a wide range of later outcomes including sound mental health, motivation to learn, achievement in school and later in the workplace, behaviors that affect physical health risks, and the ability to control aggressive impulses and resolve conflicts (Bornstein, Davidson, Keyes, Moore, & the Center for Child Well-Being, 2003; Center on the Developing Child, 2016; McClelland, Cameron, Wanless, & Murray, 2007). Developing social-emotional skills is even more critical for children facing disadvantage as they are surrounded by added stressors. The evidence suggests that children from low-income families exhibit heightened physiological indicators of stress (Blair et al., 2011; Szanton, Gill, & Allen, 2005) and exaggerated responses to perceived stress that are channeled into negative emotions into disengaged or disruptive behavior (Bradley & Corwyn, 2002; Evans, 2003). In an effort to support these vulnerable young children, the social settings in which they spend time should be targeted.

Social-Emotional Health and Well-Being of DLLs

Children growing up in a dual language context are likely to have different experiences for social and emotional development compared with their monolingual peers growing up in the U.S. These experiences could lead to different developmental outcomes with respect to regulation skills, social interactions, and relationships. Understanding the social-emotional development of DLLs is important because it is taking place within the context of learning two or more languages simultaneously (Halle et al., 2014). Children's learning occurs in the context of interactions with others within specific cultural contexts, and language operates as the means for these social interactions (Vygotsky, 1978). Their communication skills with teachers and peers may have profound implications for their adaptation to the classroom environment and thus their social-emotional well-being. Prior research has shown that DLLs have comparable or better social-emotional skills relative to their monolingual English peers (Crosnoe, 2007; Halle et al., 2014). For example, Crosnoe (2007) found that kindergarten teachers rated

Spanish-speaking children more positively than their English-only peers on self-control and externalizing and internalizing behaviors. Further, research on emotional well-being has shown that Spanish-speaking children in particular exhibit high levels of mental health (National Task Force on Early Education for Hispanics, 2007). Until recently, advancement in research on the social-emotional development DLLs has been limited because of under-sampling and a focus on the development of cognitive skills (Halle et al., 2011; 2014). Thus, there is a need for more research on the social-emotional health and well-being of this important and growing population.

Classrooms as Settings for the Development of Social-Emotional Health and Well-Being

Children's social-emotional development is fostered in an eco-logical context, with surrounding environments such as classrooms, shaping how and what children learn and experience every day. Historically, the purpose of early childhood programs has been to enhance children's social competence (Copple & Bredekamp, 2009; Shonkoff & Phillips, 2000; Zigler & Styfco, 2010). A wide range of best practices and curricula are implemented across the primary grades in an effort to promote students' enjoyment of school as well as positive emotions associated with their relationships with teachers and peers (e.g., Anderson, Christenson, Sinclair, & Lehr, 2004; Guthrie et al., 2004). Such efforts and aims are based on the premise that social-emotional well-being is a critical component of early development and that student well-being is a fundamental element of motivation for continued engagement and success in school (Finn & Zimmer, 2012; Reschly, Huebner, & Appleton, 2008). To encourage this goal, pre-K programs focus on educating the "whole child" (Copple & Bredekamp, 2009). The "whole child" approach to school readiness aims to help children at risk in the targeted domains of cognitive development, social-emotional development, health, and family functioning in order to adequately prepare children for kindergarten (Zigler & Styfco, 2010).

Given that the majority of young children are enrolled in pre-K programs (Chaudry & Datta, 2017), these early childhood settings are crucial environments for nurturing young children's social and emotional development (Denham, 2006). Innovative ways to improve the quality of these environments are necessary to effectively use the time children spend in these settings and to promote their healthy social and emotional development. Relationships with adults and other children play a central role in the development of their social and emotional regulation. The present investigation focuses on three educational assets that are social in nature and that may be of particular importance for DLL children—teacher-student interactions and relationships, and parent-teacher communication—as they relate to social-emotional functioning and well-being in first grade. Each of these assets plays a key role in high-quality early education experience and might be of particular relevance for linguistically diverse children with regard to activating the educational and developmental resources of classrooms.

Teacher-student interactions, characterized by teacher sensitivity and responsiveness to children's cues, support for engaged and positive behavior, and stimulation of language and cognitive development, are a key element of classroom experience (Ansari & Pianta, 2018; Burchinal et al., 2014; Vitiello, Bassok, Hamre, Player, & Williford, 2018; Vernon-Feagans, Mokrova, Carr, Garrett-Peters, & Burchinal, 2018). Whereas most children on average experience increases in cortisol (the principal hormone produced in response to psychosocial stress) while in nonparental childcare settings (Groeneveld, Vermeer, Van IJzendoorn, & Linting, 2010; Watamura, Kryzer, & Robertson, 2009), teachers who engage in emotionally sensitive interactions with children promote decreases in children's cortisol over the day and year (Hatfield et al., 2013; Watamura et al., 2009). Teachers can support social-emotional skill development by responding sensitively to students' emotions, providing feedback that extend their skills, and engaging them in conversations (Burchinal et al., 2010; Pakarinen et al., 2011). Further, children who display problems in self-regulation appear to benefit even more from exposure to effective teacher-child interactions (Hamre & Pianta, 2001; McCartney, Dearing, Taylor, & Bub, 2007; Vernon-Feagans, et al., 2018). Further, multiple-years of exposure to effective teacher-student interactions appears to be of additional benefit (Cash, Ansari, Grimm, & Pianta, 2018; Vernon-Feagans et al., 2018).

In terms of relationships with teachers, emotionally close relationships between children and teachers help promote emerging language skills by providing more opportunities for dyadic conversations and exposure to rich language use (Justice, McGinty, Zucker, Cabell & Piasta, 2013). Interventions designed to promote supportive and close relationships with teachers and children have shown that these relationships are also important for improving children's activity in the stress response system (Hatfield & Williford, 2017). Positive, low-conflict relationships with teachers may also provide increased opportunities for children to have their behavior guided by teachers, helping children organize and manage their emotions and behaviors, and feel a sense of security and emotional well-being (Liew, Chen, & Hughes, 2011). On the other hand, relationships characterized by teacher-child conflict can prevent a child from accessing educationally and socially supportive resources in the classroom, leading to a sense of isolation, frustration, and conduct problems that may persist across the grades (O'Connor, Dearing, & Collins, 2011).

Parent-teacher communication is also often identified as a particularly important factor for young DLL students attempting to bridge the home-school boundary. Communication between parents and teachers can be a context in which concerns about the child (e.g., school adjustment, adaptability, difficulty making friends) can be addressed constructively, particularly when such communication is sensitive to cultural and linguistic differences (Hughes & Kwok, 2007). On the other hand, language barriers between teachers and parents (Conus & Fahrni, 2019; Crosnoe, 2006; Moreno & Valencia, 2002) can make such communication challenging, and when related to children's conduct problems, more communication between parent and teacher may not necessarily signal positive engagement or outcomes for the child.

Current Study

Study context. The present study was conducted in a large, culturally and linguistically diverse mid-Atlantic school district known for success in providing strong early education programs for vulnerable children. The district serves over 186,000 students from pre-K through 12th grade, a size and scale consistent with many states, and includes a very substantial immigrant population, with 18% of families in which neither parent is a U.S. citizen. Elementary school students in the district are highly diverse ethnically, with 39% white, 26% Hispanic/Latino, 19% Asian, 10% African American, and 6% other or mixed race/ethnicity. In kindergarten, 53% of children have a home language other than English, and 38% are identified as DLLs. A substantial number of families are economically vulnerable. Ten percent have no full-time wage earner and one third of children qualify as low-income (a 40% increase in the ten years prior to 2013). Thirty-eight percent of families describe themselves as having too little income to cover household needs, while 25% receive public assistance.

The district operates a large and well-funded public pre-K program that blends funding from federal, state, and local sources to target low-income children. The vast majority (98%) of children enrolled in public pre-K attend one of two main full-day (6–6.5 hours) program types. The largest (school-based pre-K), serving over 1,500 children, consists of pre-K classrooms within the district's schools. The second largest program type (community-based pre-K), serving more than 400 children, consists of subsidized slots in private pre-K centers. Centers may be large or small, for profit or non-profit. Governance, policy, regulation, and funding of pre-K programs are all coordinated through a central authority, the Office for Children.

The district also serves as a starting point for many families new to the US and offers significant support at both the pre-k and elementary levels in English, Spanish, and several other languages. The Office for Children emphasizes support for children's home language during the pre-k years and provides professional development to child care providers. The district offers helplines in multiple languages, has bilingual staff members who help families with enrollment, integrates English for Speakers of Other Languages (ESOL) specialists into teaching and administrative teams, provides professional development to teachers on supporting DLLs, and runs two-way immersion programs. Children from families where a language other than English is spoken—over 50% of families—receive a language screener in kindergarten to qualify for ESOL services.

Research questions. In the current study, we examine differences in Spanish-speaking and English-speaking children's classroom experience in pre-K, kindergarten, and first grade, and social-emotional well-being at the end of first grade. Furthermore, in a cumulative framework that focuses on the overall amounts of accumulated assets in early schooling, we examine the extent to which these assets have similar benefits for English- and Spanish-speaking children. We consider three educational assets across preschool, kindergarten, and first grade—(1) teacher-child interactions, (2) teacher-child relationships, and (3) teacher-parent communication—and how they relate to children's social-emotional well-being at the end of first grade. We address the following research questions:

1. Do children's experiences of educational assets and social-emotional outcomes from pre-K through first grade differ for children from English- and Spanish-speaking families?

2. To what extent do these educational assets from pre-K through first grade predict social-emotional outcomes at the end of first grade among children whose families speak either English or Spanish at home?

3. How do these educational assets from pre-K through first grade differ by children's home language for their social-emotional outcomes?

To address these research questions, we consider a comprehensive set of educational assets reported by teachers and classroom observers, and social-emotional well-being outcomes reported by teachers and children. This multi-method, multi-informant approach allows for different perspectives to be considered and compared in order to gain a fuller picture of children's cumulative experiences of educational assets and subsequent well-being. Taken together, understanding these experiences can inform current efforts aimed at improving the quality of children's early schooling as a mechanism for promoting healthy child development and well-being.

Method

Recruitment and Participants

Data for this study come from a larger longitudinal study of preschool children in a large, culturally and linguistically diverse school system. Teachers were recruited in the fall of 2016 from publicly funded center-based classrooms that served children from low-income families. A total of 138 classrooms were included in the larger study. Participating teachers sent home consent forms and family demographic surveys to eligible children. Children were eligible for the larger study if they turned four by September 30, and did not have an Individualized Education Program (IEP) other than for speech. Eighty percent of parents had children who were eligible to participate and consented to allow their child's participation, resulting in 1,498 participating children.

For the current study, we selected children from the larger study who were identified as either speaking only English ($N = 309$) or only Spanish ($N = 823$) at home. Thus, of the original 1,498 children in the larger study, 1,132 were eligible to participate in our study. On average, the children in our sample were 55 months old at the start of preschool, had parents with 12.26 years of education, and were racially and ethnically diverse (11% Black, 77% Hispanic, 7% Asian or multi-racial). Income-to-needs ratios indicated that on average, families were living in poverty ($M = 0.82$, $SD = 0.55$).

Across the three years, children had teachers with 17 years of education and 11 years of experience on average. Approximately 43% of children had one teacher who spoke Spanish across the three years. On average, children's classrooms were balanced in terms of the proportion of boys and girls (50% boys) and those identified as limited English proficient (45%), and included a small proportion of students with special needs (8%). See Table 1 for descriptive statistics on children, families, teachers, and classrooms for the whole sample, and stratified by home language status.

Procedures

Data were collected through a combination of parent surveys, teacher surveys, and direct child assessments. Parents completed brief demographic questionnaires in the fall of preschool. Teachers completed rating scales about each participating child in the fall and spring. Trained data collectors conducted direct assessments of children's school enjoyment and feelings about teachers and peers in the fall (September–November) and spring (April–May). Data collectors completed a one-day training to learn the measures prior to assessing children and assessed children outside of the classroom in a quiet space, when possible. All procedures were approved by the Institutional Review Board at the University of Virginia and parents and teachers received a small stipend to thank them for their time.

Measures

Below, we describe each of our key measures, including the quality of teacher-child interactions, teacher-child relationships, teacher-parent communication, and social-emotional well-being outcomes, in turn. Reliability coefficients provided for each of the measures are specific to the study sample across the three time points. Descriptive statistics of all the key predictors and outcomes are presented in Table 2, and discussed in the Results section below.

Table One
Descriptive statistics for the study sample

	Full sample (N= 1132)		English-speaking (N= 309)		Spanish-speaking (N= 823)		ANOVA F-stat or chi-square
	M/Prop.	SD	M/Prop.	SD	M/Prop.	SD	
Child and family characteristics							
Age at preschool	55.01	3.52	55.08	3.37	54.98	3.57	0.16
Male	0.5-		0.48		0.51		0.79
Race/ethnicity							
White	0.05		0.15		0.01		78.45 ***
Black	0.11		0.41		0.00		366.84 ***
Hispanic	0.77		0.25		0.96		614.45 ***
Other	0.07		0.19		0.02		93.95 ***
Parent years of education	12.26	1.50	13.32	1.80	11.87	1.16	8.60 ***
Income-to-needs ratio	0.82	0.55	1.08	0.70	0.73	0.45	26.25 ***
Teacher and classroom characteristics							
Years of education	17.10	1.12	17.26	0.93	17.22	0.99	5.89 *
Years of teaching experience	11.01	6.68	10.89	7.18	10.92	7.05	0.06
Number of non-white teachers							
Zero	0.54		0.46		0.57		10.61 ***
One	0.38		0.43		0.37		3.98 *
Two	0.06		0.10		0.05		8.00 **

Three	0.01	0.01	0.01	0.12
Number of English-speaking teachers				
Zero	0.03	0.06	0.01	16.61 ***
One	0.22	0.26	0.21	3.32
Two	0.34	0.33	0.34	0.16
Three	0.42	0.35	0.44	6.14 *
Number of Spanish-speaking teachers				
Zero	0.43	0.53	0.39	20.00 ***
One	0.43	0.37	0.45	7.22 **
Two	0.12	0.08	0.13	4.99 *
Three	0.02	0.02	0.03	1.07
Classroom composition				
Prop. pf male	0.50	0.50	0.50	1.63
Prop. of limited English proficient	0.45	0.62	0.57	12.37 ***
Prop. of special needs	0.08	0.08	0.08	0.78

Note. All statistics were computed at the child-level. Time-varying covariates, including teacher and classroom characteristics, were averaged across the three time points. Time invariant covariates are reported at baseline. Standard deviations presented for continuous variables only. The last column represents the difference be-tween the English only and Spanish-speaking groups from an F-test. *** $p < .001$; ** $p < .01$; * $p < .05$.

Teacher-child interactions. Teacher-child interaction quality was measured with the Classroom Assessment Scoring System (CLASS; Pianta, La Paro, & Hamre, 2008). This widely-used measure assesses the average classroom quality based on 10 dimensions, each of which are rated from 1 to 7, with higher scores indicating higher-quality interactions. Dimensions are collapsed to form three domains: Emotional Support, capturing teacher sensitivity, promotion of autonomy, and climate; Classroom Organization, capturing the degree to which teachers manage behavior and use time and materials effectively to get the most out of the day; and Instructional Support, capturing teachers' promotion of higher-order thinking and language. All data collectors attended a two-day training session led by the project investigators and staff, all of whom are experts on the CLASS. Data collectors had to be deemed reliable and certified on the tool in order to conduct observations. Specifically, raters were trained to an initial level of 80% agreement (within 1-point) to be certified for data collection in the field. Observers conducted four cycles of observations (each cycle includes 15 minutes to observe, 10 minutes to score) during each classroom visit across two to three separate occasions throughout each school year. Data collector reliability was maintained with refresher training before data collection and bi-monthly calibration meetings throughout the study year. Twenty percent of all cycles were double coded to determine inter-rater reliability (ICC = .725). We composited these ratings across dimensions and across occasions of observation into a single overall domain of interaction quality across the three years.

Teacher-child closeness and conflict. Teacher-child relationship quality in terms of closeness and conflict was measured from the teachers' perspective in the fall and spring of the school year. Each participating child's relationship with his or her teacher was measured by the Student-Teacher Relationship Scale (STRS; Pianta, 2001). The STRS is comprised of 15 items, asking teachers to report from their perspectives their relationships with individual children in the classroom. We adapted this measure and asked teachers to respond to nine of the 15 items. Specifically, five items are included in the conflict score (a = .82, .81, .87, preschool, kindergarten, and first grade, respectively), where teachers are asked about the extent to which they perceive negative interactions and emotions with the child. Four items are included in the closeness score (a = .77, .71, .78, preschool, kindergarten, and first grade, respectively), where teachers report on the degree of warmth and open communication they share with the child. For the current analyses, items were averaged across the three years within their respective subscales.

Teacher-parent communication. Teachers also responded to a set of questions from the Early Education Essentials measurement system (Ehrlich et al., 2018), a set of surveys that measure organizational supports in school-based and community-based early education settings. In our larger study, teachers were asked about instructional leadership, teaching practices, professional development experiences, and teacher-parent communication. For the current study, we created a composite for two items that asked about how often "suggest ways parents can reinforce at home what their child is learning in the classroom" and "provide parents with information about their child's progression toward learning and development goals." Teachers were given six response options for these two questions: 1 = never, 2 = once or twice this year, 3 = once or twice a quarter, 4 = once or twice a month, 5 = weekly, or 6 = daily. Cronbach's alphas for the current study sample were modest for the composite score (a = .56, .67, .67, preschool, kindergarten, and first grade, respectively). These items were averaged together across the three years.

Social-emotional well-being. Children's social-emotional well-being outcomes were captured through two sources. For the first source, teachers rated each child on four general domains of social-behavioral skills using the Teacher-Child Rating Scale (TCRS; Hightower et al., 1986). Teachers were asked to indicate how well a given characteristic described the child (1 = not at all, 3 = moderately well, 5 = very well). The task orientation subscale (e.g., completes work, well organized, functions well even with distractions, and works well without adult support; $a = .84, .85, .90$ preschool, kindergarten, and first grade, respectively), peer social skills subscale (e.g., has many friends, is friendly toward peers, and makes friends easily; $a = .81, .79, .86$, preschool, kindergarten, and first grade, respectively), and frustration tolerance subscale (e.g., accepts things not going his/her way, ignores teasing, copes with failure; $a = .82, .85, .88$, preschool, kindergarten, and first grade, respectively) were comprised of five items each. The fourth and final dimension, conduct problems, was based on six items (e.g., disruptive in class, defiant, overly aggressive with their peers; $a = .84, .82, .87$ preschool, kindergarten, and first grade, respectively).

For the second source, data collectors directly assessed children in an interview format in which children were asked how they felt about their teachers and peers, and how much they enjoyed school (Ruzek et al., 2020). Assessors asked children the survey items to which they indicated their level of agreement by pointing to one of three increasingly larger circles, corresponding to less or more agreement. In terms of reliability, Ruzek et al., (2020) report modest reliability in a sample of preschool-aged children.

Covariates. To reduce the possibility of spurious associations, we control for a rich set of child, family, teacher, and classroom covariates. The child- and parent-level covariates included child gender, age at assessment, race/ethnicity, parent education, and household income-to-needs ratio. Our analytic models also included the lagged dependent variables for each of the respective outcomes as well as the time lag between assessments, which is one of the strongest adjustments in the context of a non-randomized control trial (NICHD Early Child Care Research Network & Duncan, 2003). Drawing on teacher surveys, classroom observations, and administrative data, our teacher and classroom covariates included: percent of classroom children who were male, limited English proficient, and had special needs, and teacher education, experience, and race/ethnicity. All time-varying covariates were averaged across the three time points.

Analytic Approach

Using a regression-based framework, we examined the associations between cumulative educational assets across three years and children's home language on their social-emotional outcomes at the end of first grade. Our models included clustered standard errors to account for the nesting of children in classrooms. Missing data occurred most often on our covariates (mean of 8%, range = 0% to 20%). We accounted for missing data using the Full Information Maximum Likelihood (FIML) procedure in Stata 15.0 (Enders, 2001). FIML uses all available information within cases to estimate the missing parameters so that incomplete observations can be included to calculate estimates. All key variables of interest were standardized to have a mean of zero and a standard deviation of one so that coefficients can be interpreted as effect sizes in standard deviation units.

Our first set of analyses examined the main effects of all key predictors and moderators. In separate models for each of the outcomes, we regressed the outcome of interest on the cumulative classroom asset variables and our full set of covariates. We parameterized these variables by taking the mean across preschool, kindergarten, and first grade. After establishing the main effects of these variables, we examined whether children's home language moderated the association between cumulative educational assets and children's social-emotional well-being outcomes. The interactions between educational assets and home language were each examined in separate models and also included the full set of covariates.

Results

Descriptive Statistics

We begin by discussing the descriptive patterns of children's experiences of educational assets and social-emotional well-being from preschool to first grade. Table 2 presents the means and standard deviations for these key predictors and outcomes for the whole analysis sample and by home language.

Table Two

Descriptive statistics of key predictors and outcomes.

	Full sample (N= 1132)		English only (N= 309)		Spanish-speaking (N= 823)		ANOVA F-stat or chi-square
	M	SD	M.	SD	M	SD	
Preschool educational assets							
Teacher-child interactions	4.43	0.47	4.42	0.46	4.44	0.48	0.32
Teacher-child closeness	4.19	0.73	4.24	0.73	4.18	0.73	1.55
Teacher-child conflict	1.56	0.80	1.68	0.89	1.52	0.76	8.29 **
Teacher-parent communication	3.14	0.87	3.17	0.81	3.06	0.89	3.14
Kindergarten educational assets							
Teacher-child interactions	4.10	0.49	4.02	0.48	4.13	0.49	7.45 **
Teacher-child closeness	4.09	0.75	4.20	0.71	4.04	0.77	6.26 *
Teacher-child conflict	1.57	0.76	1.67	0.86	1.53	0.71	5.28 *
Teacher-parent communication	3.20	0.92	3.24	0.84	3.18	0.95	4.29 *
First grade educational assets							
Teacher-child interactions	4.13	0.50	4.05	0.47	4.15	0.50	6.83 **
Teacher-child closeness	4.05	0.71	4.09	0.65	4.04	0.73	0.57
Teacher-child conflict	1.64	0.88	1.80	0.95	1.58	0.85	9.32 **
Teacher-parent communication	3.33	0.85	3.39	0.75	3.26	0.92	0.28

Cumulative assets from preschool to first grade						
Teacher-child interactions	4.27	0.36	4.21	0.38	4.26	0.37	7.32 ***
Teacher-child closeness	4.10	0.61	4.17	0.61	4.12	0.61	3.13
Teacher-child conflict	1.57	0.70	1.75	0.84	1.61	0.75	13.80 ***
Teacher-parent communication	3.70	0.71	3.79	0.70	3.63	0.70	7.26 **
Social-emotional outcomes in spring of first grade						
Teacher-Child Rating Scale						
Conduct Problems	1.88	0.94	1.84	0.94	1.97	1.00	2.67
Social Skills	3.88	0.90	3.91	0.90	3.77	0.95	3.27
Task Orientation	3.12	1.05	3.21	1.09	3.16	1.06	0.32
Frustration Tolerance	3.21	0.98	3.30	0.98	3.08	1.04	6.60 *
Child Interview						
School enjoyment	2.51	0.56	2.59	0.54	2.43	0.62	7.18 **
Feelings about teacher	2.65	0.42	2.65	0.42	2.64	0.41	0.01
Feelings about peers	2.46	0.46	2.54	0.44	2.38	0.54	0.55 ***

Note. CLASS scores range from 1 to 7, with higher scores indicating greater quality of interactions. The STRS scores range from 1 to 5, with higher scores indicating higher levels of closeness or conflict. The 5 Essentials items range from 1 to 6, with 1 indicating "never" and 6 indicating "every day." The Teacher Child Rating Scale subscales range from 1 to 5, with 1 indicating "not at all" and 5 indicating "very well" to describe the child's behaviors. The Child Interview questions range from 1 to 3, with higher scores indicating greater agreement. The last column represents the difference between the English only and Spanish-speaking groups from an F-test. *** $p < .001$; ** $p < .01$; * $p < .05$.

On average, Spanish-speaking children were in classrooms rated higher in the quality of teacher-child interactions than English-speaking children across all three years. Conversely, English-speaking children had higher levels of both closeness and conflict than Spanish-speaking children, as reported by their teachers from preschool to first grade. Teacher-parent communication across preschool through first grade occurred about one to two times a month, on average, with teachers reporting slightly more communication with parents of only English-speaking children than Spanish-speaking children.

In terms of children's social-emotional well-being outcomes at the end of first grade, although there was a trend toward teachers rating English-speaking children's conduct problems lower and their social skills and task orientation higher than Spanish-speaking children, these apparent differences were not statistically significant. Additionally, teachers perceived Spanish-speaking children's frustration tolerance to be significantly lower than English-speaking children. From the child interview, English-speaking children reported enjoying school and having positive feelings about their peers significantly more than Spanish-speaking children in the spring of first grade.

Associations between Educational Assets and Social-Emotional Well-Being

Results from the main effects analyses, as presented in the top panel of Table 3, revealed that the quality of teacher-child interactions experienced from preschool through first grade was not significantly related to teachers' reports of children's conduct problems, social skills, task orientation, and frustration tolerance, or children's reports of their school enjoyment and feelings about their teachers and peers, with absolute effect sizes ranging from .01–.07. In contrast, children with whom teachers reported close relationships across the preschool, kindergarten, and first grade years were reported to demonstrate greater improvements in social skills (ES = .30, p < .001) and task orientation (ES = .19, p < .01). Additionally, when teachers reported greater teacher-child conflict from preschool through first grade, children demonstrated more conduct problems at the end of first grade (ES = .81, p < .001) and less optimal social skills, task orientation, and frustration tolerance (ES = .32-.66, p < .001). Similarly, teacher-child conflict across these three years was related to children reporting less positive feelings about their teacher (ES = -.33, p < .05) and peers (ES = -.39, p < .01) at the end of first grade. Finally, teacher-parent communication from preschool through first grade was associated with an increase in teachers' reports of children's conduct problems at the end of first grade (ES = .21, p < .001).

Differences as a Function of Home Language

Having established the main effects for the key variables of interest, the next set of models tested for potential interactive effects of cumulative educational assets and home language on children's social-emotional well-being. Results for these analyses are provided in the bottom panel of Table 3. There were two significant interactions. First, teacher-parent communication was significantly less associated with conduct problems among children from Spanish-speaking families compared with children whose primary home language was English. Specifically, for every one unit increase in teacher-reported communication with parents, there is an increase of .21 teacher-reported conduct problems for children in English-speaking families, compared with a decrease of -.20 for children in Spanish-speaking families. Thus, while teacher-parent communication is associated with an increase in conduct problems for both groups, the increase is significantly stronger for children from English-speaking families. Second, teacher-reported conflict was more strongly associated with child-reported closeness with peers among children from Spanish-speaking families compared with children whose primary home language was English. For every one unit increase in teacher-reported conflict, English-speaking children's report of their feelings about their peers goes down by .39, whereas Spanish-speaking children's report of their feelings about peers goes up by .41.

Table Three
Regression coefficients from analyses predicting spring of first grade social-emotional outcomes from cumulative educational assets in pre-K, kindergarten, and first grade.

Main Effects										
Outcomes	Teacher-child interactions		Teacher-student closeness		Teacher-student conflict		Teacher-parent communication		Spanish speaker	
Teacher-Child Rating Scale										
Conduct problems	-0.07		0.11		0.81	***	0.21	***	0.04	**
	(0.06)		(0.06)		(0.07)		(0.06)		(0.06)	
Social skils	-0.01		0.30	***	-0.50	***	-0.07		0.12	
	(0.06)		(0.08)		(0.08)		(0.06)		(0.09)	
Task orientation	-0.03		0.19	**	-0.32	***	-0.08		-0.13	
	(0.06)		(0.07)		(0.06)		(0.06)		(0.08)	
Frustration tolerance	0.07		0.11		-0.66	***	-0.04		0.08	
	(0.06)		(0.06)		(0.06)		(0.06)		(0.07)	
Child Interview										
School enjoyment	-0.01		-0.06		-0.25		0.01		0.32	
	(0.12)		(0.15)		(0.14)		(0.11)		(0.17)	
Feelings about teacher	0.02		0.04		-0.33	*	-0.11		0.04	
	(0.10)		(0.10)		(0.13)		(0.10)		(0.12)	
Feelings about peers	0.04		0.04		-0.39	**	-0.02		0.44	**
	(0.13)		(0.15)		(0.13)		(0.13)		(0.15)	

Note. Interaction terms come from separate models for each respective outcome. All continuous variables have been standardized to have a mean of 0 and standard deviation of 1 and, therefore, all estimates reported above correspond to effect sizes. Clustered standard errors in parentheses. Each model includes the respective lagged dependent variable. Child and family baseline covariates include: child age,

Outcomes	Interaction terms							
	Teacher-child interactions x Spanish speaker		Teacher-student closeness x Spanish speaker		Teacher-student conflict x Spanish speaker		Teacher-parent communication x Spanish speaker	
Teacher-Child Rating Scale								
Conduct problems	0.07		-0.05		0.03		0.-0.20	**
	(0.08)		(0.07)		(0.07)		(0.06)	
Social skils	-0.04		0.06		0.00		0.05	
	(0.07)		(0.09)		(0.10)		(0.07)	
Task orientation	0.02		-0.01		-0.11		0.06	
	(0.07)		(0.08)		(0.07)		(0.07)	
Frustration tolerance	0.10		-0.02		0.02		0.03	
	(0.06)		(0.08)		(0.07)		(0.07)	
Child Interview								
School enjoyment	0.14		0.01		0.18		-0.02	
	(0.13)		(0.16)		(0.15)		(0.13)	
Feelings about teacher	0.02		-0.02		0.19		0.00	
	(0.11)		(0.11)		(0.14)		(0.11)	
Feelings about peers	0.02		-0.04		0.41	**	0.04	
	(0.14)		(0.16)		(0.14)		(0.114)	

gender, racial/ethnic minority status, parental educatior, and whether living in poverty. Teacher and classroom covariates include: percent male, percent limited English proficient, percent special needs, teacher years of education, and total class size. CLASS = Classroom Assessment Scoring System. STRS = Student-Teacher Relationship Scale. n = 1,132. *** $p < .001$; ** $p < .01$ * $p < .05$.

Discussion

Children's social and emotional experiences have been shown to influence brain development and are therefore central to their behavior, learning, and health (Center on the Developing Child, 2016; Shonkoff, 2012). Nurturing relationships generally support children's appropriate regulation and lead to the formation of brain pathways and neuroendocrine systems that are necessary for learning and good health. However, nonresponsive relationships can lead to social and emotional dysregulation and suboptimal brain development that has negative consequences for learning and health. Our study contributes to the growing literature on early education, home language, and children's development by studying how cumulative educational assets relate to social and emotional outcomes among a group of Spanish- and English-speaking children attending schools in a district that offers targeted supports to a linguistically diverse student population. Specifically, we examine the associations between children's cumulative experiences of educational assets in the early grades and their social-emotional well-being at the end of first grade among children whose home language was Spanish or English. We also examined the extent to which home language moderated these associations. In particular, this study is among the first to consider children's reports of their social-emotional well-being in early elementary school, providing an opportunity to understand the perspectives of children from a linguistically diverse sample, while also examining teacher-reported social-emotional outcomes. A strength of our study is that we focus on the cumulative aspect of children's early schooling, which examines the interactions that children and their families have with teachers in preschool, kindergarten, and first grade. Understanding these influences is important because children's behavior, capacity to learn, and health are shaped by their social surroundings.

Descriptively, we found that the children from Spanish- and English-speaking families had different assets from their early education experience. Children from Spanish-speaking families in our study experienced higher quality interactions and relationships with their teachers. Specifically, unlike other research that has shown that DLLs generally have access to lower quality classroom environments in their early education (e.g., Park, O'Toole, & Katsiaficas, 2017), children from Spanish-speaking families in our study were more likely to be in classrooms with higher levels of observer rated quality of interactions, and their teachers reported lower levels of conflict with them than their peers from English-speaking families. These strong assets for Spanish-speaking children reflect the district's targeted investments to improve education quality for dual-language learners, which research suggests would support their socioemotional development in the first few years of school (e.g., Downer et al., 2012; Moiduddin, Aikens, Tarullo, West, & Xue, 2012). At the same time that children from Spanish-speaking families had higher quality experiences with their teachers in class, their families' home language may have negative consequences for teacher communication with parents, which was significantly lower than it was for children whose families spoke English at home.

In terms of predictive associations, overall our results indicate that cumulative experiences of educational assets over the first three years of school predict children's social-emotional well-being and do so in similar ways for children from English- and Spanish-speaking families. Specifically, teacher-child relationships and teacher-parent communication are related to a number of important social-emotional outcomes at the end of first grade. The quality of teacher-child relationships is significantly associated with a wide range of child- and teacher-reported social-emotional well-being outcomes. Similar to prior studies examining relationships over the course of a single school year (Howes et al., 2008; Liew et al., 2010), teacher-child closeness was associated with greater social skills and task orientation. Also, consistent with the prior literature (Hamre & Pianta, 2005; Spilt et al., 2012), teacher-child conflict predicted higher levels of children's conduct problems and less optimal social skills, task orientation, and frustration tolerance. These findings reflect research that suggest a close- and conflict-free relationship with teachers promotes feelings of security and increases children's comfort in school, which supports the development of children's social and emotional skills during the early years of schooling (O'Connor et al., 2011).

Importantly, teacher and children's perceptions of their relationship were related. Children with teachers who reported greater conflict across the first three years of school reported more negative feelings about their teacher at the end of first grade The cumulation of conflictual interactions with teachers from preschool through first grade is related to children's maladaptive social-emotional adjustment in school, supporting previous findings that the relationship with teachers in the early years is a key influence on later social-emotional well-being (Ladd, Birch, & Buhs, 1999; O'Connor et al., 2011). These conflicted relationships with teachers may heighten the negative aspects of school for children and interfere with their enjoyment of school and how they feel about those with whom they interact. Such feelings, on the part of the child, may have considerable consequences for their motivation and engagement in subsequent years and could be a key factor for triggering interventions to reduce conflict (Williford et al., 2013).

Our findings suggest that the mechanisms by which teacher conflict shape adjustment in school could differ for children from Spanish-speaking families. For children from English-speaking families, cumulative conflict with teachers was associated with children's perceptions of closeness with their teachers and their peers, reflecting adjustment in the broader social context of school. In contrast, for children from Spanish-speaking families, cumulative conflict with teachers was associated with *increased* closeness with their peers, suggesting that the social context of school—and their adjustment in it—may be more complex for these children.

Spanish-speaking children who experience more conflict with their teachers might lean in to their peer relationships more— perhaps relationships with other children from Spanish-speaking families, who represent the majority in our sample. Shared home language background could be a key consideration for children as they select the peers with whom to engage. Indeed, past research has shown that young children tend to relate to peers who are similar in terms of a number of characteristics, including gender or race/ethnicity (Hanish, Martin, Fabes, Leonard, & Herzog, 2005; Rubin, Lynch, Coplan, Rose-Krasnor, & Booth, 1994). Language itself is also a selecting factor; children with greater fluency in spoken English are more likely to engage and socialize with English-speaking children in the same classroom (Strong, 1983; 1984). This could have complex effects on adjustment and motivation in school for these students, with the potential for either teacher or peer relationships to be a lever for supporting development and achievement in elementary school. Additionally, we found that teacher-parent communication from preschool through first grade was associated with greater teacher-reported conduct problems at the end of first grade. This finding may reflect a pattern in which teachers' perceptions of children's conduct problems trigger their communication with parents, perhaps in an effort to address the concerns in the classroom. In parallel, it may also be the case that parents who are concerned about their child (e.g., school adjustment, adaptability, difficulty making friends) are more likely to engage and communicate with teachers in an attempt to address these concerns (Hughes & Kwok 2007; Ritter, Mont-Reynaud, & Dornsbusch, 1993). For these reasons, it might be that an association between either higher levels of parent or teacher concerns about children's behaviors and high levels of teacher-parent communication is to be expected.

These reasons could also explain why, in our study, Spanish home language moderated the effects of communication on conduct problems such that there was a significantly less strong association for Spanish-speaking families compared to English-speaking families. Language barriers between teachers and parents could contribute to less frequent and less effective communication (Conus & Fahrni, 2019; Crosnoe, 2006; Moreno & Valencia, 2002). Indeed, our analyses reveal that whereas there is more communication overall related to children's conduct problems, there is significantly less communication with parents of Spanish-speaking families. If teachers or parents do not adapt their level or quality of communication in relation to child behavior, then parent communication becomes, by default, less of an asset for these children to scaffold their behavior and socioemotional development in early elementary school.

It is important to note the limitations to this study. Children's social-emotional outcomes were measured by teacher reports, which may be biased by teachers' perceptions of children. Multiple steps were taken in order to handle this bias, including adding in the child interview questions as additional measures of children's social-emotional well-being. A strength of this study is the inclusion of data from a number of sources including students, teachers, and observations. We also included child, family, and classroom characteristics in the models as control variables. These covariates help isolate the relationship between the key predictors and child outcomes. It is also important to note that although the multivariate design is strong, this is a correlational study and causal relationships cannot be inferred. Overall, this study adds to the limited empirical literature on this topic and provides further evidence that the educational assets that children experience from Spanish-speaking homes are an important area for further study.

Additionally, several factors that relate to children's home language were not examined in this study. First, we used an overall measure of the overall quality of classroom interactions and did not examine the additional interactions and practices that teachers use to accommodate the needs of children from Spanish-speaking families, like the extent to which teachers used culturally relevant materials (Castro, Páez, Dickinson, & Frede, 2011), spoke to children in Spanish (Mendez et al., 2015, Raikes et al., 2019), and focus on children developing oral language skills in Spanish and English (Buysse, Peisner-Feinberg, Paez, Hammer, & Knowles, 2014). Future research could consider children's language abilities in both the classroom language of instruction and the child's home language and could assess aspects of classroom quality specific to supporting dual-language learners (White, Fernandez, & Greenfield, 2019). Furthermore, classrooms included in this study comprised students who speak English or Spanish at home. Although the largest proportion of non-English speakers in US schools are native Spanish speakers, many classrooms are not so dichotomous, as multiple languages are likely to be represented in a classroom. Not all Spanish-speaking cultures have similar social and emotional norms and thus Spanish-speaking children may have different developmental trajectories (Halle et al., 2011). Additionally, home language prestige can impact young children's social experiences outside of the home (Fillmore, 2000; Genesee, 2008). This study should be replicated in classrooms that include children from a variety of cultures and diverse language backgrounds.

Finally, future studies might select different educational assets than those selected here. The current study used teacher-child interactions, closeness, and conflict, and teacher-parent communication, but there are other important indicators of children's educational assets. In summary, this study contributes to a growing body of work that looks specifically at preschool classrooms that serve children from linguistically diverse backgrounds and suggests some optimal paths for future research and early education programming. As the field continues to move forward in investigating the educational settings that serve DLL and Spanish-speaking children in the United States, it is important to focus on understanding how different educational assets are related to positive social-emotional development. Such information, in turn, can be used to inform interventions that promote these important outcomes and maximize children's overall well-being.

Author Note

We gratefully acknowledge the support of our many partners: school district leaders, community programs, teachers, parents and children. Their enthusiastic cooperation and participation made much of this work possible. We also extend appreciation and recognition to Marcia Kraft-Sayre, Marianna Lyulchenko, Laura Helferstay, and Brittany Rettig who each made valuable contributions to the project. The research reported here was supported by the Institute of Education Sciences (IES), U.S. Department of Education, through Grant #R305N160021 and #R305B170002 to the University of Virginia. The opinions expressed are those of the authors and do not represent views of IES or the U.S. Department of Education.

References

Anderson, A. R., Christenson, S. L., Sinclair, M. F., & Lehr, C. A. (2004). Check & Connect: The importance of relationships for promoting engagement with school. *Journal of School Psychology, 42*(2), 95–113.

Ansari, A., & Pianta, R. C. (2018). The role of elementary school quality in the persistence of preschool effects. *Children and Youth Services Review, 86*, 120–127.

Barnett, W. S. (2011). Effectiveness of early educational intervention. *Science, 333*(6045), 975–978.

Birch, S. H., & Ladd, G. W. (1997). The teacher-child relationship and children's early school adjustment. *Journal of School Psychology, 35*(1), 61–79.

Blair, C., Berry, D., Mills-Koonce, R., Granger, D., & FLP Investigators. (2013). Cumulative effects of early poverty on cortisol in young children: Moderation by autonomic nervous system activity. *Psychoneuroendocrinology, 38*(11), 2666–2675.

Bornstein, M. H., Davidson, L., Keyes, C. L., & Moore, K. A., & The Center for Child Well-Being (Eds.). (2003). Well-being: Positive development across the life course. *Adolescence, 150*, 386.

Bradley, R. H., & Corwyn, R. F. (2002). Socioeconomic status and child development. *Annual Review of Psychology, 53*(1), 371–399.

Bronfenbrenner, U., & Morris, P. A. (1998). The ecology of developmental processes. In W. Damon & R. M. Lerner (Eds.), *Handbook of child psychology: Theoretical models of human development* (p. 993–1028). John Wiley & Sons Inc.

Burchinal, M., Vandergrift, N., Pianta, R., & Mashburn, A. (2010). Threshold analysis of association between child care quality and child outcomes for low-income children in pre-kindergarten programs. *Early Childhood Research Quarterly, 25*(2), 166–176.

Buysse, V., Peisner-Feinberg, E., Páez, M., Hammer, C. S., & Knowles, M. (2014). Effects of early education programs and practices on the development and learning of dual language learners: A review of the literature. *Early Childhood Research Quarterly, 29*(4), 765–785.

Cash, A. H., Ansari, A., Grimm, K. J., & Pianta, R. C. (2019) Power of two: The impact of 2 years of high-quality teacher child interactions. *Early Education and Development, 30*(1), 60–81.

Castro, D. C., Páez, M. M., Dickinson, D. K., & Frede, E. (2011). Promoting language and literacy in young dual language learners: Research, practice, and policy. *Child Development Perspectives, 5*(1), 15–21.

Chaudry, A., & Datta, A. R. (2017). The current landscape for public pre-kindergarten programs. In K. Dodge, & D. Phillips (Eds.), *The current state of scientific knowledge on pre-kindergarten effects.* Brookings Institution.

Collaborative for Academic, Social, and Emotional Learning (CASEL). (2003). *Safe and sound: An educational leader's guide to evidence-based social and emotional learning (SEL) programs-Illinois edition.* Chicago, IL: Author.

Center on the Developing Child at Harvard University. (2016). *From best practices to breakthrough impacts: A science-based approach to building a more promising future for young children and families.* Harvard University.

Coburn, C. E., Hill, H. C., & Spillane, J. P. (2016). Alignment and accountability in policy design and implementation: The common core state standards and implementation research. *Educational Researcher, 45*(4), 243–251.

Conus, X., & Fahrni, L. (2019). Routine communication between teachers and parents from minority groups: An endless misunderstanding? *Educational Review, 71*(2), 234–256.

Copple, C., & Bredekamp, S. (2009). *Developmentally appropriate practice in early childhood programs serving children from birth through age 8.* National Association for the Education of Young Children.

Crosnoe, R. (2006). *Mexican roots, American schools: Helping Mexican immigrant children succeed.* Stanford University Press.

Denham, S. A., Blair, K. A., DeMulder, E., Levitas, J., Sawyer, K., Auerbach–Major, S., & Queenan, P. (2003). Preschool emotional competence: Pathway to social competence? *Child Development, 74*(1), 238–256.

Dong, M., Giles, W. H., Felitti, V. J., Dube, S R., Williams, J. E., Chapman, D. P., & Anda, R. F. (2004). Insights into causal pathways for ischemic heart disease: Adverse childhood experiences study. *Circulation, 110*(13),1761–1766.

Downer, J. T., López, M. L., Grimm, K. J., Hamagami, A., Pianta, R. C., & Howes, C. (2012). Observations of teacher–child interactions in classrooms serving Latinos and dual language learners: Applicability of the Classroom Assessment Scoring System in diverse settings. *Early Childhood Research Quarterly, 27*(1), 21–32.

Ehrlich, S. B., Pacchiano, D., Stein, A. G., Wagner, M. R., Park, S., Frank, E., ... & Young, C. (2019). Early Education Essentials: Validation of surveys measuring early education organizational conditions. *Early Education and Development, 30*(4), 540–567.

Enders, C. K. (2001). The impact of nonnormality on full information maximum-likelihood estimation for structural equation models with missing data. *Psychological Methods, 6*(4), 352–370.

Evans, G. W. (2003). A multimethodological analysis of cumulative risk and allostatic load among rural children. *Developmental Psychology, 39*(5), 924–933.

Fillmore, L. W. (2000). Loss of family languages: Should educators be concerned? *Theory into Practice, 39*(4), 203–210.

Finn, J. D., & Zimmer, K. (2012). Student engagement: What is it? Why does it matter? In S. L. Christenson, A. L. Reschly, & C. Wylie (Eds.), *Handbook of research on student engagement* (pp. 97–131). Springer.

Genesee, F. (2008). Early dual language learning. *Zero to Three, 29*(1), 17–23.

Groeneveld, M. G., Vermeer, H. J., Van IJzendoorn, M. H., & Linting, M. (2011). Enhancing home-based child care quality through video-feedback intervention: A randomized controlled trial. *Journal of Family Psychology, 25*(1), 86–96.

Guthrie, J. T., Wigfield, A., Barbosa, P., Perencevich, K. C., Taboada, A., Davis, M. H., ... & Tonks, S. (2004). Increasing reading comprehension and engagement through concept-oriented reading instruction. *Journal of Educational Psychology, 96*(3), 403–423.

Halle, T., Castro, D., Franco, X., McSwiggan, M., Hair, E., & Wandner, L. (2011). The role of early care and education in the development of young Latino dual language learners. *Latina and Latino Children and Mental Health, 1*, 63–90.

Halle, T. G., Whittaker, J. V., Zepeda, M., Rothenberg, L., Anderson, R., Daneri, P., ... & Buysse, V. (2014). The social-emotional development of dual language learners: Looking back at existing research and moving forward with purpose. *Early Childhood Research Quarterly, 29*(4), 734–749.

Hamre, B. K., & Pianta, R. C. (2001). Early teacher-child relationships and the trajectory of children's school outcomes through eighth grade. *Child Development, 72*(2), 625–638. doi:10.1111/1467-8624.00301

Hamre, B. K., & Pianta, R. C. (2005). Can instructional and emotional support in the first-grade classroom make a difference for children at risk of school failure? *Child Development, 76*(5), 949–967.

Hanish, L. D., Martin, C. L., Fabes, R. A., Leonard, S., & Herzog, M. (2005). Exposure to externalizing peers in early childhood: Homophily and peer contagion processes. *Journal of Abnormal Child Psychology, 33*(3), 267–281.

Hatfield, B. E., Hestenes, L. L., Kintner-Duffy, V. L., & O'Brien, M. (2013). Classroom emotional support predicts differences in preschool children's cortisol and alpha-amylase levels. *Early Childhood Research Quarterly, 28*, 347–356.

Hatfield, B. E., & Williford, A. P. (2017). Cortisol patterns for young children displaying disruptive behavior: Links to a teacher-child, relationship-focused intervention. *Prevention Science, 18*(1), 40–49.

Hertzman, C. (2012). Putting the concept of biological embedding in historical perspective. *Proceedings of the National Academy of Sciences, 109*(Supplement 2), 17160–17167.

Hightower, A. D., Work, W. C., Cowen, E. L., Lotyczewski, B. S., Spinell, A. P., Guare, J. C., & Rohrbeck, C. A. (1986). The Teacher-Child Rating Scale: A brief objective measure of elementary children's school problem behaviors and competencies. *School Psychology Review, 15*(3), 393–409.

Howes, C., Burchinal, M., Pianta, R., Bryant, D., Early, D., Clifford, R., & Barbarin, O. (2008). Ready to learn? Children's pre-academic achievement in pre-kindergarten programs. *Early Childhood Research Quarterly, 23*(1), 27–50.

Hughes, J., & Kwok, O. M. (2007). Influence of student-teacher and parent-teacher relationships on lower achieving readers' engagement and achievement in the primary grades. *Journal of Educational Psychology, 99*(1), 39–51.

Justice, L. M., McGinty, A. S., Zucker, T., Cabell, S. Q., & Piasta, S. B. (2013). Bi-directional dynamics underlie the complexity of talk in teacher-child play-based conversations in classrooms serving at-risk pupils. *Early Childhood Research Quarterly, 28*(3), 496–508.

Ladd, G. W., Birch, S. H., & Buhs, E. S. (1999). Children's social and scholastic lives in kindergarten: Related spheres of influence? *Child Development, 70*(6), 1373–1400.

Liew, J., Chen, Q., & Hughes, J. N. (2010). Child effortful control, teacher–student relationships, and achievement in academically at-risk children: Additive and interactive effects. *Early Childhood Research Quarterly, 25*(1), 51–64.

McCartney, K., Dearing, E., Taylor, B. A., & Bub, K. L. (2007). Quality child care supports the achievement of low-income children: Direct and indirect pathways through caregiving and the home environment. Journal of Applied *Developmental Psychology, 28,* 411–426.

McClelland, M. M., Cameron, C. E., Wanless, S. B., & Murray, A., Saracho, O., & Spodek, B., (2007). Executive function, behavioral self-regulation, and social-emotional competence. *Contemporary Perspectives on Social Learning in Early Childhood Education, 1,* 113–137.

McEwen, B. S. (1998). Protective and damaging effects of stress mediators. *The New England Journal of Medicine, 338*(3), 171–179.

Mendez, L. L., Crais, E. R., Castro, D. C., & Kainz, K. (2015). A culturally and linguistically responsive vocabulary approach for young Latino dual language learners. *Journal of Speech, Language and Hearing Research, 58*(1), 93–106.

Moiduddin, E., Aikens, N., Tarullo, L., West, J., & Xue, Y. (2012). *Child outcomes and classroom quality in FACES 2009* (Report No. b259d300a7764b6496a0c86 eab455781). Mathematica Policy Research

Moreno, R. P., & Valencia, R. R. (2002). Chicano families and schools: Myths, knowledge, and future directions for understanding. *Chicano school failure and success: Past, present, and future, 2,* 227–250.

National Institute of Child Health and Human Development (NICHD) Early Child Care Research Network & Duncan, G. J. (2003). Modeling the impacts of child care quality on children's preschool cognitive development. *Child Development, 74*(5), 1454–1475.

National Task Force on Early Childhood Education for Hispanics (2007). *National Task Force on Early Childhood Education for Hispanics/La Comisión Nacional para la Educación de la Niñez Hispana Executive Report: Para Nuestros Niños: Expanding and Improving Early Education for Hispanics.* National Task Force on Early Childhood Education for Hispanics. https://www.fcd-us.org/assets/2016/04/PNNExecReport.pdf

Nelson, C. A., & Bloom, F. E. (1997). Child development and neuroscience. *Child Development, 68*(5), 970–987.

O'Connor, E. E., Dearing, E., & Collins, B. A. (2011). Teacher-child relationship and behavior problem trajectories in elementary school. *American Educational Research Journal, 48*(1), 120–162.

Pakarinen, E., Kiuru, N., Lerkkanen, M. K., Poikkeus, A. M., Ahonen, T., & Nurmi, J. E. (2011). Instructional support predicts children's task avoidance in kindergarten. *Early Childhood Research Quarterly, 26*(3), 376–386.

Park, M., O'Toole, A., & Katsiaficas, C. (2017). *Dual Language Learners: A National Demographic and Policy Profile. Fact Sheet*. Migration Policy Institute.

Pianta, R. C. (2001). *STRS: Student-Teacher Relationship Scale.*

Pianta, R. C., La Paro, K. M., & Hamre, B. K. (2008). *Classroom Assessment Scoring System (CLASS): Manual K–3*. Paul H Brookes Publishing.

Pianta, R. C., Steinberg, M. S., & Rollins, K. B. (1995). The first two years of school: Teacher-child relationships and deflections in children's classroom adjustment. *Development and Psychopathology, 7*(2), 295–312. doi:10.1017/s0954579400006519

Raikes, H. H., White, L., Green, S., Burchinal, M., Kainz, K., Horm, D., ... Esteraich, J. (2019). Use of the home language in preschool classrooms and first-and second-language development among dual-language learners. *Early Childhood Research Quarterly, 47*, 145–158.

Raver, C. C., & Knitzer, J. (2002). *Ready to enter: What research tells policymakers about strategies to promote social and emotional school readiness among three- and four-year-old children.*

Reschly, A. L., Huebner, E. S., Appleton, J. J., & Antaramian, S. (2008). Engagement as flourishing: The contribution of positive emotions and coping to adolescents' engagement at school and with learning. *Psychology in the Schools, 45*(5), 419–431.

Ritter, P. L., Mont-Reynaud, R., & Dombusch, S. M. (1993). Minority parents and their youth: Concern, encouragement, and support for school achievement. *Families and schools in a pluralistic society*, 107–119.

Rubin, K. H., Lynch, D., Coplan, R., Rose-Krasnor, L., & Booth, C. L. (1994). "Birds of a feather...": Behavioral concordances and preferential personal attraction in children. *Child Development, 65*(6), 1778–1785.

Ruzek, E., Jirout, J., Schenke, K., Vitiello, V., Whittaker, J. V., & Pianta, R. (2020). Using self-report surveys to measure PreK children's academic orientations: A psychometric evaluation. *Early Childhood Research Quarterly, 50*, 55–66.

Shonkoff, J. P. (2012). Leveraging the biology of adversity to address the roots of disparities in health and development. *Proceedings of the National Academy of Sciences, 109*(Supplement 2), 17302–17307.

Shonkoff, J., & Phillips, D., National Academy of Sciences – National Research Council, W. D. B. on C. and F., & Institute of Medicine, N. W. D. (2000). From *Neurons to Neighborhoods: The Science of Early Childhood Development*.

Spilt, J. L., Hughes, J. N., Wu, J. Y., & Kwok, O. M. (2012). Dynamics of teacher–student relationships: Stability and change across elementary school and the influence on children's academic success. *Child Development, 83*(4), 1180–1195.

Strong, M. (1983). Social styles and the second language acquisition of Spanish-speaking kindergarteners. *TESOL Quarterly, 17*(2), 241–58.

Strong, M. (1984). Integrative motivation: Cause or result of successful second language acquisition? *Language Learning, 34*(3), 1–13.

Szanton, S. L., Gill, J. M., & Allen, J. K. (2005). Allostatic load: a mechanism of socio-economic health disparities? *Biological Research for Nursing, 7*(1), 7–15.

Vernon-Feagans, L., Mokrova, I. L., Carr, R. C., Garrett-Peters, P. T., Burchinal, M. R., & Family Life Project Key Investigators. (2019). Cumulative years of classroom quality from kindergarten to third grade: Prediction to children's third grade literacy skills. *Early Childhood Research Quarterly, 47*, 531–540.

Vitiello, V. E., Bassok, D., Hamre, B. K., Player, D., & Williford, A. P. (2018). Measuring the quality of teacher–child interactions at scale: Comparing research-based and state observation approaches. *Early Childhood Research Quarterly, 44*, 161–169.

Vygotsky, L. S. (1978). Interaction between learning and development. (M. Lopez-Morillas, Trans.). In M. Cole, V. John-Steiner, S. Scribner, & E. Souberman (Eds.), *Mind in society: The development of higher psychological processes* (pp. 79–91). Harvard University Press.

Watamura, S. E., Kryzer, E. M., & Robertson, S. S. (2009). Cortisol patterns at home and child care: Afternoon differences and evening recovery in children attending very high quality full-day center-based child care. *Journal of Applied Developmental Psychology, 30*(4), 475–485.

White, L. J., Fernandez, V. A., & Greenfield, D. B. (2019). Assessing Classroom Quality for Latino Dual Language Learners in Head Start: DLL-Specific and General Teacher-Child Interaction Perspectives. *Early Education and Development, 31*(2), 1–29.

Williford, A. P., Maier, M. F., Downer, J. T., Pianta, R. C., & Howes, C. (2013). Understanding how children's engagement and teachers' interactions combine to predict school readiness. *Journal of Applied Developmental Psychology, 34*(6), 299–309.

Wilson, H. K., Pianta, R. C., & Stuhlman, M. (2007). Typical classroom experiences in first grade: The role of classroom climate and functional risk in the development of social competencies. *The Elementary School Journal, 108*(2), 81–96.

Zigler, E., & Styfco, S. J. (2010). *Development at risk series: The hidden history of Head Start*. Oxford University Press.

Promoting Health and Wellness in Young Children: Preschool Assessment

Bruce A. Bracken and Lea A. Theodore

Abstract

Children's formative development is most critical during the preschool years. It is during the earliest years of a child's life when the fundamental building blocks of learning, cognitive development, academic achievement, information processing, language, and interpersonal skills are acquired and developed. Preschools are well suited to shape children's overall health and well-being, with burgeoning research demonstrating a relationship between early life experiences and subsequent adult health. Preschool and quality daycare provide rich opportunities for children's learning, yielding long-lasting and significant effects. Comprehensive preschool assessment sheds light on aspects of the whole child, providing early identification of potential problems and the subsequent development of evidence-based interventions to address delays in development. The following chapter will provide a rationale for preschool assessment, identify specific domains in need of consideration, and promote the systematic linkage of established interventions to promote children's intellectual functioning, academic achievement, information processing, and skill development.

Keywords: Preschool, Assessment, Intervention, Whole Child

Introduction

A child's formative development is most critical during the preschool years. Research outcomes and advances in the field of preschool education during the past few decades have documented the significant benefits of high-quality education and enrichment opportunities and their inextricable link to the development of productive members of society. Long-term benefits associated with quality preschool education include higher rates of high school graduation, increased matriculation in college, greater likelihood of securing skilled labor positions, and improved health as adults (Sheridan et al., 2019; Mistry et al., 2012). It is during the earliest years of a child's life when the fundamental building blocks of learning, cognitive development, academic achievement, information processing, language and interpersonal skills are acquired and developed. Assessment of these various domain-specific skills allows practitioners to evaluate children's ability to surmount curricular demands, as well as meet the behavioral expectations of formal education (Theodore, in press). For a comprehensive review of relevant preschool skill and behavioral assessment domains, investigate current preschool assessment books (e.g., Alfonso et al., in press-a; Bracken & Nagle, 2007).

Comprehensive preschool assessments reveal important aspects of the whole child, i.e., individual strengths and weaknesses, areas of development and learning delays and advances, and school readiness. Examination of these areas assist in the early identification of potential problems and the subsequent development of evidence-based interventions to address lags in development. For children who underperform in critical areas, early intervention is essential to mitigate deficits, because unresolved issues or unaddressed delays often result in an achievement gap that increases cumulatively over time (Jensen, 1974). Whether learning or developmental delays are associated with federal legislation mandating educational services, evolving political or philosophical dynamics, or individual state's early childhood educational standards, there is an increasing awareness that early childhood intervention is far more efficacious than interventions at any other age level. A direct link between assessment and intervention at every developmental level is considered essential during early childhood (Bagnato et al., 2010; Nagle et al., in press). This chapter will provide a rationale for preschool assessment and identify specific domains in need of detailed assessment to systematically link established interventions to areas of deficit, thereby promoting intellectual functioning, academic achievement, information processing, and skill development.

Legislative Mandates for Preschool Assessment and Intervention

For more than 50 years, a coalition of educators, psychologists, politicians, legislatures, and child advocacy groups have developed and promulgated sound educational standards designed to shape early educational expectations and experiences. The growing acceptance of the importance of early childhood assessment and intervention has resulted in convergent actions across organizational, state, and national levels. The recognized significance of preschool assessment, having coalesced as it has, has ascended from disparate early grass roots efforts to the enactment of state and federal legislation. To fully appreciate the current status of early childhood education, it is important to reflect on the historical changes and transformation of laws associated with early childhood initiatives. The following section provides a capsule summary of the historical timeline of early childhood legislation that has culminated in today's assessment and intervention practices for young children.

Individuals with Disabilities Education Act (IDEA)

Federal legislation (e.g., IDEA, 1975–2006) stipulated that all students with disabilities, from birth through 21 years of age, would have equal access to learning opportunities through a free and appropriate public education (FAPE). Significantly, preschool education was identified as a critical component of this law and the legislation therein set the stage for early childhood education. To this end, comprehensive preschool assessment must focus on content, process, and procedure, including an emphasis on the inclusion of parents and teachers in evaluations, as well as the assessment of authentic, developmentally appropriate abilities and behaviors that are responsive to intervention.

State and National Efforts

Nationally, the promotion of state standards from kindergarten through grade 12 was promulgated by The National Governors Association in 2003. Such an endorsement of early childhood educational standards was grounded in the belief that state standards would ensure that students, regardless of where they attended school, would receive a more uniform and stronger basic education. Special concern was expressed in the document about identifying and closing the gap between 'at-risk' students, including minority and economically disadvantaged students, and their more economically advantaged peers.

These collective efforts prompted former George W. Bush's presidential administration to introduce the *"Good Start, Grow Smart"* initiative, which emphasized the importance of cognitive development in children between the ages of birth through age five. The *Good Start, Grow Smart* program led to a downward extension of the "No Child Left Behind" legislation (Public Law 107-110), introducing accountability in early childhood education. This series of actions laid the foundation for the development of common instructional content during the preschool and the primary grades, as well as promoted the formation of early childhood educational standards in all 50 states. Significantly, these educational benchmarks addressed the "whole child," including cognitive, academic, behavioral, social/ emotional, linguistic, and physical development.

In 2009, President Barak Obama announced his support for *Race to the Top*, the nation's largest federally funded early childhood initiative, subsidized through the Department of Education. This initiative provides financial support to economically disadvantaged children and families to ensure they receive high quality education and requisite resources and services. *Race to the Top* endeavored to meet four primary goals: (1) Adopt standards, assessments, and interventions that prepare students for productive lives; (2) enhance educational data systems to measure student growth and inform teachers; (3) recruit, develop, reward, and retain effective educators; and (4) improve America's lowest-achieving schools (Bracken, 2013).

In addition to these previously mentioned goals, *Race to the Top* prioritized: (1) developing educational programs in the STEM areas (i.e., Science, Technology, Engineering, and Mathematics); (2) creating educational practices that improve school readiness (including social, emotional, and cognitive functioning), and improving the transition between preschool and kindergarten; (3) expanding statewide data systems across time that would include data from special education programs (e.g., English language learner programs, early childhood programs); and (4) improving all parts of the education system by creating a seamless transition for all preschool-through-graduate school (P-21) students.

State Standards Movement

Bracken and Crawford (2010) reviewed 5C states' early childhood educational standards and the social-political conditions that influenced the development of these standards. Notably, although the nation was beginning to employ standards for early childhood education, educational standards were inconsistent across states. The Bracken and Crawford (2010) review focused on the incidence of basic concepts in state's early childhood educationa standards, derived from the Bracken Basic Concept Scale–Third Edition (BBCS-3; Bracken, 2006a, 2006b) and the Bracken School Readiness Assessment–Third Edition (Bracken, 2007). Their review cited Scott-L ttle and researcher's work (2003) as having published an influential statement on the need for early childhood educational standards, *Standards for Preschool Children's Learning and Development: Who Has Standards, How Were They Developed, and How Are They Used?* That paper emphasized educational accountability, highlighting the "widespread growth of early childhood programs in the late 1990s" and the mounting concern about the "growing divide between the poor and non-poor" (p. 2). Also important for the formation of educational standards was the effort of the National Education Goals Panel (NEGP, 1989), formally defining what "ready to learn" actually means.

The National Association for the Education of Young Children (NAEYC), another leader in the development of early childhood educational standards, published a joint paper on the need for early childhood standards in 2004. The NAEYC and the National Association of Early Childhood Specialists in State Departments of Education (NAECS/SDE) drafted a statement elucidating a process for establishing early childhood educational standards. This statement paved the way for accreditation curriculum requirements for early childhood programs. The participating organizations approved the curriculum standards draft two years later (NAEYC, 2004).

Resulting from these combined efforts, a consensus now exists that rigorous education should occur at all levels throughout a child's educational career, the process must be uniform, lead to accountability, and comport to accepted educational standards. In response to the psychoeducational needs identified by scientists and practitioners, early childhood assessments must now match IDEA legislation mandates, states' educational standards, and current philosophical, academic, and political initiatives related to sound early childhood assessment and intervention.

Rationale for Preschool Assessment

The literature clearly demonstrates that between birth and age seven, learning and development occur at very rapid rates, with growth curves that are steeper than any age thereafter. To understand the importance of early childhood assessment and intervention, it is essential to differentiate between learned behaviors and behaviors that are developed. Development is a natural unfolding of children's abilities and characteristics that occur in a prescribed and universal sequence across race/ethnicity, sex, national origin, or any other human condition. Development occurs in the same sequence, but not at the same rate, for all individuals (e.g., all children sit before they crawl; crawl before they walk; and walk before they run). Moreover, no matter how ardently we might try, we cannot "teach" children to sit, crawl, walk, or run—they develop these functions only when they are biologically, cognitively, and physically ready.

Learning, on the other hand, is the accumulation of knowledge and abilities that result from a developing person interacting with his or her environment in a meaningful way. For example, although children acquire the ability to crawl or walk through the natural developmental process, they learn about their environments as they crawl or toddle from one place to another within their environment, and by seeing all that is present as they approach or move about. Importantly, as educators, our goal is to create stimulating and safe environments that allow children to both develop in an unrestricted manner and learn maximally. Early childhood assessment encompasses both developmental phenomena and learning outcomes in a combined manner because the two modes of behavior are inextricably linked.

Developmental psychology and educational literature have long shown that the most rapid course of physical, cognitive, motoric, linguistic, and neurological development occurs during the first few years of life. Corresponding with this period of rapid development are "critical periods," or windows of opportunity for young children to best benefit from experiences that contribute to optimal whole child development, health, and wellness. Children who are deprived of, or who have limited meaningful experiences during critical periods of development, typically lag behind their peers with respect to cognitive development, academic achievement, and behavioral comportment vis-a-vis children who have had a richer exposure to various cultural and educational opportunities. Unfortunately, remediation of children's stunted growth after these critical periods pass is much more difficult than if redress is provided while the windows of opportunity are fully opened. Therefore, identifying the need for and the provision of quality interventions during these critical periods is essential for fostering optimal learning and development in infants, toddlers, and young children.

Ideally, educators and psychologists would identify delays in children's development and learning early on and provide empirically supported interventions to overcome children's deficits during the time-period when such skills or abilities are most sensitive to growth, change, and enhancement. Educational programs such as Project Head Start or other experimental early childhood educational demonstration programs (e.g., Abecedarian Project, Perry Preschool Program) have demonstrated the benefits of early assessment, intervention, and progress monitoring. Programs such as Head Start have extended their scope of involvement to the development of requisite curricular skills that promote school readiness, including the provision of medical, dental, and mental health services and healthy eating behaviors and habits, as well as the acquisition of appropriate interpersonal skills. Thus, Head Start seeks to address the needs of the whole child, beginning in early childhood, targeting not just cognitive and academic functioning, but social and emotional functioning, behavioral comportment, and health and wellness for preschool children (Rossin-Slater, 2015; Whitcomb, 2018). Research has demonstrated the long-term well-being and health benefits of Project Head Start, including reducing the likelihood of obesity, mortality, and smoking, and enhancing nutrition and overall child health (Frisvold & Lumeng, 2011; Rossin-Slater, 2015). Similarly, The Perry Program and Abecedarian Project showed similar positive health outcomes for early childhood education, such as diminished cardiovascular and metabolic diseases and lower overall blood pressure (Currie, 2001; Masse & Barnett, 2002).

A review of successful early childhood projects reveals that learning is greatest when evidence-based interventions for young children are intensive, of high quality, employed for a reasonable duration, and consistent (Ramey & Ramey, 1998). Unlike previous funded programs with less well-defined curricula, such as Title I school-based remedial programs, focused projects like the Perry Preschool Program and the Abecedarian Project used careful developmental timing, curricular intensity, direct provision of learning experiences, program breadth and flexibility, instructional differentiation, and on-going progress monitoring.

Independent researchers, such as Wilson (2004), have demonstrated that when assessment of authentic content is followed-up with focused interventions, young children can make significant and meaningful improvements in their knowledge and skills across diverse content areas, and over brief periods of time. Bracken and Panter (Bracken & Panter, 2011; Panter & Bracken, 2000; Panter & Bracken, 2013) also highlighted the essential nature of the direct, content-focused approach to assessment, intervention, and progress monitoring for successful early childhood education, especially when the assessed and taught content is founded in well-defined early childhood states' educational standards and school curricula. These programmatic and independent findings illustrate the importance of assessing a full range of knowledge at a deep level using psychometrically sound preschool instruments (Alfonso & Flanagan, 2009; Bracken, 1987), followed by empirically-supported interventions with ongoing progress monitoring, to provide foundational support for young students' learning (Theodore, in press).

Assessment Domains

Authentic preschool assessment follows a hierarchical arrangement of domains, subdomains, and specific developmental behaviors. Each domain is composed of multiple facets or subdomains of functioning. Hierarchically, systematic early childhood assessment includes broad learning and developmental domains (e.g., language) that depict a child's current level of functioning. Moreover, within each broad communication domain there are essential subareas that collectively compose the domain (e.g., receptive and expressive language). Further, within these more specific aspects of communication, there more definitive behaviors, such as receptive and expressive vocabularies (Bracken, 2006a, 2006b; Dunn et al., 2007). The following section provides a brief description of essential early childhood assessment domains, subdomains, and a sample of specific behavioral indicators of development. Further, the core domains and subdomains of development and learning that comprise a thorough and complete preschool assessment, are delineated in multiple sources (e.g., Alfonso et al., in press-b; Bracken, 2013).

Cognitive

The cognitive domain addresses behaviors associated with learning and development in the most global sense; that is, development of cognitive functioning and experiential learning drawn from the environment and every day events, as well as from formal settings (e.g., preschools, daycare centers). In order for children to learn effectively, their cognitive skills must include well developed short-term (i.e., immediate) and long-term memory (i.e., memory of more distant experiences and facts) and sustained attention. The early childhood assessment of cognition (i.e., intelligence), including reasoning, memory, and quantitative skills can be conducted with traditional language- and culturally-loaded intelligence tests (e.g., Wechsler Preschool and Primary Scale of Intelligence–Fourth Edition, Wechsler, 2012) or through totally nonverbal and culturally fair intelligence tests (e.g., Universal Nonverbal Intelligence Test, Bracken & McCallum, 1998, 2016).

Additionally, sound cognitive functioning includes the ability to differentiate the hierarchical arrangement of percepts and concepts; that is, the ability to perceive important conceptual characteristics of objects (e.g., blue color, small size, square shape, smooth texture) and group those characteristics conceptually with into categories (e.g., colors, sizes, shapes, textures) (Bracken, 2006, 2007, in press). Using percepts and concepts, children begin to reason with the knowledge they have accumulated. For example, they may begin to deduce that most plant leaves are green — and begin to inquire why leaves are generally green. Attentive children may notice that cubes provide better building blocks than balls or oddly shaped objects and develop a sense of how objects can be combined to form wholes greater than their respective parts (e.g., several blocks combined might represent a fort, bridge, or vehicle.). Finally, among the most important cognitive skills are attention and executive functioning—skills needed to sustain attention long enough to complete an activity while attending to important details, features, and relationships and subsequently use that information collectively to generalize an effective approach and plan for similar future situations.

Memory

Memory consists of short-term immediate recall, long-term delayed recall, and working memory (i.e., the ability to retain information in memory while using it simultaneously to solve a problem). Accurate and useable memory also requires effective and non-impaired use of basic channels of communication (e.g., auditory, visual, tactile), as well as the nature of the material to be recalled (e.g., verbal, spatial, numerical); hence, the importance of visual and auditory screenings before conducting assessments. Memory can be simple (e.g., recalling a single object or number) or it can be complex, using combined channels of communication and dissimilar content. For example, a teacher's simple question to a child, "How many red, tall flowers did you see on the picture?" is a question presented aurally. The child must respond orally, after recalling previously viewed multicolored flowers on a page, and then count the number of red flowers that were tall, as opposed to those that were short, all from memory.

Percepts and Concepts

Children begin to differentiate objects in their environment, and they do so because of dominant characteristics they perceive. Those objects may have no inherent meaning to the child initially—they are just sights the child notices (e.g., chair, table, bed). The sight of these objects initially represents percepts because the objects are perceived through the senses but have no special meaning to the child; that is because they have not yet acquired the status of becoming concepts. Once these objects develop meaning and their salient characteristics are used to define them, they attain the status of being concepts (i.e., multiple salient features that in combination define the object as fitting into a specific category). As concepts, they can be categorized according to their salient features, which then classifies them within different conceptual categories. For example, a blue bowl might be categorized with other dishes used in the kitchen; it might be grouped with other objects that hold a substance (e.g., soup, cereal) or are used for mixing (e.g., mixing bowl); it could be classified among other objects that are blue. As such, percepts represent what the child notices as a single object; concepts are what the child organizes and generalizes into meaningful categories based on the features that were initially perceived (Bracken, 1984, 2006a, 2006b, in progress).

Reasoning

Reasoning combines recalled information that might be perceptual or conceptual to solve problems, see relationships, create new combinations, and so on. When a child recalls that steam locomotives have loud whistles, tea kettles whistle on stovetops, and both of these disparate objects make a similar high-pitched noise, the child might begin to reason that steam, when passing through a small hole, is what makes the whistling sound. Moreover, through reasoning, the child might also see that if one regulates the volume of steam passing through the hole, they can vary the intensity of sound produced.

Attention and Executive Functioning

The ability to attend with intention is essential for memory, perception, conceptualization, and reasoning. Children must sustain attention long enough to discern relevant from irrelevant features of objects or a situation to the point of understanding associations, relationships, or utility. Further, children must attend with sufficient focus and time to effectively comprehend and solve problems. Without effective attention and awareness, children flit from experience to experience without discriminating relevant from irrelevant information. Executive functioning is the ability to make a plan, organize time and material effectively, execute the plan, and then evaluate how well the plan worked. Attention and executive functioning are central to children effectively organizing their lives, planning for future events, following through on their plans, and anticipating how to approach future situations. Children's ability to focus their thinking and to concentrate are essential components of wellbeing throughout life (Thompson, 2014).

Communication Domain

Communication involves receiving and expressing information through multiple channels of communication. At a foundational level, children hear (i.e., aural communication mode) and speak (i.e., oral communication mode); however, children also communicate non-verbally (e.g., pointing, shrugging, sign language), which employs a tactile channel of communication. As children participate in school-related activities, they begin to employ cross-modal communications based on combinations of these fundamental channels of communication. For example, when children learn to read, even silent reading, they "hear" what their eyes are viewing. Similarly, children may feel an object with their eyes closed, and "see" a ball in their hands. In addition, children might provide text in printed form, using the tactile mode of communication. Although sophisticated communication is complex and can cross modalities, we generally think of communication as either receptive or expressive in nature. The assessment of speech and communication and speech requires a comprehensive array of approaches, methods, and instruments (Crais, 2011).

Receptive Language. Although a child can receive communicated information through their eyes, ears, hands, and so on, communicated information for the preliterate child is largely spoken. The extent to which children perceive aural communications accurately depends on their hearing acuity, the volume they can effectively hear, how well they attend, how expansive their vocabulary is, or their ability to comprehend and make sense of what they hear. Children with receptive communication difficulties may have encountered the limitation due to any number of conditions (e.g., deafness or hard of hearing at birth, injury, infection), and children with limited receptive abilities generally experience mild to significant delays in language development.

Expressive Language. Expressive language consists of the extent to which a child can express their needs, wants, or desires effectively. At a basic level, a young children's expression might consist of shrugs, points, or grimaces, but typically, expressive communication is a function of how well children articulates their message verbally. Children with expressive language delays may have any number of physical, psychological, or personal/cultural overlays (e.g., tied frenulum, shyness, cultural expectations that children should be seen and not heard) that limit their expressive abilities.

Academic Domain

Once children are exposed to pre-academic experiences, they begin to develop pre-literacy skills and specific knowledge about numbers and counting, science, social studies, technology, the arts, and so on. Caregivers and teachers begin to introduce children to basic facts and experiences (e.g., mathematics, science, art) and begin teaching them pre-literacy skills such as number and letters recognition. This broad academic domain comprises all topical and subject matter that reflects accepted beliefs about what is important for children to know to prepare them to engage their academic K-12 careers.

Literacy Knowledge and Skills. Literacy and pre-literacy skills are typically taught in a systematic manner in preschools by exposing children to letter identification and sounds, and number identification and counting, and through a broad exposure to books and other print material. As children develop, their vocabularies grow rapidly and begin to become specialized; their interests also become more divergent (e.g., interest in dinosaurs, the heavens above, plants); and they begin to seek picture books and textual books of interest that foster interest in reading and enhance their literacy and general knowledge.

Math Knowledge and Skills. Beginning with fundamental concepts such as "more," children increasingly become aware of math related concepts, such as numbers, counting, volume, size, and other quantity, measurement, and volume concepts and knowledge. Starting with rote counting, followed by place counting (i.e., one to one correspondence), children begin to develop a sense of numerosity and quantitative values, as well as a global number sense (e.g., more, less, same).

Science. Children's wonderment about basic science facts, such as why the sky is blue or why leaves turn colors initiates many young children's interest in science. Animal husbandry, plant life, geological structures and formations, and all such natural phenomena have scientific explanations that many young children seek to understand. Children's innate sense of curiosity causes them to seek explanations of common events and relationships, and as they begin to ask and learn about science content, their understanding about the inter-relationships between organisms and systems begins to develop.

Social Studies. When children ask why one child is black, another yellow, and yet another is white, they are expressing an awareness of fundamental social/cultural and individual differences in people; differences which may not be evident within their own family, unless of course their families are multi-racial. In multi-racial families, children's perceptions about human differences will likely blossom at an even younger age. Social studies provide many opportunities for educators to explain individual and group differences, and the importance and foundations of cultural beliefs, gender roles, societal expectations, and so on. Linked with these foundational human characteristics are other aspects of society that are important, such as education, economy, religious beliefs, health and social welfare, and related cultural issues that are dominant in the local and national media.

Technology and Engineering. In an ever-increasingly technological world, children learn about technology at increasingly younger ages, as they are exposed to home computers, tablets, calculators, telephones, televisions, and the many electronic devices common in many households. As children begin to playfully build structures, dam streams, move earth, build sand castles, erode or wash away surfaces with water, create levers and ramps, play with magnets, and replace batteries, they begin to develop an emerging understanding of civil, mechanical, and electrical engineering. Their innate curiosity encourages a natural comprehension of engineering concepts and laws; however, systematic exposure to these phenomena as part of the preschool experience fosters this interest in a much more direct manner.

Arts. Children are also naturally drawn to sounds, sights, and textures that in combination create art. This interest begins to develop not only a sense of aesthetic awareness, but also a deeper appreciation of music, dance, visual arts, and the production of artistic products. Importantly, art can easily be found in the previously mentioned academic and cultural areas (i.e., literacy, math, science, social studies, engineering).

Adaptive Functioning

Children typically develop adaptive skills in tandem with their cognitive functioning, but not always. In cases where children are overly protected and have much done for them, their adaptive skills are often slower to develop. Some children, due to lack of exposure to cognitively stimulating environments, may develop adaptive skills at a faster rate out of necessity than more advantaged children; however, for most normally developing children, their adaptive skills generally develop at a rate commensurate with their cognitive skills. Adaptive functioning includes the child's ability to take care of themselves and perform basic routines (e.g., dressing, toileting, self-feeding, hygiene, making transitions in daily routines) (Harrison & Oakland, 2015; Sparrow et al., 2016). As children grow older and are coached or taught basic self-care skills, their abilities and adaptation increase to the point of becoming relatively independent in their daily functioning, with less and less reliance on adults to care for them. Similarly, as they increase in independence, children are often assigned responsibilities that contribute to maintaining the home or classroom, such as performing chores, duties, or meeting expectations that help others, and keep an orderly, safe, and kempt setting.

Self-Care

Children demonstrate increasingly complex self-care skills as they assume responsibility for meeting their own personal needs. They rely less on adults to feed them, or provide food for them, and begin to make their own snacks or vocalize eating preferences. They dress themselves little by little by first pulling on or off clothing, and later snapping snaps, buttoning buttons, zipping zippers, and tying or fastening their shoes. As young children develop, they become reliable users of the toilet, and assume the full range of toileting behaviors. Similarly, they increasingly bathe themselves, get themselves ready for bed, and prepare for upcoming events (e.g., putting on coats, boots, mittens, hats). Children who are fully developed in their self-care behaviors are free of adult support, except for parental or caregiver suggestions or guidance as to what clothing or outerwear is appropriate for the weather, event, or situation.

Personal Responsibility. As children develop self-care behaviors, they also contribute to or assist in activities that maintain overall order, cleanliness, or orderly functions For example, they may make their own beds, roll up their nap mats, pour drinks for themselves and others, set tables, pick up litter and put away toys, and in general help clean up before or after an event.

Motor Skills

Monsma and colleagues (in press) identify three important findings from decades of motor skill development research: (1) most children, with and without disabilities are delayed in their gross motor skills; (2) motor skills can be significantly improved with just minimal intervention (Logan et al., 2012; Morgan et al., 2013; Taunton et al., 2017); and, (3) the relationships between motor skills, perceived motor skill competence, physical fitness, and physical activity in childhood convey to adolescence and early adulthood (Sackett & Edwards, 2019). Importantly, early years of motor development set the foundation for neuromuscular coordination used by the individual throughout life.

Motoric activity mostly includes the child's ability to use fingers, hands, feet, and legs in a coordinated manner to take on academic and nonacademic physical activities; activities, such as cutting, pasting, coloring, picking up small objects, snapping fasteners, walking, kicking or striking balls, running, skipping, balancing, and jumping. Fine motor activities are those that require the use of fingers and hands to hold, manipulate, carry, or handle objects. Academic fine motor skills include the ability to effectively use pencils, crayons, pens, scissors, rulers, paintbrushes, and the like. Non-academic fine motor skills include the dexterity to do such things as zip zippers, fasten snaps, use dining utensils, pick up small objects, etc. In contrast to fine motor skills, gross motor behaviors typically require the use of legs and arms to accomplish tasks, but also includes the balance and coordination of the entire body in activities (e.g., kicking, running, striking, dancing, climbing, jumping).

Fine Motor. As mentioned previously, fine motor skills require small muscle movements of the fingers and hands in a coordinated manner. Fine motor behaviors may be classified as academic or non-academic. Children who come to school from homes in which parents encourage and make available school-like activities (e.g., coloring, book handling, cutting and pasting), often demonstrate better academic fine motor abilities in the classroom than children with limited exposure to school-related activities. On the other hand, some children lack those pre-academic opportunities and develop non-academic fine motor abilities, but they lack the dexterity to effectively manipulate scissors, pencils, crayons, and so on due to a lack of previous exposure to these objects, not an inability to do so.

Gross Motor. Children's gross motor development, like fine more skills, is dependent on both developed abilities as well as experience. Children who come from homes that emphasize athletic development or creative movement (e.g., dance), will typically demonstrate smoother gross motor coordination that children from homes that are overall less physically oriented.

Perceptual Motor. Perceptual motor skills include the combination of sight or sound, and a corresponding fine motor response to that which is seen or heard. For example, many academic fine motor skills fit this description—cutting, pasting, coloring, require that the child have both adequate fine motor skills and the ability to respond appropriately to what they see or hear (e.g., drawing through a maze, producing recognizable drawings, cutting along lines, tying shoe laces). Using other perceptual channels of communications, children also develop the ability to respond across modalities (e.g., hearing and responding to auditory stimuli), such as swatting away an unseen buzzing insect, or locating by sound and physically stopping a ringing bell or buzzer.

Personal/Social Skills

As children mature, they become ever more social and begin to interact more effectively with other people, including older individuals (e.g., older children, adolescents, and adults), as well as children their own relative age (i.e., peers). Children's effective interactions with adults and peers are based on different behavioral and cultural expectations (e.g., showing deference, respect, and following the lead of responsible adults versus sharing and playing cooperatively with children their own age). As children refine their social skills, they are better able to initiate and respond to others in a socially acceptable manner. In contrast, children who lack social skills tend to be more isolated from others, either by choice (e.g., shy children) or because of how others view and respond to them (e.g., children who are shunned by their peers). Social skills and healthy interpersonal relations are essential elements of happiness and overall well-being.

Adult Interaction. Children with well-developed social skills have a balanced approach in their interactions with adults—that is, they respond appropriately to the authority of adults (e.g., follow adult directions, seek adult assistance when in need, ask adults opinions or permission), but they also must discern and respond differentially when adults lack true authority (e.g., knowing to not accept invitations from strangers, avoiding adults who might be behaving irresponsibly or dangerously). In general, as children develop, they learn manners (e.g., to be polite, respectful, and respond to the directions of adults), but they also begin to learn which adults they must be responsible to or wary of, and make choices about what they should do with each adult.

Peer Interaction. Children initially learn to play among other children without interacting (e.g., parallel play), and then increasingly learn to incorporate their peers into collaborative or interactive play (e.g., games, joint activities). When engaged in joint activities, children further learn how to share, cooperate, and lead activities or follow their friends' lead. Learning to take turns in conversation, play, and group activities, and showing empathy for other children who are upset, hurt, or sick are higher order social skills that develop after children progress past parallel and cooperative or interactive play and move toward fully integrated activities.

Self-Concept and Social Role. Children's social self-concepts, their overall self-concepts, and their personal sense of self, are often tied into their self- or other-perceived role. When children are effective in their interactions, they gain confidence; when they are timid or afraid to interact with others, or when others reject them, they tend to develop fewer positive self-images. Caregivers shape children's self-concepts by their actions, words, and the manner in which they support and encourage children in their da ly functioning and interactions. For a discussion on the formulation and development of self-concept, see Bracken (1996, 2009, 2017) and Theodore and Bracken (in press).

Preschool Assessments Issues

As a developmental and learning assessment process, examiners assess behaviors that virtually all preschool children will eventually master; therefore, mastery of specific skills is the criterion of successful growth, regardless of when that mastery occurs. Thus, a typically developing child will master the specified milestone behaviors on or about the age at which other normally developing children have been found to master the same behavior. Whether the child is behind or ahead of his or her normally developing peers, mastery of finely sequenced learning and developmental behaviors is the goal, or the criterion for rate of growth comparisons.

Criterion-Referenced Versus Norm-Reference Assessment. In a criterion-referenced approach to assessment, examiners seek to determine where on the continuum of development or learning children were at the beginning of their educational programming. Moreover, progress monitoring is important for assessing the child's rate and level of progress throughout the academic year or intervention period. Such direct evaluation, like measuring a child's height over a period, is useful for assessing the child's current level of development, as well as assessing the child's ongoing rate of growth.

Norm-referenced assessment is especially useful for determining lags in development across domains as compared to other children of the same age. Norm-referenced assessments allow for the identification of developing delays that without intervention may result in persistent delay of an ability or the ear y identification of a diagnosed condition. However, because the rate of development is variable during this period of rapid growth, normative comparisons may only be an indication of a slower rate of development, not terminal outcomes within domains.

It is sometimes difficult for examiners unfamiliar with early childhood behavior to determine what behaviors are typical or normally developing versus those behaviors that are problematic or even advanced. For example, when a child is described as distractible, impulsive, and easily frustrated, educators often consider possible disabilities associated with those behavioral characteristics (e.g., Attention Deficit Hyperactivity Disorder). Although behavioral descriptors of this sort are frequently associated with disorders among older children, the same behaviors often characterize many normal children between the ages of two and eight (Bracken & Theodore, in press). As such, these behaviors are only problematic because of the difficulties the behaviors cause caregivers and teachers who must deal with the child.

Normalcy is especially difficult to define among young children, and frequently even parents differ dramatically in their perceptions of their children's behavior (e.g., Bracken et al., 1998; however, empirically constructed early childhood rating scales with strong psychometric qualities like the *Clinical Assessment of Behavior* (Bracken & Keith, 2004) ease these concerns to a large extent.

During the preschool years social, motor, language, and cognitive development occur at rapid rates and the range of development among normal preschool children across and within these domains is great. As children increase in age, their rate of development slows and the range of behaviors among normal children likewise narrows. Because of this developmental phenomenon, it is sometimes difficult to differentiate mildly impaired preschool children from normal preschoolers due to variable rates of "normal" development. The task for psychologists conducting norm-referenced and criterion-referenced preschool assessments is to determine when a preschooler ceases to be considered within the normal range and begins to be considered abnormal (i.e., significantly delayed or advanced). As these early childhood years are a time of rapid development, children's overall health, including the brain, nervous and central nervous systems, endocrine, and immune systems, are particularly salient to a child's early experiences and environments, when the foundation of lifelong health is established.

Observing and Interpreting Preschool Behavior

Educators often assume that a child's behavior in school is similar to the same child's behavior at home. In many cases this assumption may not be appropriate. A young child's behavior in one context should never be interpreted unconditionally as being representative of his or her typical behavior in another setting (Bracken & Theodore, in press). The dynamics of a classroom are often much different from the child's home environment, resulting in a wide range of behaviors across contexts. Thus, the preschool child's classroom behavior may be specific to a group setting and academic context, and generalize less well to other solitary, non-academic settings. It is common for parents to claim that their child often performs some specific behavior at home, but school-based caregivers or teachers contend they have not seen the same behavior within the academic setting. While the educational context provides enough structure, personal attention, and peer influence to keep some children eagerly on task, other youngsters resist the structure and formality of a classroom, are more timid and refuse to participate or join in activities only half-heartedly. To develop a better understanding of the child's typical behavior, the examiner should observe the child in a variety of situations and contrast the child's behavior across contexts, time, and activities. Observations should also be made while the child is involved in free play on the playground and during structured educational activities for a more complete picture of the child's typical behavior. If developmental observations are made within a variety of settings, the examiner will have a greater sample of behavior from which inferences can be made more reliably and validly.

To effectively evaluate a child's development and learning, the examiner must be aware of the child's full range of behavior and integrate those observations into meaningful behavioral trends. One distinction that should be made with observations is determining whether a child failed to perform individual activities due to an inability to complete the task successfully or because of an unwillingness to attempt the task. It is common for shy preschoolers to refuse to attempt some educational tasks for fear of failure or to avoid unwanted attention being drawn to them. In such instances, in addition to noting the detrimental effects of the child's limited participation in the educational setting, the examiner has identified potential behaviors in another domain for intervention (e.g., self-confidence or self-regulation).

Cognitive and Academic Behaviors

Preschool evaluations include a wide variety of academic related behaviors, including functioning in each of the previously identified Cognitive and Academic domains and subdomains. Caregivers and teachers should be watchful for how children approach educational opportunities, including their interest in print material (e.g., books, magazines); recognition of text (e.g., uppercase and lowercase letters); recognition of numerals and understanding of number values; awareness of letter sounds, phonemic analysis of words, reading level, and so on. Teachers should also pay close attention to the academic subjects that children express curiosity about and choose to engage in on their own initiative. Children who choose specific subject matter typically are more advanced in those subjects than are other children.

Within the classroom, teachers are typically aware of those students who need more help in performing daily routines (e.g., toileting, lunch or snack time, getting dressed to go outside), or transitioning from one routine to another (i.e., some children respond better to changes in routines than others). These behaviors are related to a child's adaptive functioning, and many opportunities occur throughout the day (e.g., snack time, bathroom time, dressing to go outdoors) to observe how well children adapt to their environment and demonstrate personal self-care skills.

During classroom activities, teachers or examiners are in an excellent position to notice children's cognitive functioning. They see how well children sustain attention during classroom lessons; how well they remember and follow directions, instructions, or receive admonitions; how well they reason during problem-solving activities; and, how they perceive and understand slight differences in concepts (e.g., differences between *cold, cool, lukewarm, warm, hot*).

Communication Behaviors

In the broad area of communications, it is easy to misunderstand a child's true cognitive skills or language abilities because the child may not be very good at expressing himself or herself. For example, children who are shy or who have articulation difficulties may not appear to be very intelligent or may seem to have poor language skills, yet they may be brighter than anticipated and *understand* language at a very high level. In contrast to children who have well-developed receptive language skills, children who are hard of hearing or have even periodic hearing loss due to otitis media (i.e., inner ear infections) may develop both poor reception, comprehension, expression and articulation. Observers must attend to how well the young child: (1) hears or receives what is spoken, both in group and individual settings; (2) understands what they hear and do not hear (e.g., accuracy at following directions or responding to prompts); and (3) expresses themselves, either vocally or using words and gestures in combination. To fully understand a child's communication skills, the examiner must consider the full channel of communication, including hearing, understanding, and expressing.

Motoric Behaviors

Teachers can readily identify those children in the classroom who are the coordinated ones and those who are typically clumsy, drop things, and make messes. Fine and gross motor skills require the delicate balance of combining eyesight with the movement of fingers, hands, arms, legs, and whole bodies in a coordinated manner. Teachers should seek to differentiate between classroom accidents that were due to a child's inattention or impaired vision, gross motor clumsiness (e.g., tripping, falling, tumbling), and his or her fine motor awkwardness (e.g., breaking pencil points due to too much pressure, difficulty zipping zippers, spilling drinks at the table). Moreover, within the fine motor domain, teachers should be observant of academic versus nonacademic fine motor functioning. That is, some children lack prior educational experiences and may be awkward when printing, coloring, or using scissors, but may be able to zip zippers, snap or button clothing, and pick up and manipulate small objects with ease. In such a case, the teacher should note the differences in skills and abilities, and attribute the differences to a lack of academic experience as opposed to limited fine motor ability.

Social Skills and Adjustment

Within the social arena, teachers have ample opportunity to watch children interact with their peers of both genders, as well as their interactions with teachers and other caregivers (e.g., classroom aids). Recognizing that children are socialized with adults and other children to differing degrees, and are exposed to group activities at different rates, teachers should be careful about judging whether a child is "well-behaved" or "misbehaved." Rather, teachers should focus on specific behaviors that are appropriate or inappropriate and note what the child does and does not do to facilitate effective social interactions. Similarly, teachers should make note of those children who tend to be leaders in the classroom (e.g., organizing events, assigning roles) and those who are more passive and simply go along. Related to taking a dominant or passive role may be how the child feels about himself or herself – that is, their self-concept. Not all shy or passive children, however, have poor self-concepts; they very well might feel good about themselves across core self-concept domains (e.g., social, physical, academic, family, competence, affect), yet have no desire to assume leadership roles (Bracken, 1996; Theodore & Bracken, in press). To be effective evaluators, psychologists must look beyond global areas of functioning (e.g., global self-concept) and consider clues that reveal how children feel about themselves within specific areas or domains of functioning (e.g., specific domains of self-concept), as well as each child's idiosyncratic ecological systems.

Conclusion

Preschool assessment includes a diverse array of methods, procedures, instruments, and behavioral domains. During the preschool years, more so than any other age level, examiners must attend to both developmental and learning-based assessments. Development includes the natural unfolding of behaviors (e.g., motor, speech), whereas learning-based assessments are focused on what children acquire from exposure to their environments. The two assessment foci are interrelated and must be considered together using both norm-referenced and criterion-referenced formal and informal assessment approaches.

Author Note

We have no known conflict of interest to disclose. Correspondence concerning this article should be sent to Bruce A. Bracken, The College of William and Mary, P.O. Box 8795, Williamsburg, VA 23187-8795. Email: babrac@wm.edu

References

Alfonso, V. C., Bracken, B. A., & Nagle, R. J. (Eds.) (In press-a). *Psychoeducational assessment of preschool children* (5th ed.). Routledge.

Alfonso, V. C., Engler, J. R., & Lapore, J. (in press-b). What areas of development should be assessed and how? In V. C. Alfonso & G. J. DuPaul (Eds.), *Promoting healthy growth and development in young children: Bridging the science-practice gap in early education settings*. American Psychological Association.

Alfonso, V. C., & Flanagan, D. P. (2009). Assessment of preschool children: A framework for evaluating the adequacy of the technical characteristics of norm-referenced instruments. In B. Mowder, F. Rubinson, & A. Yasik (Eds.), *Evidence based practice in infant and early childhood psychology* (pp. 129–166). John Wiley & Sons.

Bagnato, S. J., Neisworth, J. T., & Pretti-Frontczak, K. (2010). *LINKing authentic assessment and early childhood intervention: Best measures for best practices* (2nd Ed.). Paul H. Brookes Publishing.

Bracken, B. A. (1984). *Bracken basic concept scale*. Psychological Corporation.

Bracken, B. A. (1987). Limitations of preschool instruments and standards for minimal levels of technical adequacy. *Journal of Psychoeducational Assessment, 5*(4), 313–326.

Bracken, B. A. (1996). Clinical applications of a context-dependent, multidimensional model of self-concept. In B. A. Bracken (Ed.). *Handbook of self-concept: Developmental, social, and clinical considerations,* 463–505.

Bracken, B. A., Keith, L. K., & Walker, K. C. (1998). Assessment of preschool behavior and social-emotional functioning: A review of thirteen third-party instruments. *Journal of Psychoeducational Assessment, 16*(2), 153–169.

Jackson, L. D., & Bracken, B.A. (1998). The relationship between Bracken, B. A. (2006a). *Bracken basic concept scale – receptive 3rd edition*. Pearson.

Bracken, B. A. (2006b). *Bracken basic concept scale – expressive*. Psychological Corporation.

Bracken, B. A. (2007). *Bracken school readiness assessment – 3rd edition*. Psychological Corporation.

Bracken, B. A. (2009). Growing healthy self-concepts. *Promoting wellness in children and youth: A handbook of positive psychology in the schools,* 89–106.

Bracken, B. A. (2013). *Riverside early assessments of learning*.

Bracken, B. A. (2017). Evidence-based interventions for self-concept in children and adolescents. *Handbook of evidence-based interventions for children and adolescents,* 337–386.

Bracken, B. A., & Crawford, E. (2010). Basic concepts in early childhood educational standards: A 50-state review. *Early Childhood Education Journal, 37*(5), 421–431.

Bracken, B. A., & Keith, L. K. (2004). *Clinical assessment of behavior.* Psychological Assessment Resources.

Bracken, B. A., & McCallum, R. S. (1998). *Universal nonverbal intelligence test* (UNIT).

Bracken, B. A., & McCallum, R. S. (2016). *Universal nonverbal intelligence test–2nd edition* (UNIT-2).

Bracken, B. A., & Nagle, R. (2007). *Psychoeducational assessment of preschool children–4th edition.* Lawrence Erlbaum Associates.

Bracken, B. A., & Panter, J. E. (2011). Using the bracken basic concept scale and Bracken concept development program in the assessment and remediation of young children's concept development. *Psychology in the Schools, 48*, 465–475.

Bracken, B. A., & Theodore, L. A. (in press). Observing preschool assessment-related behavior. In V. Alfonso, B. Bracken and R. Nagle (Eds.) *Psychoeducational assessment of preschool children, 5th edition* (in progress). Routledge

Crais, E. R. (2011). Testing and beyond: Strategies and tools for evaluating and assessing infants and toddlers. *Language, Speech and Hearing Services in Schools, 42*, 341–364.

Currie, J. (2001). Early childhood education programs. *Journal of Economic Perspectives, 15*(2), 213–238.

Dunn, L. M., Dunn, L. M., & Williams, K. T. (2007). *PPVT-4*: Peabody picture vocabulary test. Pearson Assessments.

Frisvold, D. E., & Lumeng, J. C. (2011). Expanding exposure: Can increasing the daily duration of Head Start reduce childhood obesity? *Journal of Human Resources, 46*(2), 373–402.

Harrison, P. L., & Oakland, T. (2015). ABAS-3: Adaptive behavior assessment system. Western Psychological Services.

Individuals with Disabilities Education Improvement Act, 20 U.S.C. § 1400 (2004).

Jensen, A. R. (1974). Cumulative deficit: A testable hypothesis? *Developmental Psychology, 10*(6), 996–1019.

Logan, S. W., Robinson, L. E., Wilson, A. E., & Lucas, W. A. (2012). Getting the fundamentals of movement: A meta-analysis of the effectiveness of motor skill interventions in children. *Child: Care, Health and Development, 38*(3), 305–315.

Masse, L. N., & Barnett, W. S., (2002). A benefit cost analysis of the abecedarian early childhood intervention. In H. M. Levin & P. J. McEwan (Eds.), *Cost-effectiveness and educational policy* (pp. 157–173). Eye on Education.

Mistry, K. B., Minkovitz, C. S., Riley, A. W., Johnson, S. B., Grason, H. A., Dubay, L. C., & Guyer, B. (2012). A new framework for childhood health promotion: The role of policies and programs in building capacity and foundations of early childhood health. *American Journal of Public Health, 102*(9), 1688–1696.

Monsma, E. V., Miedema, S. T., Brian, A. I., & Williams, H. G., (in press). Assessment of gross motor development in preschool children. In V. Alfonso, B. Bracken and R. Nagle (Eds.), *Psychoeducational assessment of preschool children, 5th edition.* Routledge.

Morgan, P. J., Barnett, L. M., Cliff, D. P., Okely, A. D., Scott, H. A., Cohen, K. E., & Lubans, D. R. (2013). Fundamental movement skill interventions in youth: A systematic review and meta-analysis. *Pediatrics, 132*(5), 1361–1383.

Nagle, R. J., Gagnon, S. J., & Kidder-Ashley, P. (in press). Issues in preschool assessment. In V. Alfonso, B. Bracken and R. Nagle (Eds.) *Psychoeducational assessment of preschool children – 5th edition.* Routledge.

National Association for the Education of Young Children. (2004). NAEYC *early childhood program standards and accreditation criteria:* Curriculum.

National Education Goals Panel, Washington DC. (1997). *Special early childhood report, 1997.* National Education Goals Panel.

No Child Left Behind Act of 2001, 20 U.S.C. 20 U.S.C. § 6319 (2001).

Panter, J. E., & Bracken, B. A. (2000). Promoting school readiness. In K. M. Minke & G. C. Bear (Eds.), *Preventing school problems - promoting school success: Strategies and programs that work,* 101–142.

Panter, J. E., & Bracken, B. A. (2013). Preschool Assessment. In Bracken, B. A. *Testing and Assessment in School Psychology and Education*, B. A. Bracken (Vol. Ed.); K. F. Geisinger (Editor-in-Chief), *APA handbook of testing and assessment in psychology (Vol. 3B, pp. 21–37).* American Psychological Association.

Ramey, C. T., & Ramey, S. L. (1998). Early intervention and early experience. American *Psychologist, 53*(2), 109–120.

Rossin-Slater, M. (2015). Promoting health in early childhood. *Future of Children, 25,* 35–64.

Sackett, S. C., & Edwards, E. S. (2019). Relationships among motor skill, perceived self-competence, fitness, and physical activity in young adults. *Human Movement Science, 66,* 209–219.

Scott-Little, S., Kagan, S. L., & Frelow, V. S. (2003). *Standards for preschool children's learning and development: Who has standards, how were they developed, and how are they used.* University of North Carolina, *SERVE.*

Sheridan, S. M., Witte, A. L., Wheeler, L. A., Eastberg, S. R. A., Dizona, P. J., & Gormley, M. J. (2019). Conjoint behavioral consultation in rural schools: Do student effects maintain after 1 year? *School Psychology, 34*(4), 410–420.

Sparrow, S. S., Cicchetti, D. V., & Saulnier, C. A. (2016). Vineland adaptive behavior scales, (Vineland-3). *Antonio: Psychological Corporation*

Taunton, S. A., Brian, A., & True, L. (2017). Universally designed motor skill intervention for children with and without disabilities. *Journal of Developmental and Physical Disabilities, 29*(6), 941–954.

Theodore, L. A. (in press). Linking assessment results to evidence-based interventions. In V. Alfonso, B. Bracken and R. Nagle (Eds.) *Psychoeducational assessment of preschool children, 5th edition.* Routledge.

Theodore, L. A., & Bracken, B. A. (in press). *Positive psychology and multidimensional adjustment.* In Perfect, M., Phelps, L., Riccio, C., & Bray, M.A. *Health-related disorders in children and adolescents* (2nd ed.). American Psychological Association.

Thompson, R. A. (2014). *Stress and child development. The Future of Children, 24*(1), 41–60.

Wechsler, D. (2012). *Wechsler preschool and primary scale of intelligence–4th edition.* The Psychological Corporation.

Whitcomb, S. A. (2018). *Behavioral, social, and emotional assessment of children and adolescents* (5th ed.). Routledge.

Wilson, P. (2004). A preliminary investigation of an early intervention program: Examining the intervention effectiveness of the Bracken concept development program and the Bracken basic concept scale-revised with Head Start students. *Psychology in the Schools, 41*(3), 301–311.

Assessing Social-Emotional Abilities of Preschool-Aged Children Within a Social-Emotional Learning Framework

Joseph R. Engler, Vincent C. Alfonso, Jenna M. White, and Cory D. Ray

Abstract

During the past decade, there has been an increasing amount of research demonstrating a positive relationship between early childhood social-emotional abilities and later life outcomes. As such, practitioners who work with preschool-aged children are called to understand the social-emotional abilities that constitute healthy development. Doing so provides practitioners with a social-emotional framework from which to work so that they may efficiently assess and intervene in these abilities. This manuscript grounds social-emotional abilities within the Collaborative for Academic, Social, and Emotional Learning's (CASEL) Framework for Social-Emotional Learning (SEL). We describe the need for a multi-method, multi-sourced, multi-setting comprehensive social-emotional assessment of preschool-aged children and describe a rating scale that can be used as a part of the assessment process. The manuscript concludes with a discussion regarding the importance of intervening early to prepare preschool-aged children for future academic and life success.

Keywords: *Social-emotional Learning, Preschool Assessment, and Collaborative for Academic, Social, and Emotional Learning*

The developmental period associated with preschool-aged children (i.e., ages 3:0 to 5:11 years) is an ideal time for them to develop social-emotional abilities that set the stage for later learning of myriad skills (Blair & Raver, 2015; Hojnoski & Missall, 2020). For example, during this time period preschool-aged children may gain their first life experiences outside of their nuclear family where they are in social settings (e.g., daycare, preschool, etc.) that require them to interact with peers and adults. The hope is that during this time, preschool-aged children learn how to develop healthy social relationships through awareness of self and others, while effectively understanding and managing their emotional responses to situations and circumstances. For most preschool-aged children, the acquisition of social-emotional abilities occurs with minimal disruptions. In contrast, approximately 10-15% of preschool-aged children will likely experience social-emotional difficulties to some degree (Qi & Kaiser, 2003). As such, it seems incumbent upon practitioners who work with preschool-aged children to understand the abilities that are part of healthy social-emotional development of these children as well as know how to assess and intervene in these areas when needed.

This manuscript begins with an overview of a Social-Emotional Learning (SEL) Framework that can be broken down into the following measurable social-emotional abilities: self-awareness, self-management, social awareness, relationship skills, and responsible decision-making. Specifically, we define and describe each of these abilities. Then we discuss the increasing support for conducting social-emotional assessments of preschool-aged children. Next, we briefly describe how to conduct a comprehensive assessment of preschool-aged children that addresses the aforementioned abilities. The manuscript concludes with a review of a rating scale that can be used to measure social-emotional abilities of preschool-aged children as part of a comprehensive assessment followed by a discussion of how the data obtained from the assessment can be used for intervention planning.

SEL Framework

In order to assess the social-emotional abilities of preschool-aged children, practitioners must first have a clear understanding of what SEL is and how to measure it. Perhaps the most well-known organization that provides guidance in the assessment of social-emotional abilities is the Collaborative for Academic, Social, and Emotional Learning (CASEL). As such, CASEL published a guide on an effective social-emotional learning program for preschool and elementary schools (CASEL, 2013). In the guide, CASEL defined SEL as, "The processes through which children and adults acquire and effectively apply the knowledge, attitudes, and skills necessary to understand and manage emotions, set and achieve positive goals, feel and show empathy for others, establish and maintain positive relationships, and make responsible decisions" (CASEL, 2013, p. 4). Specifically, there are abilities within an overall SEL framework of particular importance that can be taught and measured in preschool-aged children. These abilities are self-awareness, self-management, social awareness, relationship skills, and responsible decision-making and they contribute to an individual's overall social-emotional development.

Self-Awareness

The first ability within the SEL framework is self-awareness, or the ability to recognize one's own thoughts and emotions and how these thoughts and emotions influence one's own behavior (CASEL, 2013). Self-awareness is critically important at the preschool ages. There are several key indicators that suggest healthy development of self-awareness in preschool-aged children, which includes establishing personal likes and dis-likes, understanding personal strengths and weaknesses, and completing tasks independently (Ng & Bull, 2018). For example, discussing and connecting personal emotions with specified behaviors is an important step in the development of self-awareness for preschool-aged children. When preschool-aged children recognize and communicate personal emotions, they are correspondingly able to pay introspective attention to their immediate states (Lambie & Lindberg, 2016). In turn, this introspection aids in their ability to connect emotions with behaviors.

Additionally, Zeidner and colleagues (2003) found that preschool-aged children who begin verbalizing their emotions by three years of age have a better emotional understanding by six years of age. Another indicator of healthy self-awareness by preschool-aged children is comprehending how others think of them, which helps facilitate the experiencing of secondary emotions, such as pride or shame (Rochat, 2003). Preschool-aged children who lack self-awareness may have difficulties understanding how their own behaviors contribute to the peer development process. As such, preschool-aged children who lack self-awareness may experience more challenges creating and maintaining appropriate peer groups within the preschool setting.

Self-Management

The second ability within the SEL framework is self-management, or the ability to control impulses, manage stress, and motivate oneself. Thus, preschool-aged children with good self-management regulate their thoughts, emotions, and behaviors at different locations and across divergent social situations (CASEL, 2013). This includes expressing negative emotions appropriately, as well as setting goals and then working independently to meet those goals (Dettmer et al., 2020). Self-management requires mastery of complicated processes beyond simply recognizing or expressing thoughts and emotions. Good self-management requires the preschool-aged child to organize their emotions in a way that facilitates other processes such as focusing attention, problem solving, and building relationships (Cole et al., 2004). In fact, substantial research illustrates the positive influence emotion regulation has on children's later emotional well-being (e.g., mood and self-esteem), cognitive mastery, school readiness, and academic success (Djambazova-Popordanoska, 2016).

Two further indicators suggesting the healthy acquisition of self-management in preschool-aged children are the sharing of positive feelings and the appropriate expression of anger. Further development of these skills includes preschool-aged children understanding the causes of personal anger/frustration, and the awareness of how individual actions impact themselves and others around them (Ng & Bull, 2018). For example, preschool-aged children with poor self-management abilities might react to a situation by tantruming, yelling, kicking, or sulking after negative social interactions with others (Whitcomb, 2018). Negative verbal behaviors from preschool-aged children with poor self-management could result in name calling, bossing others, taunting, criticizing, or threatening others, which ultimately may lead to diminished peer relationships.

Pretend play is a promising opportunity for preschool-aged children to develop self-management. Through pretend play, preschool-aged children can use planning, monitoring, and controlling one's own behavior (e.g., either verbally or non-verbally) to develop self-management that can be used when playing with peers (Slot et al., 2017). At the preschool age range, self-management gradually begins to replace reliance on parental support for regulatory strategies, largely due to increasing social demands (Sameroff & Fiese, 2000). Thus, developing strong self-management is a critical contributing factor in children's growing levels of independence (Dettmer et al., 2020) and should be prioritized in early childhood settings.

Social Awareness

The third ability within the SEL framework is social awareness, or the ability to understand social and cultural norms (CASEL, 2013) which is accomplished through empathy, awareness of other perspectives, and identification of available supports (i.e., family). Indications that preschool-aged children are developing appropriate social awareness can be seen in those who wait their turn to speak or play (instead of interrupting), add their own ideas to a discussion, and/or recognize the celebrations of other ethnic groups (Ng & Bull, 2018). Appropriate social awareness is very important at the preschool age range because children lacking social awareness tend to have difficulties processing and interpreting social cues of others, overestimate their own competence, and misattribute the intent of others (Webster-Stratton & Lindsay, 2009), which may result in conduct/behavioral problems later on in development. In contrast, a higher capacity for empathy, increased ability to comfort, and more willingness to compromise in conflict are positively correlated with understanding the connections between what people want or believe and their behavior (Dunn & Cutting, 1999), a skill which aids in the development of healthy relationships later in life.

Relationship Skills

The fourth ability within the SEL framework is relationship skills, or the ability to display socially acceptable behaviors while working with others, which can then lead to the development of healthy relationships with other individuals (CASEL, 2013). Behaviors needed to maintain healthy relationships include initiating and building relationships, taking turns, and sustaining conversations. (Denham et al., 2014). Indications that preschool-aged children are developing healthy relationship skills include displaying appreciation for others, asking for and providing assistance to others, ensuring positive working relationships with others through cooperation and conflict resolution, and thinking interdependently (Alexander & Vermette, 2019; Ng & Bull, 2018).

Collectively, these skills are core characteristics of communication and social-engagement, which, in turn, lead to working successfully with peers in groups and teams. A main difference between relationship skills and the other abilities discussed is that relationship skills require interacting in social situations (Alexander & Vermette, 2019). Therefore, adequate social opportunities are necessary for the development of relationship skills. Provided ample social opportunities, relationship skills develop rapidly throughout the preschool years as peer groups become more structured, children experience acceptance or rejection by peers, and higher-level relationship processes emerge (Hay et al., 2004). As such, strong development in relationship skills is imperative to young children's successful transition into their school-aged years.

Responsible Decision-Making

The final ability within the SEL framework is responsible decision-making, or the ability to make personal behavioral decisions based on defined ethical standards, social norms, and concerns for the safety of others (CASEL, 2013). Evaluating the realistic consequences of one's actions by determining the impact those actions will have on others is the basis for responsible decision-making. Children as young as three years of age have demonstrated reasoning collaboratively, providing compelling reasons behind their decisions, and adapting their justificatory speech in a cooperative manner when engaging in joint decision making (Dunn & Munn, 1987; Köymen et al., 2014, 2016). To make such decisions, preschool-aged children must recognize their own thoughts and emotions, take social cues from others, and act on the collectivity of that information (Alexander & Vermette, 2019). Indications that preschool-aged children are appropriately developing responsible decision-making include following rules, considering cause and effect when exploring options for solving problems, and apologizing to others when necessary (Ng & Bull, 2018). Humor is also an indication that children are developing appropriate responsible decision-making because the use of humor is a universal method of safely communicating without putting down oneself or others (Alexander & Vermette, 2019).

The five core abilities previously described contribute to the development of SEL competence for preschool-aged children. As such, practitioners who may be conducting comprehensive social and emotional assessments of preschool-aged children should be familiar with the five abilities within CASEL's SEL Framework. In recent years there has been a heightened awareness regarding the need for accurately assessing, and intervening in the lives of preschool-aged children (Alfonso et al., 2020).

Support for Assessing Preschool-Aged Children's Social-Emotional Abilities

Research has continued to demonstrate the many positive outcomes associated with preschool-aged children's increased social and emotional abilities (Cristofaro & Tamis-LeMonda, 2012; Duff et al., 2015). Therefore, comprehensively assessing such abilities has been prioritized by federal mandates and national organizations. This is reflected in the Individuals with Disabilities Education Improvement Act (IDEIA; 2004) and the Every Student Succeeds Act (ESSA; Pub. L. 114–95). Between 1986 and 2004, regulations expanded mandatory assessment practices to apply to preschool-aged children, required that comprehensive assessments take place in children's natural environment, and charged local education agencies with the task of utilizing a variety of preventative measures (e.g., Response to Intervention) to identify students with special needs as early as possible (Nagle et al., 2020). IDEIA Part B focuses on ensuring preschool-aged children receive free and appropriate special education services by assessing a variety of developmental domains including cognitive, communication, social or emotional, behavior, and adaptive areas. Assessing this breadth of domains facilitates the identification of preschool-aged children who may require extra supports to enter kindergarten prepared to succeed.

IDEIA Part C is designed to reduce infants' and toddlers' potential for subsequent developmental delay, reduce overall special education and related service costs, and enhance educational agencies' capacity to evaluate and serve the varying needs of children effectively (Jacob et al., 2016). IDEIA Part C makes early intervention mandatory and incentivizes states to provide comprehensive identification services (e.g., Child Find), appropriate and early diagnostic testing, and family-directed assessments. Implemented together, these legislatively-driven practices and developmental screenings help to identify children at risk for disabilities and provide corresponding early intervention services.

With a growing body of research demonstrating the influence of early development on later outcomes, preschool assessment has become a priority not only in the area of special education, but in general education as well. The ESSA aims to close educational achievement gaps by ensuring all children begin kindergarten ready and equipped to access their education and learn. The focus on academic readiness has driven many early childhood education initiatives and has led to subsequent increases in publicly funded preschool programs. However, addressing academic readiness in early childhood education settings may not be sufficient. For example, kindergarten teachers may perceive appropriate social-emotional development as important as, or perhaps more important than, early academic skill acquisition (Curby et al., 2017). With funding comes the need for accountability measures; therefore, most constituents use some form of preschool assessment to measure preschool-aged children's readiness to begin kindergarten. Knowing the influence of social and emotional competencies on preparedness to enter the K-12 school system, such comprehensive assessments must measure these competencies in preschool-aged children and then use these data to inform early intervention. Legislators continue to develop additional policies centering around early intervention as additional evidence of long-term benefits for children is discovered (Raines et al., 2020).

Beyond federal regulations, a variety of professional organizations have asserted their support for preschool assessment practices. One such organization, the National Association for the Education of Young Children (NAEYC), provides accreditation programs, advocacy efforts, position statements, conferences, and professional development resources to bolster early childhood educators' support for preschool-aged children and increase their readiness to enter kindergarten. Standard 4 of NAEYC's Early Learning Program Accreditation Standards and Assessment Items guide, *Assessment of Child Progress*, emphasizes the importance of utilizing systematic assessment to identify children who require more intensive instruction or intervention or who may require further developmental evaluation (NAEYC Early Learning Program Accreditation Standards and Assessment Plan, 2018). In their guide, NAEYC outlines best practices in creating assessment plans, using appropriate assessment methods, identifying children's interests/needs and describing children's progress, adapting curriculum, individualizing teaching, and informing program development. Similar to the aforementioned federal regulations, NAEYC also underscores the importance of communicating with families and involving families in the comprehensive assessment process. Truly comprehensive assessment involves employing a wide range of strategies, individuals, and data-collection methods to describe the most accurate picture of a preschool-aged child.

Conducting a Comprehensive Assessment of Social-Emotional Abilities

A properly conducted comprehensive assessment of social-emotional abilities typically begins with a referral question where a teacher, parent, or other caregiver may have noticed a deficit or concern with their preschool-aged child. The referral question is often given to a practitioner with the credentials and competencies necessary to conduct a comprehensive assessment and evaluation (e.g., school psychologist). For example, a preschool teacher may have noticed that a preschool-aged child has extreme difficulties with self-management and has therefore been isolated amongst their peers warranting a referral for an assessment. The preschool teacher may then refer the preschool-aged child for an assessment to identify the problem and consequently intervene early, if needed, so that difficulties do not persist into the future. Then the practitioner responsible for conducting a social-emotional assessment often seeks to clarify the initial concerns and develop an assessment plan for proceeding (Alfonso et al., 2020).

In order to understand a preschool-aged child's difficulties, it is the authors' recommendation that a comprehensive social-emotional assessment should be multi-method, multi-sourced, and occur across multiple settings (Alfonso et al., 2020). This is necessary because social-emotional abilities are not an all-or-nothing phenomenon (Dettmer et al., 2020). Rather, they occur across a continuum of ability levels. Social-emotional abilities, or lack thereof, may also occur differently across various situations. To complicate matters further, social-emotional abilities may be a result of what has or has not been taught or modeled by peers and adults. Several of the abilities previously discussed (e.g., relationship skills) require opportunities to practice skills in order to develop appropriately. Therefore, the practitioner conducting the assessment must take the opportunities to learn skills and abilities into consideration when interpreting assessment data. As a result, a comprehensive social-emotional assessment needs to be mult modal to provide the best or most thorough understanding of the preschool-aged child's difficulties.

A social-emotional assessment should use multiple methods for collecting data. Multiple methods include, but are not limited to, systematic direct observations (SDO), interviews, and norm-referenced measures (e.g., tests and rating scales). Each method of assessment has identifiable strengths and limitations (Hojnoski & Missall, 2020). Within a preschool social-emotional assessment, the authors of this manuscript suggest utilizing SDOs, interviews, and ratings scales.

SDOs are a necessary component of a social-emotional assessment in that they provide rich information regarding the contexts in which the referral concern is occurring. Moreover, SDOs provide the practitioner with the opportunity to see the nature of the problem first hand. During the observations, for example, the practitioner may better identify contextual variables that may contribute to the problem. Interviews, while providing different assessment data than SDOs, are also necessary for multiple reasons. First, referrals for preschool-aged children often come from adult caregivers. Thus, conducting an interview with that caregiver provides the opportunity to develop rapport. Second, conducting an interview gives the practitioner an opportunity to clarify the overall goals of the assessment. In this way, the practitioner can make sure they meet the expectations of the caregiver. Third, gathering information through an interview can provide necessary data regarding how past incidents and/or histories may contribute to the referral question. Rating scales are also recommended for collecting social-emotional assessment data due to their ease of use and comparability to a normative sample (National Research Council, 2008). Because social-emotional problems occur across a continuum, rating scales also provide an assessment of the gradation, or relative frequency, of a problem. That is, a rating scale may capture data regarding a low frequency behavior that may be missed through conducting SDOs. Taken together, these three methods of assessment should provide a great deal of breadth and depth of data to a comprehensive social-emotional assessment.

In addition to multiple methods, multiple sources of information should be used to gather social-emotional assessment data. For example, preschool teachers, parents, daycare providers, and other adult caregivers can provide valuable assessment data. Each of the caregivers adds different perspectives to the comprehensive assessment. From gathering information from multiple sources, the practitioner can look for convergent or divergent data, which assists in determining whether problems are consistently identified across sources. Lastly, a comprehensive social-emotional assessment should occur across multiple settings. Preschool-aged children may display different social-emotional responses dependent on the setting in which they are interacting with peers and adults. For example, a preschool-aged child may display different social-emotional responses inside a preschool classroom as compared to a playground. While these variations may be attributed to the structural differences between each setting, the data obtained can be valuable as part of the assessment nonetheless.

Along with a multimodal comprehensive social-emotional assessment, we recommend that practitioners focus on the strengths of the preschool-aged child. Moreover, measuring the strengths of a child can provide useful, meaningful data as well (Lappalainen et al., 2009). These data can be used to inform interventions by helping to determine the preschool-aged child's developmental progress and existing skills, while providing a roadmap for future growth (Hojnoski & Missall, 2020). Understand ng areas of strength can also help to enhance the motivation and engagement of parents, teachers, and caregivers when working with preschool-aged children (Cress et al., 2015). Furthermore, including strengths in the assessment can provide advantages to the preschool-aged child, such as enhancing the child's sense of empowerment, as well as identifying behavioral/academic traits that are more easily applied when in non-treatment settings (LeBuffe & Shapiro, 2004).

In sum, a comprehensive social-emotional assessment of preschool-aged children must be multi-method, multi-sourced, and occur across multiple settings to provide a context for understanding the problem(s) for which the child was referred. By using methods such as SDOs, interviews, and rating scales, practitioners conducting comprehensive social-emotional assessments can gather multiple perspectives from multiple contexts to understand social-emotional problems more thoroughly. In addition, social-emotional assessments should be strength-based so that practitioners assessing preschool-aged children can identify strengths in an attempt to overcome difficulties, which is necessary for intervention planning.

We now discuss one of many available rating scales and tools (see Denham, 2006; McCabe & Altamura, 2011 for a further discussion) that can be used as part of a comprehensive social-emotional assessment for preschool-aged children; namely, the Social Skills Improvement System-Social-Emotional Learning Edition (SSIS-SEL; Gresham & Elliott, 2017a). This rating scale was chosen because it specifically targets the five social-emotional abilities discussed in this manuscript consistent with CASEL's SEL Framework, and the assessment data collected can be used for intervention planning for preschool-aged children.

Social Skills Improvement System–Social-Emotional Learning Edition

One response from test developers and publishers to the increasing emphasis on the development of preschool-aged children's social-emotional abilities was the creation of the SSIS-SEL which is a rating scale that can be used to evaluate the social and emotional abilities of preschool-aged children through young adults (i.e., 18 years of age). For the purpose of this manuscript, the authors focus the discussion on the preschool-aged components of the SSIS-SEL (i.e., 3:0 to 5:11). The SSIS-SEL is comprised of the following scales: Self-Awareness, Self-Management, Social Awareness, Relationship Skills, Responsible Decisions Making, SEL Composite, and Core Skills. These scales directly align with CASEL's overall SEL Framework. The SSIS-SEL includes several interrelated components that can be used as a part of a comprehensive evaluation to assess and intervene in the five social-emotional abilities for preschool-aged children described earlier in this manuscript. These components include the SSIS-SEL Screening/Progress Monitoring Scales, Teacher and Parent Rating Forms, and a Classwide Intervention Program that is designed for children 4 to 14 years of age.

When choosing a rating scale to use, it is necessary to evaluate its psychometric properties to determine whether it is suitable or valid for use with preschool-aged children. The psychometric evaluation of preschool instruments is not new. Rather, researchers have spent decades determining evaluative criteria for preschool instruments across various domains (e.g., cognitive, adaptive, social-emotional/ behavioral, language, and motor). Readers who are interested in a further discussion of the evaluative criteria for preschool instruments are encouraged to see Alfonso and Flanagan (2009) and Alfonso and colleagues (2020). While a thorough review of the SSIS-SEL's psychometric properties is precluded from this manuscript due to space limitations, a brief overview is provided.

When evaluating the psychometric rigor of a social-emotional rating scale, there are certain characteristics that should be examined.

In particular, the standardization, reliability evidences, and validity evidences are of particular importance when assessing social-emotional abilities (see Table 1.1 in Alfonso et al., 2020). That is, these are the three psychometric characteristics that have been subjected to evaluative criteria by researchers most often. Evaluating the standardization, reliability evidences, and validity evidences can be accomplished through examining information in the SSIS-SEL *Manual* (Gresham & Elliott, 2017b) and comparing it to criteria set forth by Alfonso and Flanagan (2009) and more recently Engler and Alfonso (2020). The standardization sample for the SSIS-SEL consisted of 600 children ages 3 through 5 years. The standardization sample was compared to the U.S. Census Data with regard to race/ethnicity, socioeconomic status, and geographic region. The 3- to 5-year-old sample was representative in regards to race/ethnicity and socioeconomic status. There was a slight geographic underrepresentation from the Northeast and West on the Teacher Rating Form. As such, those testing preschool-aged children should consider this information to assure that the preschool-aged child they are assessing is adequately represented in the standardization sample.

The authors provided three evidences for reliability of the SSIS-SEL: internal consistency reliability, test-retest reliability, and interrater reliability. The internal consistency was measured using coefficient alpha for the Teacher and Parent Rating Form. For the preschool age range, coefficient alphas ranged from 0.70 to 0.97 on the Teacher Rating Form and .74 to .96 on the Parent Rating Form across gender specific scales. In general, most coefficient alphas were in the .80s with the exception of the Self-Awareness scale which consistently fell in the .70s to low .80s. This suggests that the internal consistency for the SSIS-SEL is generally adequate (Alfonso & Flanagan, 2009; Engler & Alfonso, 2020); however, practitioners should use caution when interpreting the Self-Awareness scale for preschool-aged children. Moreover, those assessing Self-Awareness of preschool-aged children would want to ensure that there are corroborating evidences using multiple methods prior to making high stakes decisions based upon a low score in this area.

The SSIS-SEL *Manual* (Gresham & Elliott, 2017b) provided test-retest reliability data for the Screening/Progress Monitoring Scales as well as the Teacher and Parent Rating Forms. The test authors, however, did not differentiate the test-retest reliability data between age groups. Therefore, no conclusions can be drawn regarding the adequacy of these data for preschool-aged children. The final evidence of reliability was interrater reliability. Similar to the test-retest reliability data, the test authors did not disaggregate the data based upon age. Thus, no evaluative conclusions can be drawn regarding the adequacy of these data for preschool-aged children.

The SSIS-SEL authors provide validity evidence based on scale content, intercorrelations between rating forms, correlations with other acceptable measures, and evidence based upon a special group study. The authors reported that items were created for the SSIS-SEL based upon a review of the literature and also theoretical and statistical derivations. The test authors also provided evidence for validity based upon intercorrelations between rating forms. While some correlations between forms are low to moderate, the two composite scale scores (SEL Composite Scale and Core Skills Scale) demonstrated the strongest correlations. The SEL Composite Scale and Core Skills Scale are derived from several scales; therefore, it makes sense that these have the highest intercorrelations. The authors also provided correlations between the SSIS-SEL and other behavioral assessments such as the Behavior Assessment System for Children, Third Edition (Reynolds & Kamphaus, 2015) and the Vineland-II (Sparrow et al., 2005, 2006). In general, the correlations between the SSIS-SEL and other similar measures are generally high. Lastly, the authors of the SSIS-SEL provided validity evidence based on a special group study with a population of children with autism spectrum disorder. In general, children diagnosed with autism spectrum disorder were rated significantly lower than a matched control group. It should be noted that validity evidence is something that must continue to be accumulated through independent reviews and research. Therefore, those considering using the SSIS-SEL should monitor the professional literature as more information becomes available.

The SSIS-SEL is one of many tools that can be used as part of a comprehensive social-emotional assessment for preschool-aged children. It is directly aligned with CASEL's SEL Framework and can provide multiple perspectives (i.e., Teacher and Parent Rating Forms) regarding a preschool-aged child's social-emotional abilities. In addition, the SSIS-SEL also provides af (CIP) that can be used to intervene with preschool-aged children. The CIP is a viable tool that is relatively easy to implement and is grounded in instructional approaches that have been shown to be effective when teaching preschool-aged children.

Intervening with Preschool-Aged Children

At the preschool age range, children are subject to myriad influences. Preschool teachers, daycare providers, and parents may all utilize varying skillsets in their work with preschool-aged children and their influence remains with children well beyond their preschool years. With the increased emphasis on kindergarten readiness, the number of children attending preschool or other early childhood programs is increasing (Conroy et al, 2019), and as a result, more credence is being given to the influence of preschool programs and preschool educators on children's current and future successes. However, certification requirements for preschool teachers are generally less rigorous and formalized than requirements placed on those pursuing a K-12 certification. This contributes to early childhood teachers finding themselves less equipped to intervene effectively with preschool-aged children's social or behavioral challenges (Stormont et al., 2008), resulting in increasing numbers of behavioral problems in their classrooms (Conroy et al., 2019). In fact, preschool teachers cite student discipline as their primary concern (Ingersoll, 2001) and often times resort to more reactive or punitive disciplinary measures (e.g., suspension or expulsion, which are negatively correlated with access to behavior professionals or behavioral consultation) (Gilliam, 2005). Unfortunately, these measures show little positive impact on the long-term development of preschool-aged children, primarily in the area of self-regulation, and do not set these preschool-aged children up for smooth transitions into their K-12 educational careers.

In contrast, research illustrates a positive correlation between preschool teacher knowledge of behavior management and preschool-aged children's prosocial behavior (LeBel & Chafouleas, 2010), allowing teachers and children the opportunity to spend more time engaging in educational material and less time managing interfering behavior. Taken together, growing class sizes, lack of training in behavior management, and increasing numbers of behavioral problems create an imminent need for preventative and targeted interventions to mitigate the number of challenges preschool-aged children experience upon entering the K-12 school system. When preschool-aged children receive interventions early and in the appropriate area, receive interventions that are based upon data, and are taught skills generalizable to other settings, they enter their educational journey better prepared to learn and experience the greatest success long-term.

Up until several decades ago, interventions were determined based largely upon practitioners' philosophical or clinical beliefs rather than on formative data; however, interventions rooted in subjective beliefs showed little effectiveness and therefore did not appropriately address children's difficulties (Riley-Tillman & Burns, 2009). Presently, ESSA requires interventions to be evidence-based; that is, they must demonstrate a statistically significant effect on improving student outcomes based on varying degrees of methodological rigor (Grant et al, 2017). Part of what makes assessment so valuable is that, when conducted comprehensively, it can identify a preschool-aged child's most significant challenges and areas of need for subsequent intervention. Allowing assessment data—rather than subjectivity—to guide intervention decisions ensures that preschool-aged child receives support in the most critical areas unique to them and shows greater likelihood for success when implemented with integrity (Riley-Tillman & Burns, 2009). In addition, interventions designed and implemented based on data can be formalized, researched and replicated for use with other preschool-aged children, allowing impact on a larger scale. As such, should practitioners wish to fulfil their ethical and legal responsibilities to provide appropriate education to preschool-aged children, it is critical that they utilize comprehensive assessment data to inform and evaluate the effectiveness of interventions. CASEL's (2013) Effective Social and Emotional Learning Programs: Preschool and Elementary School Edition provides a more detailed review of various evidence-based programs. A review of preschool programs published after 2013 may be found on CASEL's website, www.casel.org/guide/programs/.

In addition to using data to guide intervention planning, data should be collected and analyzed to evaluate the progress of interventions. While interventions may be adjusted according to the preschool-aged child's needs, progress and circumstances, any intervention put in place should be paired with a corresponding method of measuring outcomes. For preschool-aged children, these measures may include SDOs, daily behavior report cards, rates of behaviors or pre- and post-ratings on a behavior rating form (Hale & Fiorello, 2004). A plan should be set in place for data collection and progress should be monitored frequently given the rapid changes that occur throughout a preschool-aged child's early development. If outcome data reflect a lack of growth, interventions should be intensified or changed accordingly, and should always take into consideration the learning environment in which the child is developing.

Several instructional methods have been shown to be effective in mitigating social or behavioral concerns for preschool-aged children in a class-wide setting. According to the National Association of School Psychologists' Position Statement on Early Childhood Services (2015), specific learning goals promoting interactions, paired with instruction and interventions across various social and emotional domains, provide a focused and intentional learning environment and provide preschool-aged children with ample opportunities to practice new skills and respond in various environments.

Teachers who establish rules and expectations clearly and early, create emotionally warm and safe environments for all students, offer brief and succinct instructions, provide diverse opportunities for students to receive, engage with, and present information, and embed student interests into lessons enjoy decreased behavioral challenges when teaching preschool-aged children (DuPaul & Cleminshaw, 2020). Teacher-directed instruction allowing preschool-aged children the opportunity to play, explore and discover with increasing levels of independence has also been shown to be effective in teaching social and emotional skills to preschool-aged children.

At the individual level, socially appropriate communication and other prosocial skills can be taught and maintained by implementing interventions utilizing direct instruction, modeling, rehearsal, and reinforcement (Steege et al, 2019). Finally, it is important to understand that the behavior management skills displayed by teachers and other influential adults are internalized by preschool-aged children. That is, by observing and internalizing prosocial emotion and behavior regulation, preschool-aged children become more self-regulated themselves (Rimm-Kaufman et al., 2009). As such, perhaps one of the most effective ways to increase social-emotional abilities in preschool-aged children is for adults to model their own behavior and communication.

While there are many available intervention programs focusing on teaching social-emotional abilities to preschool-aged children (see McCabe & Altamura, 2011), the SSIS-SEL's CIP is one tool which utilizes several of the aforementioned strategies via its Tell, Show, Do, Practice, Monitor, Generalize model of teaching skills consistent with the five SEL abilities (Elliott & Gresham, 2017). Each of these instructional phases (Tell, Show, Do, etc.) provides preschool-aged children with new ways to engage with the material and when implemented together, allow children to apply their new skills with increasing degrees of independence. This format is consistent with the scaffolding approach wherein instructors teach at a level just above what children are able to do independently, allowing them to reduce supports gradually until children demonstrate abilities completely independently. Further, the SSIS-SEL's CIP graduated format allows the intervention to focus on preschool-aged children's prior knowledge rather than their learning style, which has been shown to maximize engagement in lessons (Willingham, 2009). Skill units may then be tailored to each preschool-aged child's area of need, while assessment data are used to inform subsequent intervention units (e.g., Listening to Others, Saying Please and Thank You, Following Rules, etc.).

Given the variety of influences on preschool-aged children, effective interventions must include collaboration with families, early childhood educators, community resources and physicians. Working collaboratively with these stakeholders increases the likelihood that skills learned throughout interventions will be consistently applied, and eventually generalized across settings. Generalizability, which refers to a child's ability to apply a skill learned in one setting to new, diverse settings, contributes positively to a preschool-aged child's more seamless transition to elementary school and subsequently reduces the amount of behavioral and academic difficulties they may experience later in their educational career and beyond.

Summary

In summary, a well-designed social-emotional assessment for preschool-aged children should be grounded in an SEL framework. One of the most widely recognized frameworks was designed by CASEL (2013). The CASEL Framework provides direction for practitioners conducting comprehensive social-emotional assessments for preschool-aged children regarding the most salient abilities to measure. These abilities are self-awareness, self-management, social awareness, relationship skills, and responsible decision-making. Each of the abilities can be measured using a multi-model approach to assessment that also focuses on the strengths of a preschool-aged child. One particular tool, of many, that can be used as part of a comprehensive social-emotional assessment is the SSIS-SEL.

The SSIS-SEL was described in this manuscript because of its alignment with CASEL's SEL Framework and also because it was designed with an intervention component (i.e., CIP) that is consistent with instructional strategies and opportunities necessary to promote social-emotional development in preschool-aged children.

References

Alexander, K., & Vermette, P. (2019). Implementing social and emotional learning standards by intertwining the habits of mind with the CASEL competecies. *Excelsior: Leadership inTeaching and Learning, 12*(1), 3–16. https://doi.org/10.14305/jn.19440413.2019.12.1.03

Alfonso, V. C., Engler, J. R., & Lepore, J. C. (2020). Assessing and evaluating young children: Developmental domains and methods. In V. C. Alfonso & G. J. DuPaul (Eds.), *Healthy development in young children: Evidence-based interventions for early education* (pp.13–44). American Psychological Association.

Alfonso, V. C., & Flanagan, D. P. (2009). Assessment of preschool children: A framework for evaluating the adequacy of the technical characteristics of norm-referenced instruments. In B. Mowder, F. Rubinson, & A. Yasik (Eds.), *Evidence based practice in infant and early childhood psychology* (pp. 129–165). John Wiley & Sons, Inc.

Blair, C., & Raver, C. C. (2015). School readiness and self-regulation: A developmental psychobiological approach. *Annual Review of Psychology, 66*, 711–731. http://dx.doi.org/ 10.1146/annurev-psych-010814-015221

CASEL – Collaborative for Academic, Social, and Emotional Learning. (2013). *Effective social and emotional learning programs: Preschool and elementary* (School edition).

Cole, P. M., Martin, S. E., & Dennis, T. A. (2004). Emotion regulation as a scientific construct: Methodological challenges and directions for child development research. *Child Development, 75*(2), 317–333. https://doi.org/: 10.1111/j.1467-8624.2004.00673.x

Conroy, M. A., Sutherland, K. S., Algina, J., Ladwig, C., Werch, B., Martinex, J., Jessee, G., & Gyure, M. (2019). Outcomes of the BEST in CLASS intervention on teachers' use of effective practices, self-efficacy, and classroom quality. *School Psychology Review, 48*(1), 31–45. https://doi.org/: 10.17105/SPR-2018-0003.V48-1.

Cress, C., Lambert, M. C., & Epstein, M. H. (2016). Factor analysis of the preschool behavioral and emotional rating scale for children in Head Start programs. *Journal of Psychoeducational Assessment, 34*(5), 473–486. https://doi.org/10.1177/0734282915617630

Cristofaro, T. N., & Tamis-LeMonda, C. S. (2012). Mother–child conversations at 36 months and at pre-kindergarten: Relations to children's school readiness. *Journal of Early Childhood Literacy, 12*(1), 68–97 http://dx.doi.org/10.1177/1468798411416879

Curby, T. W., Berke, E., Alfonso, V. C., Blake, J. J., DeMarie, D., DuPaul, G. J., Flores, R., … & Subotnik, R. F. (2017). Kindergarten teacher perceptions of kindergarten readiness: The importance of social-emotional skills. *Perspectives on Early Childhood Psychology and Education, 2*, 117–137.

Denham, S. A. (2006). Social-emotional competence as support for school readiness: What is it and how do we assess it? *Early Education and Development, 17*(1), 57–89.

Denham, S. A. Bassett, H. H., Zinsser, K., & Wyatt, T. M. (2014). How preschoolers' social-emotional learning predicts their early school success: Developing theory-promoting, competency-based assessments. *Infant and Child Development, 23*(4), 426–454. https://doi.org/10.1002/icd.1840

Dettmer, A. M., Clinton, A. B., & Mildon, H. A. (2020). Self-regulation in young children. In V. C. Alfonso & G. J. DuPaul (Eds.), *Healthy development in young children: Evidence-based interventions for early education*. American Psychological Association, 131-150.

Djambazova-Popordanoska, S. (2016). Implications of emotion regulation on young children's emotional wellbeing and educational achievement. *Educational Review, 68*(4), 497–515. https://doi.org/:10.1080/00131911.2015.1144559

Duff, F. J., Reen, G., Plunkett, K., & Nation, K. (2015). Do infant vocabulary skills predict school-age language and literacy outcomes? *The Journal of Child Psychology and Psychiatry, 56*(8), 848–856. http://dx.doi.org/10.1111/jcpp.12378

Dunn, J., & Cutting, A. L. (1999). Understanding others, and individual differences in friendship interactions in young children. *Social Development, 8*(2), 201–219.

Dunn, J., & Munn, P. (1987). Development of justification in disputes with mother and sibling. *Developmental Psychology, 23*(6), 791–798. https://doi.org/: 10.1037/0012-1649.23.6.791

DuPaul, G. J., & Cleminshaw, C. L. (2020). Principles and practices that promote positive guidance in early childhood. In V. C. Alfonso & G. J. DuPaul (Eds.), *Healthy development in young children: Evidence-based interventions for early education* (pp. 193–210). American Psychological Association. http://dx.doi.org/10.1037/0000xxx-010

Elliott, S. N., & Gresham, F. M. (2017). *SSIS SEL–Social skills improvement system–Social-emotional learning edition classwide intervention program* (CIP manual). Pearson Assessments.

Engler, J. R., & Alfonso, V. C. (2020). Cognitive assessment of preschool children: A pragmatic review of theoretical, quantitative, and qualitative characteristics. In V. C. Alfonso, B. A. Bracken, & R. J. Nagle (Eds.), *Psychoeducational assessment of preschool children* (5th ed., pp. 226–249). Routledge.

Every Student Succeeds Act, 20 U.S.C. § 6301 (2015).

Gilliam, W. S. (2005). *Prekindergarteners left behind: Expulsion rates in state prekindergarten systems.* NY: Foundation for Child Development (Policy Brief No. 3). https://medicine.yale.edu/childstudy/zigler/publications/briefs

Grant, S., Hamilton, L. S., Wrabel, S. L., Gomez, C. J., Whitaker, A., Leschitz, J. T., … & Harris, M. (2017). *Social and emotional learning interventions under the Every Student Succeeds Act: Evidence review.* Research Report, RR-2133-WF. RAND Corporation.

Gresham, F. M., & Elliott, S. N. (2017a). *SSIS SEL–Social skills improvement system–Social-emotional learning edition* (Brochure). Pearson Assessments.

Gresham, F. M., & Elliott, S. N. (2017b). *SSIS SEL–Social skills improvement system–Social-emotional learning edition* (Manual). Pearson Assessments.

Hale, J. B., & Fiorello, C. A. (2004). *School neuropsychology: A practitioner's handbook.* Guilford Press. https://www.guilford.com/excerpts/hale.pdf?t

Hay, D. F., Payne, A., & Chadwick, A. (2004). Peer relations in childhood. *Journal of Child Psychology and Psychiatry, 45,* 84–108.

Hojnoski, R. L. & Missall, K. N. (2020). Considerations and methods in assessing earlylearning and social emotional development in young children. In V. C. Alfonso & G. J. DuPaul (Eds.), *Healthy development in young children: Evidence-based interventions for early education* (pp. 45–64). American Psychological Association.

Individuals with Disabilities Education Improvement Act, 20 U.S.C. § 1400 (2004).

Ingersoll, R. (2001). Teacher turnover, teacher shortages, and the organization of schools. CPRE Research Reports. https://repository.upenn.edu/cpre_researchreports/12

Jacob, S., Decker, D. M., & Lugg, E. T. (2016). *Ethics and law for school psychologists* (7th ed.). John Wiley & Sons, Inc.

Köymen, B., Rosenbaum, L., & Tomasello, M. (2014). Reasoning during joint decision-making by preschool peers. *Cognitive Development, 32,* 74–85. https://doi.org/: 10.1016/j.cogdev.2014.09.001

Köymen, B., Mammen, M., & Tomasello, M. (2016). Preschoolers use common ground in their justificatory reasoning with peers. *Developmental Psychology, 52*(3), 423–429. https://doi.org/: 10.1037/dev0000089

Lambie, J. A., & Lindberg, A. (2016). The role of maternal emotional validation and invalidation on children's emotional awareness. *Merrill-Palmer Quarterly, 62*(2), 129–157. https://doi.org/: 10.13110/merrpalmquar1982.62.2.0129

Lappalainen, K., Savolainen, H., Kuorelahti, M., & Epstein, M. H. (2009). An international assessment of the emotional and behavioral strengths of youth. *Journal of Child and Family Studies, 18*(6), 746–753. https://doi.org/10.1007/s10826-009-9287-5

LeBel, T. J., & Chafouleas, S. M. (2010). Promoting prosocial behavior in preschool: A review of effective intervention supports. *School Psychology Forum, 4*(2), 25-38.

LeBuffe, P. A., & Shapiro, V. B. (2004). Lending "strength" to the assessment of preschoolsocial-emotional health. *The California School Psychologist, 9,* 51–61.https://doi.org/10.1007/bf03340907

McCabe, P. C., & Altamura, M. (2011). Empirically valid strategies to improve social and emotional competence of preschool children. *Psychology in the Schools, 48*(5), 513–540. https://doi.org/: 10.1002/pits.20570

Nagle, R. J., Gagnon, S. G., & Kidder-Ashley, P. (2020). Issues in preschool assessment. In V. C. Alfonso, B. A. Bracken, & R. J. Nagle (Eds.), *Psychoeducational assessment of preschool children* (5th ed., pp. 3–31). Routledge.

National Association for the Education of Young Children. (n.d.). *NAEYC early learning program accreditation standards and assessment items.* https://www.naeyc.org/accreditation/early-learning/standards.

National Association of School Psychologists. (2015). Early childhood services: Promoting positive outcomes for young children. [Position Statement].

National Research Council. (2008). *Early childhood assessment: Why, what, and how.* Committee on Developmental Outcomes and Assessments for Young Children, C. E.

Ng, S. C., & Bull, R. (2018). Facilitating social emotional learning in kindergarten classrooms: Situational factors and teachers' strategies. *International Journal of Early Childhood, 50*, 335–352. https://doi.org/10.1007/s13158-018-0225-9

Qi, C. H., & Kaiser, A. P. (2003). Behavior problems of preschool children from low-income families: Review of the literature. *Topics in Early Childhood Special Education, 23*(4), 133–139. https://doi.org/10.1177/02711214030230040201

Raines, T. C., Malone, C., Beidleman, L. M., & Bowman, N. (2020). National policies and laws affecting children's health and education. In V. C. Alfonso & G. J. DuPaul (Eds.), *Healthy development in young children: Evidence-based interventions for early education* (pp. 319–336). American Psychological Association.

Reynolds, C. R., & Kamphaus, R. W. (2015). *Behavior assessment system for children, BASC-3* (Manual) (3rd ed.). Pearson.

Riley-Tillman, T. C., & Burns, M. K. (2009). *Evaluating educational interventions: Single-case design for measuring response to interventio*n Guilford Press.

Rimm-Kaufman, S. E., Curby, T. W., Grimm, K. J., Nathanson, L., & Brock, L. L. (2009). The contribution of children's self-regulation and classroom quality to children's adaptive behaviors in the kindergarten classroom. *Developmental Psychology, 45*(4), 958–972. http://dx.doi.org/10.1037/a0015861

Rochat, P. (2003). Five levels of self-awareness as they unfold early in life. *Consciousness and Cognition, 12*(4), 717–731. https://doi.org/10.1016/s1053-8100(03)00081-3

Sameroff, A. J., & Fiese, B. H. (2000). Transactional regulation: The developmental ecology of early intervention. In J. P. Shonkoff & S. J. Meisels (Eds.), *Handbook of early childhood intervention* (2nd ed., pp. 135–159). Cambridge University Press.

Slot, P. L., Mulder, H., Verhagen, J., & Leseman, P. P. (2017). Preschoolers' cognitive and emotional self-regulation in pretend play: Relations with executive functions and quality of play. *Infant and Child Development, 26*(6), 1–21. https://doi.org/10.1002/icd.2038

Sparrow, S. S., Cicchetti, D. V., & Balla, D. A. (2005). *Vineland Adaptive Behavior Scales: Parent/Caregiver rating form* (2nd ed.). Pearson Assessments.

Sparrow, S. S., Cicchetti, D. V., & Balla, D. A. (2006). *Vineland Adaptive Behavior Scales: Teacher rating form* (2nd ed.). Pearson Assessments.

Steege, M. W., Pratt, J. L., Wickerd, G., Guare, R., & Watson, T. S. (2019). *Conducting school-based functional behavioral assessments: A practitioner's guide* (3rd ed.). Guilford Press.

Stormont, M., Lewis, T. J., Beckner, R., & Johnson, N. W. (2008). *Implementing positive behavior support systems in early childhood and elementary settings.* Corwin Press.

Webster-Stratton, C., & Lindsay, D. W. (1999). Social competence and conduct problems inyoung children: Issues in assessment. *Journal of Clinical Child Psychology, 28*(1), 25–43. https:// doi.org/10.1207/s15374424jccp2801_3

Whitcomb, S. A. (2018). *Behavioral, social, and emotional assessment of children and adolescents* (5th ed.). Routledge. https://doi.org/10.4324/9781315747521

Willingham, D. T. (2009). *Why don't students like school?: A cognitive scientist answers questions about how the mind works and what it means for your classroom.* Jossey-Bass.

Zeidner, M., Matthews, G., Roberts, R. D., & MacCann, C. (2003). Development of emotional intelligence: Towards a multi-level investment model. *Human Development, 46*(2-3), 69-96. https://doi.org/10.1159/000068580

Understanding Basic Relational Concepts in Directions: A Study of Native Mexican and U.S. Children in Early Elementary Grades

Adrian E. Tovar and Zheng Zhou

Abstract

The present study uses both quantitative and qualitative approaches to examine: (1) U.S. and Mexican children's ability to understand basic relational concepts in directions; and (2) to analyze language arts and math textbooks to determine the levels of complexity in directions (i.e., number of qualifiers or concepts embedded in the directions). A total of 265 first grade (n = 128) and second-grade (n = 137) children in Mexico were assessed using the Boehm Test of Basic Concepts-Revised (BTBC-R) Applications Booklet. Their performance was compared to the U.S. standardized sample of the BTBC-R to make cross-cultural comparisons. Results from the quantitative study suggest that U.S. children at both grade levels outperformed Mexican children on direction following tasks. Furthermore, both cultural groups demonstrated developmental progression from first to second grade. Qualitative analysis of language arts and mathematics textbooks in both U.S. and Mexico revealed that the majority of instructions had "no complexity." Mexico's first grade language arts textbooks had significantly more "no complexity" directives than the U.S. textbooks; whereas first grade math textbooks in Mexico had significantly more "moderately complex" directives than in the U.S. The "very complex" directives were minimal in both cultures. Cross-cultural differences were discussed in terms of linguistic transparency, conceptual complexity, item biases, and the education system.

Keywords: *Basic Relational Concepts, Cross-cultural, Mexican Children*

Boehm (1991) asserts that knowledge of the basic relational concepts allows children to comprehend and describe relationships between objects, distance in relation to the object and the person, and to describe characteristics of objects (e.g., dimensions, positions, movements, quantity, and presence). Children can use their understanding of concepts to make orders, initiate and engage in dialogue with their peers, make comparisons, categorize objects, and problem solve (Boehm, 1991; Zhou & Boehm, 2004). Developing these skills by the time a child enters school is crucial, as linguistic and instructional demands increase significantly. Kaplan (1980) speculated that as children develop, their ability to understand complex directions increases. A child's ability to follow directions in the classroom is often seen as a complex cognitive process which tests their ability to process, comprehend, maintain, manipulate, and recall verbal information that is presented (Zhou & Boehm, 2004). If children do not acquire the foundational knowledge pertaining to relational concepts, they may have difficulty following directives in the classroom.

Cultural implications have also been investigated regarding basic concept acquisition. Specifically, researchers noted that relational concepts develop among children from all cultural backgrounds and are influenced by their language and culture (Siegler, 1998; Zhou & Boehm, 2001, 2004). For example, Spanish-speaking children's performance on *Pureba Boehm de Conceptos Basicos* (PBCB) (Form A, 1971; Form B, 1973) revealed both a similar order of concept difficulty and an increasing mastery with age (Preddy et al., 1984). However, both linguistic complexity and language characteristics interact to influence young children's acquisition of the basic relational concepts (Zhou & Boehm, 2001, 2004).

Defining Basic Relational Concepts

A child's acquisition of basic relational concepts involves their ability to make relational judgments and problem solve, between objects, persons, or sequence of events (Boehm, 1991). Boehm (2004) used the term "basic relational concepts" to describe size (small-medium-large), distance (near, far), position in space (above-below, left-right, between), time (before-after), and quantity (equal, few, whole). For example, when a teacher asks a child to "look *under* the chair for the pencil," or to "place the assignment *on* your desk;" they use relational concepts to describe the task they would like the child to complete.

Acquiring basic concepts early on is essential for children to communicate with their peers; make decisions, solve problems, and accomplish tasks presented by school staff and administrators. These tasks include, but are not limited to: following instructions (e.g., "John, please move to the *back* of the line); comprehending stories (e.g., "When the girl was excited, she jumped *on* the bed"); describing a series of events to others (e.g., "*After* school I went to the park and played *on* the playground"); making commands (e.g., "Can I have *more* food please?"); and describing individual thoughts and feelings (e.g., "I feel sad because I'm *always* last"). By assessing a child's ability to understand basic relational concepts, teachers are able to identify which concepts are difficult for children, who face challenges mastering these skills, and what strategies to use in teaching these concepts (Preddy et al., 1984). Based on these assessments, teachers can modify their instructional materials to promote the development and knowledge of basic concept attainment (Boehm, 2004).

Basic Relational Concepts and Direction Following

According to Kaplan & White (1980), a direction is defined as a statement or command that prompts a behavior or response from another individual(s). A direction has been successfully completed once the behavior matches the directive administered by another person (Kaplan & White, 1980). Basic relational concepts in direction following have been found in textbook materials, as well as in the administration directions of intelligence and achievement test batteries (Flanagan et al., 1995; Zhou & Boehm, 2004). Other researchers, such as Flanagan and researchers (1995), reported that if directions on intelligence tests were too complex or too long, children may have difficulty understanding the directives, perform poorly, and the assessment will not be an accurate representation of the child's overall ability. In addition, researchers found that directions that contain negative qualifiers or negatively worded questions (e.g., "mark all of the items *except…*") are more challenging for children to understand and hinder their ability to execute a command with accuracy (Chiavaroli, 2017; Jones, 1966). Chiavorili (2017) also emphasized that non-native, English language learners have greater difficulties with these types of questions. Furthermore, directions may be presented in a variety of ways and may differ in complexity. They can be presented both orally and in written form. Some directions may be long or short, while others may include multi-step instructions, and consist of one or more relational concepts in a given instruction (e.g., pick up the book to your *right*, and place it *under* your chair) (Zhou & Boehm, 2004).

In general, limited research has been conducted in understanding basic relational concepts in direction following. With Spanish-speaking children, the studies are extremely scarce. According to the National Center for Education Statistics, in the U.S., Spanish was the primary language spoken at home for 3.7 million "English Language Learner's" (ELL's) in 2014-2015, which represents 77.1% of all ELL children nationwide, and 7.6 percent of all public K-12 children (NCES, 2017). Due to the significant increase of Spanish speaking children entering U.S. public and private schools across the country, it is critical for educators to have an understanding on children's language development and their ability to follow instructions in the classroom. Furthermore, cross-cultural studies on how the textbooks influence children's learning of the basic relational concepts and their ability to follow instructions are nonexistent. Research shows that supporting a bilingual child's learning at an early age can have academic, cognitive and social advantages (U.S Department of Health and Human Services, 2017).

The present study uses qualitative and quantitative methods to 1) assess both monolingual English-speaking (U.S.) and Spanish-speaking (Mexico) children's performance on direction following (directions that contain basic relational concepts), and 2) examine the presence of the basic relational concepts in the textbooks (math and language arts) in U.S. and Mexico, as well as the nature of complexity of the instructional directions (defined by number of concepts embedded in the directions).

Methods

Study 1 (Quantitative Study)

Participants

Participants from this study were selected from three elementary schools in Celaya, the third largest city in the state of Guanajuato, Mexico. With approximately 494,304 inhabitants, Celaya's growing economy has led to an increase in job opportunities (approximately 77% of the population are employed), and the development of new schools. Most families from Celaya are of average income; working primarily for large industrial/commercialized companies such as Honda and/or own their own family businesses. Children were selected from this major city in particular as it serves as a general representative sample of other urban/suburban cities throughout Mexico. Both parental consent and consent from school administrators were obtained prior to testing. A total of 265 children were assessed ($n = 128$ for First grade, $n = 137$ for Second grade).

In order to make comparisons between children from Mexico to those of the U.S., the present study used data from a standardized sample (U.S. First grade, $n = 2196$; Second grade, $n = 2208$) collected by Boehm (1986). Although the "middle-class" status is not comparable between the U.S. and Mexico, the overall status of the two samples in comparison to their own country were similar. Although the Applications Booklet of the BTEC-R has not yet been re-normed, Zhou and Boehm (2004) collected a sample of 95 U. S., middle class children at the end of Spring 2001 and compared them to the 1986 sample and found no significant statistical difference (interpreted in terms of effect size, $d > 0.5$) between both groups.

Assessment Materials

A translated Spanish version of the Applications Booklet of the Boehm Test of Basic Concepts-Revised (BTBC-R) (*Prueba Boehm de conceptos básicos- Edición revisada*) (Boehm, 1986b) was used. The BTBC-R Applications Booklet consists of 26 items that include the following qualifiers: size, direction, position in space, quantity, time, classification, temporal order, and others (Zhou & Boehm, 2004). The types of tasks included in the Applications booklet consisted of the following direction types: (a) one or more qualifying feature (e.g.,"Mark the *longest* key in the *top* row"); (b) two or more qualifying features (e.g.,"Mark *all* the bugs that are *big* and *black*,"); (c) equal numbers of objects (e.g.,"Mark the pictures that have *equal* number of lolli-pops."); (d) comparisons involving intermediate position (e.g.,"Find the tree that is *taller* than one but not the *tallest*."); (e) temporal order (e.g.,"Mark the picture needed to keep the story in order."); and (f) a series of commands (e.g.,"Begin at the *left*. Mark an X on the *first* square. *Skip* a square and make an X on the *next* square.") (Boehm, 1986; Zhou & Boehm, 2004).

Procedures

The first author fluent in both English and Spanish traveled to Celaya, Guanajuato, Mexico, toward the end of the 2018 academic school year and administered the Prueba Boehm de Conceptos Básicos–Edición Revisada in three different schools. Each school had two first-grade and two second-grade classes in both the morning and afternoon. Children were assessed in groups of 15 to 20. They were evenly dispersed throughout the classroom in order to prevent them from looking at each other's response booklets. Classroom teachers (one teacher per class) served as proctors to ensure children were not cheating.

Data Analysis

Due to the significant difference between sample sizes (U.S. standardized sample versus the Mexican sample). the current study used Cohen's (1988) recommendation by calculating and reporting effect sizes for differences between proportions in terms of specific values of "h." Cohen used "h" as an indicator of effect size to describe the following: small effect size (h = 0.20), medium effect size (h = 0.50), and large effect size (h = 0.80). For the purposes of this study, only medium and large effect sizes were interpreted. An 80% passing rate, as used by Zhou & Boehm (2004) was also used as the criterion for mastery of the concepts, where percentage passing was calculated using the formula below:

$$\% \text{ PASSING} = \frac{\text{The total number of children who answered an item correctly}}{\text{the total number of children assessed}} \times 100$$

Results (Study 1)

Performance Scores on BTBC-Application

Based on the 80% passing rate, U.S. first graders mastered 10 out of the 26 items (38%), while second graders mastered 17 of the 26 items (65%). In comparison, Mexican children mastered 4 of the 26 items (15%) at the first-grade level and 12 out of 26 items (46%) at the second-grade level. The statistical analyses were significant at both first (h = .53) and second-grade levels (h = .38), suggesting that U.S. children outperformed Mexican children. The analysis also showed that the progression from first to second grade were statistically significant for both U.S. (27% increase, h = .54) and Mexican children (31% increase, h = .70).

Analyses of the Nature of Directions

In order to understand children's direction following, it is important to analyze the directions in terms of conceptual complexity.

Position-in-space. Although both first and second grade U.S. children performed slightly better than Mexican children on items related to position-in-space (e.g., *below, above, outside, inside, etc.*), both cultural groups had difficulty identifying the concepts *above* and *below* at the first grade level (e.g., "Mark the drawing where a ball is *below* a shoe and a ball is *above* a glove") (78% passing for U.S.; 54% passing for Mexico; $h = 0.51$). The data also reveal that there were an increase in developmental progression of 20% for children from Mexico, while U.S. children made an 8% gain for the item related to the concepts *above* and *below*.

At both first and second-grade levels, U.S. children had a better understanding of the qualifiers *outside* and *inside* ("Mark the drawing where a star is *outside* of a circle, and a star is *inside* of a box") (Grade 1, 92% passing for U.S. and 66% passing for Mexico, $h = 0.67$; Grade 2, 96% passing for U.S. and 72% passing; $h = 0.71$). In addition, U.S. first graders had a better understanding of the concepts *across* and *bottom* than Mexican children (e.g., "Mark the arrow that is going *across* in the *bottom* row") (96% passing for U.S. and 74% passing for Mexico, $h = 0.67$). By the second grade, Mexican children made a 10% gain in their understanding of the concepts across and bottom (84% passing, $h = 0.24$), catching up with their U.S. counterparts.

Intermediate point comparisons. In comparison to their U.S. counterparts, both first and second-grade children from Mexico had difficulty understanding intermediate point comparisons that include the negative qualifier, "not" with three additional qualifying attributes (e.g., "Mark the automobile that is *not* the *farthest* from the stop light, but it is *farther* than *another* automobile") (Grade 1, 36% passing for Mexico, 79% passing for U.S., $h = 0.90$; Grade 2, 60% passing for Mexico, 82% passing for U.S., $h = 0.49$).

U.S. children also performed better than Mexican children, at both grade levels, in their ability to follow directions that contained the concepts *more-less-another* (e.g., "Mark the bowl that has *more* ice-cream than one bowl, but *less* ice-cream than *another*) (Grade

1 76% passing for U.S., 40% passing for Mexico, $h = 0.75$; Grade 2, 86% passing for U.S., 58% passing for Mexico, $h = 0.64$). For first graders, both cultural groups had difficulty understanding the concepts *taller-shorter-another*, (e.g., Mark the tree that is *taller* than one tree, but *shorter* than *another*) (77% passing for U.S., 52% for Mexico, $h = 0.53$). Developmental progression was observed from first to second-grade for both cultural groups; an 8% increase for U.S. children, and a 12% increase for Mexican children.

Concept of "equal." Mexico children outperformed their U.S. counterparts at both first and second-grade levels on the concept of *equal* (e.g., "Mark the pictures that have an *equal* number of lollipops") (Grade 1, 62% passing for U. S., 90% passing for Mexico; $h = 0.68$; Grade 2, 76% passing for U.S., 90% passing for Mexico; $h = 0.38$). On item 15 (e.g., "Mark the pictures that have *equal* numbers of stars"), Mexican children also performed better (84% passing) than U.S. children (66% passing) at the first grade ($h = 0.42$), and second grade (88% passing for Mexico and 78% passing for U.S.; $h = 0.27$).

Objects with three qualifying attributes. With regard to directives that contain three qualifying attributes, both first and second-grade children from Mexico had significant difficulties. Specifically, Mexican children had trouble understanding the concepts *large-over-small*, when presented in a single directive (e.g., "Mark the *large* box that is *over* the *small* ball") (Grade 1, 80% passing for U.S., 42% passing for Mexico; $h = 0.80$; Grade 2, 85% passing for U.S., 34% passing for Mexico, $h = 1.10$). There was no developmental progression observed for following *large-over-small* direction, but rather, Mexican children regressed 8% at the end of second grade.

A medium difference ($h = 0.60$) was observed between Mexican (73% passing) and U.S. first graders (94% passing) in their ability to follow directions containing the concept, "*all*," and two other qualifiers (*big-black*) (e.g., "Mark *all* of the insects that are *big* and *black*"). First grade Mexican children also had more difficulty than U.S. children following directions that contained the concepts *all-wide-up* (e.g., "Mark *all* the arrows that are *wide* and pointing *up*") (85% passing for U.S., 52% passing for Mexico, $h = 0.74$). Despite the observed difficulties, Mexican children made a 30% increase from first to second grade in their understanding of the concepts *all-wide-up* (from 52% to 81% passing; $h = 0.65$).

On directions that included the qualifiers *shortest-between-tall* (e.g., Mark the *shortest* flower, that is *between* two *tall* flowers), first graders from the U.S. (90% passing) outperformed their Mexican counterparts (42% passing, $h = 1.09$). However, by the end of second grade, Mexican children made a 46% increase in their understanding of the qualifiers *shortest-between-tall* (from 42% to 88% passing; $h = 1.02$).

Following multistep directions. Using the 80% passing rate as the criterion, both U.S. and Mexican first and second-grade children had difficulty following a series of multistep commands. Specifically, U.S. children had difficulty following the multi-step direction, "Mark an X on the *first* square. *Skip* a square and mark an X on the *next* square" (Grade 1, 60% passing for U.S., 23% passing for Mexico; Grade 2, 73% passing for U.S., and 36% passing for Mexico). On item 25 (e.g., "Mark the *second pair* of shoes"), both U.S. and Mexican first and second graders had difficulty (Grade 1, 33% for U.S., 33% for Mexico; Grade 2, 47% for U.S., 25% for Mexico).

In summary, overall, U.S. children outperformed Mexican children on the BTBC-R direction following assessment. U.S. children at both first and second grades also outperformed their Mexican counterparts in following directions with three qualifying attributes, intermediate point position, and directions relating to space (outside-inside, across-bottom). Mexican children outperformed U.S. children in their ability to follow directions involving the concept of *"equal"* (*igual*). Developmental progression from first to second grade was observed among U.S. children across all items. Developmental progression was also observed on 24 out of the 26-item assessment for Mexican children. Finally, both cultural groups had difficulty following multi-step directions.

Methods

Study 2 (Qualitative)

The purpose of the Study was to: (1) examine the type of basic relational concepts (qualifiers) identified by Boehm (1986) embedded in the instructional materials of math and language arts in both the U.S. and Mexico; and (2) the complexity of directions (the number of qualifiers or concepts found in each directive) present in the instructions in the textbooks. The term "qualifier" and "concept" are sometimes used interchangeably in this sect on to be consistent with the term used in the extent literature.

Materials

U.S. Math and English Language Arts Textbooks.

For Mathematics, the following textbooks from the United States were analyzed: *Math in Focus 1A and 1B: Singapore Math (Grade 1)*, and *Math in Focus 2A and 2B: Singapore Math (Grade 2)*, by Marshall Cavendish Education (Fong et al., 2009). The Singapore Math program was originally developed in Singapore, publishing its first Primary Mathematics (grades 1-6) textbooks in 1982. In 1984, Singapore scored 16th out of 26 nations in the Second International Science Study (SSIS) and in 1995, their children placed first in the Trends in International Mathematics and Science Study (TIMSS). In 2007, Houghton Mifflin Harcourt worked with Marshall Cavendish to produce a Singapore Math program for the United States. *The Math in Focus* textbooks supports the goals of the Common Core State Standards for Mathematics and is widely used across the United States (Clark et al., 2019).

For English Language Arts, the present study analyzed the following textbooks: *Adventures of the Superkids First Grade*, and *The Superkids Hit Second Grade*, by Pleasant Rowland (Rowland Reading Foundation, 2017a, 2017b, 2017c, 2017d). The Superkids Reading program is a core literacy textbook for grades K-2 that teaches all aspects of reading in combination with the language arts and is widely used across the United States.

Mexico's Math and language Arts Textbooks. For the text-books selected from Mexico, the following textbooks were analyzed: *Español: Primer Grado* (Spanish 1st grade), *Español: Segundo Grado* (Spanish 2nd grade), *Desafíos Matemáticos: Primer Grado* (Mathematics 1st grade), *Desafíos Matemáticos: Segundo Grado* (Mathematics 2nd grade), (SEP, 2016a, 2016b, 2016c, 2016d). These textbooks were cre-ated and developed by the Secretary of Public Education (Secretario de Educación Publica–SEP), the General Direction of Textbooks Development (Dirección General de Desarrollo Curricular), and the Assistant Secretary of Basic Education (Subsecretaria de Educación Basica). Similar to the United Stated, according to Article 3 of the Constitution of Mexico, children and families have the right to a free and appropriate public education. This includes access to educational materials, such as textbooks. Furthermore, the textbooks being used for this study are considered to be part of the national textbooks in Mexico that were developed by the government and provided to public schools across the country (WENR, 2016). As stated by the Secretary of Public Education in Mexico, the hope is that by providing a free and appropriate public education, as well as education mate-rials, millions of Mexican children who are traditionally marginalized from proper educational services will have an equal opportunity. The four textbooks selected for the present study, serve to be an accurate representation of the textbooks for first and second grade children across Mexico.

Coding Procedures

Identifying concepts (Qualifiers). A total of 72 Boehm basic relational concepts were used as the criteria for identifying the con-cepts in the textbooks. Of the 72 concepts, 50 concepts were adopted from Boehm-3 (Boehm, 2001) and an additional 22 concepts were derived from the teacher observation form of Boehm-3. However, only 66 basic relational concepts were used for the Spanish version (50 concepts from the Boehm-3 and 16 of 22 concepts were translated from the teacher observation form (Thorne & Narváez, 1987). The lower number of Spanish concepts were a result of the differences in language characteristics. For example, while the English language uses the words "each" and "every" for different purposes, the Spanish language uses only one word "cada" for these two English terms.

Identifying instructions. The teacher manuals and student textbooks were analyzed to identify the concepts corresponding to the core list. The directions in the textbooks started with the word "**Say**" (English) and "**Diga**" (Spanish) were examined. Each identified concept was organized by grade and subject area (i.e., Math, ELA, Spanish) in an excel spreadsheet.

Identifying the Complexity of Directions. Due to inconsistencies and flexibility in teachers' use of the instructions allocated to them in the textbooks, only children's textbooks were used for this part of the analyses. The complexity of each directive (i.e., the number of concepts or qualifiers found within a single direction) was based on a classification system: *No Complexity* (i.e., containing zero concepts or qualifiers), *Low Complexity* (i.e., containing one qualifier), *Moderately Complex* (i.e., containing two qualifiers), and *Very Complex* (i.e., containing three or more qualifiers). For example:

Directions:
      "You read about an experiment in "3, 2, 1…Liftoff."
      (0 Qualifiers, No Complexity)

      "Read the sentences at the bottom of the page, cut them out, and glue them into the chart in the *order* they happened." (2-Qualifiers (*bottom, order*), Moderately Complex-two qualifiers)

Results (Study 2)

Concepts Identified in the U.S. and Mexico Textbooks

Forty-one concepts of the 72 English (57% for U.S) and 66 Spanish concepts (62% for Mexico) identified by Boehm were present in both cultures' textbooks. Results in this section are presented in Table 1.

Table One
Basic Relation Concepts Found in U.S. and Mexican Textbooks

	Basic Relational Concepts (Englsih/Spanish)	U.S. Textbooks				Mexican Textbooks			
		English		Math		Spanish		Math	
		1st grade	2nd grade	1st grade	2nd grade	1st grade	2nd grade	1st grade	2nd grade
1	Most/Mas	√	√	√	√	√	√	√	√
2	Next/ Mas Cerca, Siguiente	√	√	√	√	√	√	√	√
3	Other/Otro	√	√	√	√	√	√	√	√
4	Top/Mas Alto	√	√	√	√	√	√	√	√
5	All/Todos	√	√	√	√	√	√	√	√
6	Before/Antes	√	√	√	√	√	√	√	√
7	Last/Ultimo	√	√	√	√	√	√	√	√
8	First/Primero	√	√	√	√	√	√	√	√
9	Each/Cada	√	√	√	√	√	√	√	√
10	Same/Mismo	√	√	√	√	√	√	√	√
11	Tall,Taller/Alto, Mas Alto	√	√	√	√	√	√	√	√
12	More/Mas	√	√	√	√	√	√	√	√
13	Order/En Orden	√	√	√	√	√	√	√	√
14	Shortest/Mas Corto	√	√	√	√	√	√	√	
15	End/Final	√	√	√	√	√		√	√
16	Beginning/ Empezando	√	√	√	√	√	√	√	
17	Different/Diferente	√	√	√	√	√	√	√	
18	After/Despues	√	√	√	√	√	√	√	
19	Right/ Derecho	√	√	√	√		√		√
20	Below/ Debajo	√	√	√			√	√	√
21	Second/ Segundo	√	√	√		√	√	√	√
22	Pair/ Par	√	√	√	√		√	√	√
23	Under/Debajo	√	√	√	√		√		√
24	Least/Menos	√	√	√	√			√	√
25	Left/ Izquierda	√	√	√	√	√	√		
26	Match/Une	√	√	√	√	√	√		
27	Part/ Parte	√	√	√	√	√	√		

Table One
Basic Relation Concepts Found in U.S. and Mexican Textbooks (cont.)

Basic Relational Concepts (Englsih/Spanish)		U.S. Textbooks				Mexican Textbooks			
		English		Math		Spanish		Math	
		1st grade	2nd grade	1st grade	2nd grade	1st grade	2nd grade	1st grade	2nd grade
28	Front/En Frente	√	√	√	√		√	√	
29	Above/Arriba	√	√	√	√	√	√		
30	Big/Bigger/ Grande, Mas Grande	√	√	√	√	√			√
31	Large/Grande	√	√	√	√	√			√
32	Small/Pequeno	√	√	√	√				√
33	Between/Entre-Adentro	√	√	√	√			√	
34	Across/Atravesada, Atraves De	√	√	√	√				
35	Third/Tercero	√	√	√	√				√
36	Whole/Completa	√	√	√	√				
37	Some/Algunos	√	√	√	√				
38	Few/Pocos	√	√	√	√				
39	Away/Retirado	√	√	√	√				
40	Back/ Detras, De Atras	√	√	√	√				
41	Half/Mitad	√	√	√	√				
42	Long/Longest/Largo, Mas Largo		√	√	√	√		√	
43	Starting/Empezando		√	√	√	√	√	√	
44	Alike/Igual	√	√	√		√	√	√	√
45	Down/Hacia Abajo	√	√	√				√	√
46	Middle/Medio	√	√	√		√	√	√	√
47	Up/ Hacia Arriba	√	√	√				√	√
48	Every/ Cada	√		√	√	√	√	√	√
49	Medium-sized/ Tamano-Mediano	√	√		√				√
50	Bottom/Mas Abajo	√	√		√				
51	Side/Al Lado	√		√	√				
52	Less/Menos		√	√	√			√	√
53	Fewest/Menor Cantidad	√		√	√				

Table One
Basic Relation Concepts Found in U.S. and Mexican Textbooks (cont.)

Basic Relational Concepts (Englsih/Spanish)		U.S. Textbooks				Mexican Textbooks			
		English		Math		Spanish		Math	
		1st grade	2nd grade	1st grade	2nd grade	1st grade	2nd grade	1st grade	2nd grade
54	Outside/Fuera	√	√						
55	Inside/ Dentro, Adentro	√	√					√	√
56	Always/Siempre	√	√						
57	Behind/Detras	√		√					
58	Backward/Hacia Atras		√		√				
59	Center/ Centro	√	√					√	√
60	Corner/Esquina			√	√				
61	Equal/ Igual			√	√	√	√	√	√
62	Near/Nearest/Cerca, Mas Cerca			√	√			√	
63	Widest/Mas Ancha	√			√				
64	Through/A Traves	√	√						
65	Over/Sobre	√	√						
66	Forward/Hacia Adelante	√	√					√	
67	Row/ En Linea	√	√						
68	Farthest/ Mas Lejos			√	√			√	
69	Skip/Saltando				√		√		
70	As Many/ Tantos				√				
71	Never/Nunca								
72	Separated/ Separado								

Concepts Found in U.S. Textbooks

English Language Arts. Using the concepts from the Boehm Test of Basic Concepts as the criteria, 60 concepts were found in the first-grade English Language Arts (ELA) textbooks, while 59 concepts were found in second-grade textbooks. Fifty-six (56) concepts were found to overlap in both first and second grade textbooks except for three concepts: *side*, *every*, and *wide*. Additionally, there were three new concepts that were introduced at the second-grade level: *backward, long,* and *up.*

Mathematics. Fifty-five (55) relational concepts were found in the first-grade textbooks, while 57 concepts were found in second grade. Five concepts found in first grade were not found in second grade: *alike, behind, down, middle, up.* Seven (7) concepts were introduced in the second grade only: *another, as many as, backward, bottom, medium-sized, skip,* and *wide.*

Concepts Found in Mexican Textbooks

Spanish Language Arts. Twenty-seven (27) relational concepts were identified in first grade and 29 concepts in second-grade textbooks. There were 24 concepts that overlapped between first and second grade. Three concepts were found in the first grade but not in second-grade textbooks: *final* (ending), *grande* (big), *mas largo* (longest). Five concepts were introduced in the second-grade textbooks only: *saltado* (skip), *segundo* (second), *terminar* (finish), *debajo* (below), and *frente* (in front).

Mathematics. Thirty-one (31) concepts were identified in the first grade and 32 concepts were found in the second-grade textbooks. There is a total of 27 concepts overlapping between first and second grades. Four concepts were found only in the first grade: *corto* (short), *frente* (front), *mas cerca* (near), *mas largo* (longest). Six concepts were only identified in the second-grade textbooks: *hacia arriba* (up), *derecha* (right), *mediano* (medium), *par* (pair), *pequeño* (small), and *tercera* (third).

Cross-Cultural Overlap/Absence in Relational Concepts.

Cross-Cultural Similarities. Some cross-cultural similarities were also observed between textbooks. Specifically, the following concepts were observed in both Mexican and U.S. textbooks: *double/doble, greater/mayor que, complete/completo, missing/falta, faster/mas rapido, little/chico, total/en total,* and *only/solo.*

Concepts present in U.S. but not in Mexico textbooks. There were 26 concepts observed in the U.S. textbooks not found in Mexico's textbooks. These concepts include: *across, alike, always, as many as, away,* *back, backward, beginning, behind, bottom, center, corner, few, half, least, most, other, outside, over, row, side, some, through, top, whole, wide.* On the other hand, all concepts found in Mexico's instructional materials were also found in the U.S. textbooks.

Concepts Rarely Appeared in the U.S. and Mexico Textbooks. Two concepts of *farther/farthest* and *skip* only appeared in 25% of the U.S. textbooks. The concepts that appeared in only 25% of the Mexican textbooks are as follows: *adelante* (forward), *más cerca* (nearest), *más lejos* (further/furthest), *pequeña* (smaller/smallest), *tamaño mediano* (medium sized), *tantas como* (as many as), and *tercero* (third).

Concepts not found in any culture. The concepts of *never/nunca*, and *separated/separados* were not observed in the any of the directions analyzed in the textbooks from both countries.

Concepts other than Boehm's. In addition to Boehm's 72 concepts, other concepts were also found in both U.S. and Mexico's first and second grade Mathematics and English/Spanish textbooks. Specifically, 29 new concepts were found in the U.S. textbooks, while 15 new concepts were observed in the Mexican textbooks. These additional concepts are organized in the following categories:

Space. New concepts found in the U.S. textbooks included: *lower/lowest, opposite, straight*, and *missing*. New concepts from the Spanish Language textbooks include: *horizontal, vertical*, and *falta* (missing).

Quantity. In the U.S. textbooks, the following new concepts were identified: *altogether, as much as, both, even, exactly, greater/greatest, how many, similar.* In the Mexican textbooks, the new concepts of *mayor que* (more than), *menor que* (less than), and *muchos* (a lot). The following new concepts were observed in both U.S. and Mexican textbooks: *complete/completo, double/doble, greater/mayor que, total/en total,* and *only/solo.*

Time. In the U.S. textbooks, the new concepts of *repeating* and *again* were observed. No new concepts were observed in this area for the Mexican textbooks.

Speed. The new concepts of *faster/fastest* and *slower/slowest* were identified in the U.S. textbooks. Similarly, the new concept of *mas rapido* (faster) was identified in both U.S. and Mexican textbooks.

Size. The new concept of "little" was found in the U.S. textbooks. Similarly, the concepts of *chico* (small/little), *chiquito* (tiny), and *enorme* (huge) were found in the Mexican textbooks.

Mass. The concepts of *heavier/heaviest* and *lighter/lightest* were identified in the U.S. textbooks.

Complexity of Directions in The Textbooks

The complexity of directions is defined as the number of qualifiers (concepts) found in each directive presented in the instructions. *No complexity* directives (i.e., no qualifiers) have no qualifiers found in a directive; *low complexity* directives (e.g., "Fill in the blanks with the words from the box *above*") have only one qualifier; *moderately complex* directives (e.g., "Complete the *first* column on the *left*") have two qualifiers; and *very complex* directives have three or more qualifiers (e.g., "Use the words *above*, to complete *each* sentence on the lines *below*"). The results for this section are summarized in Table 2.

Level of Complexity	Subject							
	ELA				Math			
	1st Grade		2nd Grade		1st Grade		2nd Grade	
	US (%)	Mexico (%)	US (%)	Mexico (%)	US (%)	Mexico (%)	US (%)	Mexico (%)
No Complexity	**49**	**73***	55	64	**73**	**43***	67	**45***
Low Complexity	28	22	31	29	25	39	27	35
Moderately Complex	13	4	12	5	3	**15***	6	16
Very Complex	10	1	2	2	1	3	1	4

*medium effect size

English Language Arts Textbooks (U.S.)

In the U.S., 49% of first grade and 55% of second-grade instructions contained "no complexity," whereas 28% of first and 31% of second-grade directives are "low complexity." Furthermore, 13% of first-grade material and 12% of second-grade material were "moderately complex," while 10% of first-grade material and 2% of second-grade material were "very complex."

Spanish Language Textbooks (Mexico)

In Mexico, 73% of first and 64% of second-grade instructions are "no complexity," whereas 22% of first grade and 29% of second-grade instructions have "low complexity." Furthermore, 4% of first and 5% of second-grade directives were "moderately complex," while 1% of first and 2% of second-grade instructions are "very complex."

Analyses indicated that in language arts textbooks, the Mexico first-grade textbooks (73%) had significantly more "no complexity" directives than the U.S. textbooks (49%) ($h = 0.498$), but not at the second-grade level.

Math textbooks (U.S.)

In the U.S. textbooks, 73% of the first, and 67% of the second-grade instructions were identified as having "no complexity" (i.e., no qualifiers). Twenty-five (25) percent of the first grade and 27% of second-grade instructions are identified as "low complexity." Three percent of first grade and 6% of second-grade directives are identified as "moderately complex." One percent of instructions found across both grade levels were "very complex" directives.

Math textbooks (Mexico)

In Mexico, 43% of first grade and 45% of second-grade instructions found in student textbook contained "no complexity," whereas 39% of first and 35% of second-grade directions were "low complexity." In addition, 15% of first grade and 16% of second-grade instructions were "moderately complex," and 3% of first and 4% of second-grade directives were "very complex."

Analyses indicated that at both first ($h = 0.618$) and second-grade ($h = 0.447$) levels, U.S. math textbooks had significantly more "no complexity" directives than found in Mexico math textbooks. However, at the first-grade level, Mexico math textbooks had significantly more "moderately complex" directives than found in U.S. math textbooks ($h = 0.447$). The "very complex" directives were minimal in both cultures.

Discussion

This study was conducted in order to gain a more comprehensive understanding of direction following among the Spanish-speaking children in Mexico in comparison to their English-speaking counterparts in the United States. In addition, the language arts and math textbooks from each country were analyzed to determine the role that teaching materials play in a child's understanding of basic relational concepts and their ability to follow directions.

Conceptual Complexity, Linguistic Transparency and Direction Following

Cross-cultural differences and similarities were identified. U.S. children at both grade levels outperformed Mexican children on direction following tasks. Furthermore, developmental progression was observed among both cultural groups from first to second grade. This finding is consistent with previous research (Kaplan & White, 1980; Zhou & Boehm, 2004), that children were better able to process increasingly complex directions as they got older.

Although overall, the U.S. children outperformed the Mexican children on the direction following test, it is interesting to note that Mexican children performed better than their U.S. counterparts on some specific directions. For example, Mexican children had a better understanding of the concept of *equal* at both grade levels. It could be that the Mexican children took advantage of the transparency of the Spanish language. For example, the English language uses the concepts of *equal, alike,* and *same* to describe quantity, whereas the Spanish uses the single term *igual* to describe quantity. Therefore, there was less ambiguity or confusion about the concept for the Spanish-speaking children. According to Evans (2017), there are many reasons why English is a more complex language in comparison to other languages in terms of difficult spelling system, complex grammatical patterns, phrasal verbs (i.e., run, run up, run over, run something down), and idioms. Furthermore, Mexican children better understanding the concept of *equal* may also be attributed to the amount of exposure they receive from the school textbooks. Based on our textbook analyses, the concept of *igual* (equal) was consistently found across all subjects (Math and Language Arts), all grades (first and second), and appeared more frequently in Mexico, while it was observed in the U.S. only in Math textbooks across grades.

Mexican children also outperformed their U.S. counterparts on the concept of *longest/mas largo*. We speculate that linguistic transparency in Spanish could have helped Mexican children in their demonstrated mastery of this concept. Specifically, the English language uses the suffix "-est" to form superlatives at the end of one or two syllable adjectives (Bos & Nissim, 2006; Zhou & Boehm, 2004). The Spanish language, similar to Chinese, uses the adverb mas (i.e., more or most) before the adjective to form the comparatives and superlatives. For example, the concept of *mas largo* is directly translated in English as the "the most long" (i.e., longest) and the English concept of *furthest* is translated as *mas lejos* or "the most far." Understanding and using the suffix "-est" is linguistically more complex and demanding (Zhou & Boehm, 1999), while adding a word like *mas* is simple and straight forward. However, despite the transparency of the Spanish language, Mexican children had difficulty at both grade levels with *furthest* and *further* (e.g., "Mark the automobile that is not the furthest from the stoplight, but is further than another automobile"), as well as *taller* and *shorter* (e.g., "Mark the tree that is taller than one tree, but shorter than another"). One of the explanations could be that these directions are conceptually more complex because they involved relativity in the comparison, that is, one could be taller or shorter depending on what it is being compared to.

Difficulty with conceptually complex concepts is also revealed in U.S. and Mexican children's understanding of the concepts *left-right* (e.g., "Mark the cat that is to the *right* of the table, and to the *left* of the basket"), *second pair* (e.g., "Mark the *second pair* of shoes") and a combination of the concepts *left, first, skip, next* (e.g., "Begin at the *left*. Mark an X on the *first* square, *skip* a square, and mark an X on the *next* square"). Zhou and Boehm (2004) purported that children who had difficulty understanding the left-right perspective could be a reflection of the "egocentric representations" (p.). Siegler (1998) further pointed out that children were better able to identify visual-spatial perspectives if provided with the opportunity to shift their bodies in the direction the presented object is facing. As for the concept of "skip," our analyses of the textbooks in both cultures revealed that children were not exposed to this concept as much as other ones, which could have impacted on their mastery of this concept.

In addition to the conceptual complexity inherited in the concepts, the complexity in the directions (number of qualifiers embedded in the direction) could have also played a role in a child's ability to execute the tasks. In our study, U.S. children outperformed their Mexico counterparts on direction following tasks at both first and second-grade levels. This performance discrepancy parallels our analyses of the nature of directions embedded in both countries' textbooks. We found that Mexico first-grade language arts textbooks had significantly more "no complexity" directives than in the U.S. textbooks. Consistent with previous studies, our findings seemed to support that the more exposure children had to relational concepts, the better they were at following complex directions (Boehm, 1991; Kaplan & White, 1980). Furthermore, the more complex directives in the U.S. language arts textbooks used in the "Superkids" program could also suggest emphasis on familial and teacher support in children's learning. Researchers have identified positive associations between higher school-based parent involvement and improved student success, particularly in the early years of school (Daniel et al., 2016). Equally important is the positive influence of textbook materials on student learning through teacher and child interactions with those specific materials in the classroom (Stein et al., 2007). Although Mexican textbooks also require familial support, factors such as family SES levels and parental education could limit a parent's resources and ability to support their child academically (Schalla, 2015).

U.S. math textbooks had significantly more "no complexity" directives than found in Mexico's math textbooks. However, at the first-grade level, Mexico's math textbooks had significantly more "moderately complex" directives than found in U.S. math textbooks.

Perhaps Mexican educators do not recognize that "complex" directions can inhibit or interfere with a child's learning and make it more difficult for a child to understand what is being asked of them. The complexity of directions may also be contributory factors of low-test scores in the area of math in Mexico. Specifically, research shows that 86.2% of Mexican elementary and secondary school children fall in the "basic" or "insufficient" range in the area of math (Vila Rosado et al., 2018).

More broadly, there are also cross-cultural similarities regarding the levels of complexity in directions in the textbook's materials. Overall, directions in both U.S. and Mexican textbooks contained more concise directions that had no qualifiers ("no complexity") or low complex directions. From an information processing perspective, in order for children to execute any directive presented, instructions should be kept short, simple, and with low complexity (e.g., one to two qualifiers used). Perhaps, overelaborated directions do hinder compliance (Kaplan, 1978; Kounin, 1970). This is because there are connections between memory and a child's ability to follow written direction (Engle et al., 1991). Engle and colleagues (1991) reported developmental differences in the relationship between working memory capacity and directions following. Other researchers found that the more complex the information in textbooks materials is, the more difficult it is to process which can lead to misinterpretations of the information presented (Martiniello, 2009; Mestre, 1988). Thorndike and Lorge (1944) emphasized that how teachers present information to children impacts the way children learn and understand the material being presented to them.

Traditional Concepts, Newly Emerged Concepts, and Cultural Biases

An overlap in many concepts was observed in both cultures' textbooks. This suggests a similar instructional approach that focuses on measurement (e.g., longest vs. shortest), comparisons between objects, and teaching concepts relating to position in space (e.g., near vs. far).

Perhaps at the elementary level, "all" academic coursework presented to children is "mostly common" (Brown, 2014). Meaning, that what is taught at the first-grade level in one country, may parallel instructional materials in another. In most countries, all children pursue and complete a "common curriculum" up through secondary school (Schwarts, 2014).

Also worthy of attention are several qualifiers outside of Boehm's typical concepts that the author identified. These concepts include: *double/doble* (e.g., "Draw a circle around the bag with *double* the amount of candy"), *complete/complete* (e.g., "Write the letters that are missing to *complete* the words"), *missing/falta* (e.g., "Write the *missing* numbers in the shapes below"), *fastest/mas rapido* (e.g., "Circle the object moving *fastest*"), *little/chico* (e.g., "Draw a circle around the tree that is *little*") and *only/solo* (e.g., "Mark *only* the numbers"). These concepts were important to add to the assessment tools because they appear frequently in modern textbooks and entire lessons were based on some of these concepts. As knowledge and technology evolve, additional concepts emerge. It is important for educators and researchers to understand and keep up the new educational demands (Thomas et al., 2016).

Possible cultural bias and cultural loading on the BTBC-R direction following test was identified on two items: items 12 (e.g., "Mark the pumpkin needed to keep the story *in order*") and 14 (e.g., "Mark the toy robot needed to keep the story *in order*"). While the United States celebrates Halloween and uses pumpkins, vampires. ghosts, and goblin costumes, etc., the Mexican culture does not. Similarly, understanding toy robots is crucial for any student to answer item 14 with accuracy. It is possible that not all children from Mexico have been exposed to *toy robots* or know how they are made. Such "culturally loaded" items may put children from different cultural background at a disadvantage (Reynolds & Suzuki, 2012).

Implications of the Study

Several implications can be made from the present study. First, it is important to keep cultural and ecological factors in mind when interpreting children's performance. Mexican children's difference in performance on BTBC-R Application test could be partly attributed to challenges and/or differences in Mexico's education system. These speculations are consistent with the findings from the Program for International Student Assessment (OECD, 2019), where Mexican children scored well below other countries involved. Guichard (2005) indicated that although education has been a priority for several decades in Mexico, "teaching is still largely based on rote learning rather than comprehension skills and communication." In addition, teachers within the same school seldom interact and cooperate with one another (Guichard, 2005; Ministry of Education, 2004). Further, schools in Mexico run on a schedule that is considered a double-shift system (e.g., morning and afternoon sessions, or *vespertino y matu-tino*). Studies show that children enrolled in the afternoon program may receive a poorer education due to tiredness (Sagyndykova, 2013) or the diminishing productivity of teachers, which negatively impacts the quality of instruction (García Garduño, 2004). In addition, a child's concentration may be lower in the afternoon, which impacts their ability to learn new material, resulting in lower academic performance (Sagyndykova, 2013). Other researchers have also discovered that children who attend later shifts (e.g., afternoon sessions) have significantly lower grades in Spanish than children who attend morning sessions (Denham, 2011; Travino & Travino, 2004). Teachers who work in the afternoon sessions have a greater number of children from low socioeconomic homes and are often criticized and harassed by the directors of the "morning shifts" (Denham, 2011).

Researchers, psychologists, and test publishers responsible for developing assessment tools for early childhood (e.g., achievement and cognitive batteries) should be mindful of cultural practices, linguistic demands, and level of complexity in test instructions. This would reduce the amount of test bias, cultural loading, and would improve the overall quality and fairness of the assessment.

Children from Mexico, as well as those from other Spanish-speaking countries, are not exposed to the same number of relational concepts as their monolingual counterparts from the United States.

Therefore, it may be difficult for them to follow directions in the classroom. With the growing number of ethnic minorities entering the U.S., it is essential for educators to have an awareness of this and to address the cultural and linguistic differences these children face (Lasagabaster, 2017; Souto-Manning, 2018). Research also stresses the importance of understanding the impact acculturation and socialization can have on an immigrant child's education, language development, and their overall emotional well-being (Souto-Manning, 2018; Yousef, 2019).

References

Boehm, A.E. (1986a). *Boehm* Test of Basic Concepts-Revised. The Psychological Corporation.

Boehm, A.E. (1986b). *Prueba Boehm de conceptos basicos (Edición revisada).* The Psychological Corporation.

Boehm, A. E. (1991). Assessment of basic relational concepts. In B. A. Bracken (Ed.), *The psychoeducational assessment of preschool children* (pp. 241–258). Erlbaum.

Boehm, A.E. (2001). *Boehm Test of Basic Concepts-3.* The Psychological Corporation. https://www.pearsonassessments.com/store/usassessments/en/Store/ Professional-Assessments/Academic-Learning/Brief/Boehm-Test-of-Basic- Concepts-|-Third-Edition/p/0158020995.html

Bos, J., & Nissim, M. (2006, July 22). *An empirical approach to the interpretation of superlatives.* [Conference proceedings]. Conference on Empirical Methods in Natural Language Processing, Sydney, Australia (pp. 9–17). *Association for Computational Linguistics* (ACL).

Brown, C. (2014). *All Children Need Common Foundational Skills* (Vol. 14, No. 3). Education Next. https://www.educationnext.org/children-need-common-foundational-skills/.

Chiavaroli, N. (2017). Negatively-worded multiple-choice questions: An avoidable threat to validity. *Practical Assessment, Research, and Evaluation, 22*(3) 1–14.

Clark, A., Coyne, C., Resnick, S., & Gifford, L. (2019). Math in Focus: Singapore Math: K-8 Curriculum & Assessment: Houghton Mifflin Harcourt. https://www.hmhco.com/ programs/math-in-focus

Cohen, J. (1988). *Statistical power analysis for the behavioral sciences* (2nd ed.). Erlbaum.

Daniel, G. R., Wang, C., & Berthelsen, D. (2016). Early school-based parent involvement, children's self-regulated learning and academic achievement: An Australian longitudinal study. *Early Childhood Research Quarterly, 36*, 168–177.

Denham, S. (2011). *Escuelas de doble turno en México: Una estimación de diferencias asociadas con su implementación* (Revista Mexicana de investigación educative), *16*(50), 801–827.

Engle, R. W., Carullo, J. J., & Collins, K. W. (1991). Individual differences in working memory for comprehension and following directions. *The Journal of Educational Research, 84*(5), 253–262.

Flanagan, D. P., Kaminer, T., Alfonso, V. C., & Raderc, D. E. (1995). Incidence of basic concepts in the directions of new and recently revised American intelligence tests for preschool children. *School Psychology International, 16*(4), 345–364.

Fong, H. K., Ramakrishnan, C., Wah, B. L. P., Bisk, R., Clark, A., & Kanter, P. F. (2009). *Math in focus: The Singapore approach.* Marshall Cavendish Education.

García Garduño, J. M. (2004). La administración y gestión educativa: Algunas lecciones que nos deja su evolución en los Estados Unidos y México. *Revista Interamericana de Educación de Adultos, 26*(1), 11–52.

Guichard, S. (2005). *The Education Challenge in Mexico: Delivering Good Quality Education to All.* OECD Economics Department Working Papers, No. 447. OECD Publishing (NJ1).

IES – Institute of Education Sciences, & NCES – National Center for Education Statistics. (n.d.). *IES & NCES Fast Facts website: Elementary and Secondary: English language learners.* U.S. Department of Education. (n.d.). https://nces.ed.gov/fastfacts/display.asp?id=96

Jones, S. (1966). The effect of a negative qualifier in an instruction. *Journal of Verbal Learning and Verbal Behavior, 5*(5), 497–501.

Kaplan, C.H. (1978). *A developmental analysis of children's direction following behavior in grades K-5.* [Unpublished doctoral dissertation]. Columbia University.

Kaplan, C. H., & White, M. A. (1980). Children's direction following behavior in grades K–5. *The Journal of Educational Research, 74*, 43–48.

Kounin, J. S. (1970). *Discipline and group management in classrooms.* Holt, Rinehard & Winston.

Lasagabaster, D. (2017). Language learning motivation and language attitudes in multilingual Spain from an international perspective. *The Modern Language Journal, 101*, 583–596.

Martiniello, M. (2009). Linguistic complexity, schematic representations, and differential item functioning for English language learners in math tests. *Educational Assessment, 14*(3-4), 160–179.

Mestre, J. (1988). The role of language comprehension in mathematics and problem solving. In R. Cocking & J. Mestre (Eds.), *Linguistic and cultural influences on learning mathematics* (pp. 201–220). Erlbaum.

OECD – Organisation for Economic Co-operation and Development. (2019). Mexico: Student performance PISA 2015. http://gpseducation.oecd.org/CountryProfile?primaryCountry= MEX&treshold=10&topic=PI

Preddy, D., Boehm, A. E., & Shepherd, M. J. (1984). PBCB: A norming of the Spanish translation of the Boehm Test of Basic Concepts. *Journal of School Psychology, 22*(4), 407–413.

Reynolds, C. R., & Suzuki, L. A. (2012). Bias in psychological assessment. *Handbook of psychology, Second edition.* doi: 10.1002/9781118133880.hop210004

Rowland Reading Foundation. (2017a). Adventures of the Superkids (1st grade). *First semester teacher materials.* Zaner-Bloser, Inc.

Rowland Reading Foundation. (2017b). More adventures of the Superkids: (1st grade) *Second semester teacher materials.* Zaner-Bloser, Inc.

Rowland Reading Foundation. (2017c). The Superkids hit second grade (2nd grade). *First semester teacher materials.* Zaner-Bloser, Inc.

Rowland Reading Foundation. (2017d). The Superkids take off (2nd grade). *Second semester teacher materials.* Zaner-Bloser, Inc.

Sagyndykova, G. (2013). Academic Performance in Double-shift schooling. Nazarbayev University.

Schalla, L. K. (2015). Family-school collaboration in Mexico: perspectives of teachers and parents. [Unpublished doctoral dissertation]. University of Minnesota Digital Conservancy. http://hdl.handle.net/11299/171715.

Schwarts, R. (2014). Multiple Pathways Can Better Serve Children. (Vol. 14, No. 3). Education Next. https://www.educationnext.org/multiple-pathways-can-better-serve-children/.

Secretario de Educación Publica (SEP) (2016a). Español (1st grado). *Libro para el maestro.* Impreso en Mexico.

Secretario de Educación Publica (SEP) (2016b). Español (2nd grado). *Libro para el maestro.* Impreso en Mexico.

Secretario de Educación Publica (SEP) (2016c). Desafíos Matemáticos (1st grado). *Libro para el maestro.* Impreso en Mexico.

Secretario de Educación Publica (SEP) (2016d). Desafíos Matemáticos. *Libro para el maestro* (2nd grado). Impreso en Mexico.

Siegler, R. S. (1998). *Emerging minds: The process of change in children's thinking.* Oxford University Press.

Souto-Manning, M. (2018). Disrupting Eurocentric epistemologies: Re-mediating transitions to centre intersectionally-minoritised immigrant children, families and communities. *European Journal of Education, 53*(4), 456–468.

Stein, M. K., Remillard, J., & Smith, M. S. (2007). How curriculum influences student learning. In F. Lester (Ed.), *Second handbook of research on mathematics teaching and learning* (pp. 319–370). Information Age.

IES – Institute of Education Sciences, & NCES – National Center for Education Statistics. (n.d.). *IES & NCES Fast Facts website: Elementary and Secondary: English language learners.* U.S. Department of Education. (n.d.). https://nces.ed.gov/fastfacts/display.asp?id=96

Thorndike, E. L., & Lorge, I. (1944). *The teacher's word book of 30,000 words.* Bureau of Publications, Teachers Co.

Thorne, C., & Narváez, A. (1987). La Prueba de Conceptos Básicos de Boehm: Adaptación y elaboración de baremos para Lima y Callao. *Revista de Psicología, 5*(2), 135–148.

Thomas, P. A., Kern, D. E., Hughes, M. T., & Chen, B. Y. (2016). *Curriculum development for medical education: A six-step approach.* Johns Hopkins University Press.

Treviño, E., & Treviño, G. (2004). Estudio sobre las desigualdades educativas en México: La incidencia de la escuela en el desempeño académico de los alumnos y el rol de los docentes. *Colección Cuadernos de investigación.* (No. 5).

Vila Rosado, D. N., Duran, M. M. G., & Riera, J. L. R. (2018, August 22-27). *Development of mathematical skills like a support to executive functions in Mexican students and the psycho-pedagogical benefits.* [Conference proceedings]. Conference on Social Sciences and Humanities, Princeton, NJ. (pp. 21-23). Research Association for Interdisciplinary Studies (RAIS).

World Education News Review (2016). Education System Profiles: Education in Mexico. https://wenr.wes.org/2016/08/education-in-mexico

Yousef, N. (2019). Prejudices and Obstacles Immigrant Students Face in the Los
  Angeles Unified School District. *Aleph, UCLA Undergraduate Research
  Journal for the Humanities and Social Sciences, 16.* https://escholarship.org/uc/
  item/3742m8cd

Zhou, Z., & Boehm, A. E. (2004). American and Chinese children's understanding of
  basic relational concepts in directions. *Psychology in the Schools, 41,* 261–272.

Zhou, Z., & Boehm, A. E. (2001). American and Chinese children's knowledge of basic
  relational concepts. *School Psychology International, 22*(1), 5–21.

Zhou, Z., & Boehm, A. E. (1999). Chinese and American children's knowledge of basic
  relational concepts.

Mind Body Health Interventions in Preschoolers

*Melissa Bray, Emily Winter, Aarti P. Bellara,
Johanna deLeyer-Tiarks, Jessica Dirsmith, Adeline Bray,
and Sai Aravala*

Abstract

There are myriad of mind body health (MBH) interventions that are effective for the preschool population. Supports may include, yet are not limited to, journal expression, yoga, music therapy, mindfulness, video self-modeling, and muscle relaxation. These particular interventions have resulted in positive changes for preschoolers with anxiety, depression, stress, and attention, as well as various physical conditions. Benefits of these MBH interventions include being effective with respect to teacher time, economically feasible, and are well-received by parents, teachers, and preschoolers.

Keywords: *Physical Health, Mental Health, Interventions, Children, Preschool*

Introduction

Mind body health interventions, including positive psychological interventions, are increasingly being applied in school settings to sustain and improve health and well-being in children and adolescents (Campion & Rocco, 2009; Froh et al., 2008; Huppert & Johnson, 2010). While large amounts of present research have centered on school-aged populations, several researchers are beginning to study the impact of mind body health interventions in preschoolers (e.g. Cohen et al., 2018; Flook et al., 2015). This piece provides an overview of the literature on mind body health interventions in preschool populations, including: mindfulness, yoga, relaxation and progressive muscle relaxation (PMR), expressive arts, physical activity, music, gratitude writing, bibliotherapy, and video self-modeling. Following the scientist-practitioner model, school psychologists are well-equipped to implement research-based mind body health interventions for preschool populations. They are also ideally suited to provide educators with the research and professional development needed to assist in intervention planning, implementation, and service delivery.

What is Mind Body Health?

Mind body health may be applied to all age groups, including preschool. The techniques derived from the conceptualization of mind body health are rooted in psychology, education, and the health sciences. Individuals of all ages benefit from a holistic framework using interdisciplinary collaboration to effect change and preschoolers are no exception. The developing psyche evidences aspects of positive psychology such as feelings of gratitude and acceptance. The mind interacts with the physical body producing various psychological and physical outcomes. This is evident in preschoolers with somatic complaints, heightened visits to school nurses, bathrooms, absenteeism, and tardiness (Berk, 2012).

To impact change with the preschool population, techniques derived from the mind body health paradigm include such interventions as yoga (Kim et al., 2016), relaxation and guided imagery

(Kohen & Wynne, 1997), mindfulness (Zelazo & Lyons, 2012), video self-modeling (Buggey et al., 2011; Buggey, 2012; Buggey et al., 2018; Lemmon & Green, 2015), and meditation (Campion & Rocco, 2009). These are all easily implemented in the preschool setting, are economically feasible, and enjoyable for preschoolers and their teachers alike. These treatments are gaining in popularity and effectiveness in terms of supporting experimental data mounting (Inagaki & Hatano, 1993).

Interventions

Mindfulness

Research on mindfulness, which encompasses the practice of focusing intently on processes in the moment using intention, attention, and attitude, has gained recent traction in popular culture and in the present state of the academic literature (Shapiro et al., 2006; Zelazo & Lyons, 2011). Much research has demonstrated the positive impact that mindfulness may have on adults in various realms of functioning, such as enhancing self-regulatory abilities, decreasing medical symptoms, and reducing symptoms of stress, amongst a variety of other mind body health benefits (Baer, 2003; Grossman et al., 2004)

When considering the role of mindfulness specifically for preschool aged populations, research is not as robust as it is for adults; thus, there is a deficiency in findings for this age group (Flook et al., 2015). However, some research has demonstrated promising preliminary findings (Zelazo & Lyons, 2012). Recent findings from Flook and colleagues (2015) examined a kindness curriculum intervention in a preschool classroom. The curriculum, which encompassed mindfulness as the core underlying principle of the multi-dimensional program, aims to teach prosocial skills to preschool children. Preschool students in the intervention demonstrated increases on measures of social competence as well as had higher grades on report cards for daily skills such as ability to learn, overall health, as well as social-emotional skills. In contrast, the control group demonstrated an increase in selfish behaviors (e.g., lack of sharing). Students also demonstrated growth in executive functioning skills as measured by inhibitory control and cognitive flexibility. Overall, moderate effects were noted for students in the intervention, who had lower baseline levels of executive functioning as well as social ability. This improvement demonstrates the students' growth in such domains after completing the intervention, as compared to students in the control.

Researchers Lim and Qu (2017) noted that after one brief mindfulness intervention (a mere 15-minutes in length), their research identified enhanced attention in children's. Further, the authors noted that mindfulness practices may espouse the potential to "de-automatize habitual responses." Such deautomatization looked at preschooler's abilities to control impulses and disengage responses that are habitual, instead examining their abilities to access appropriate responses, oversee attention, as well as self-regulate their behaviors (Lim & Qu, 2017, p. 308). Additional research examining interventions for mindful eating children from preschool through early elementary grades, indicated that students who participated in mindful eating increased their food consumption, particularly for foods that the child did not generally prefer (Hong et al., 2018). However, enjoyment ratings for such foods did not differ from the controls (Hong et al., 2018).

Overall, literature for MBH interventions looks promising, and showcases the need for additional focused research for the preschool population (Zelazo & Lyons, 2012). More research is needed to create developmentally appropriate and empirically based interventions targeted for preschool aged students.

Yoga

Preschool children have benefited from yoga in the areas of physical development, academic achievement, and social emotional and cognitive functioning (Cohen et al., 2018; Wolff & Stapp, 2019). Social emotional improvements have been shown for anxiety, stress,

self-regulation, attention, and cognitive relative to executive functioning (Cohen et al., 2018; Razza et al., 2015; Wolff & Stapp, 2019).
Physical outcomes have included improvements in heart rate variability (Cohen et al., 2018), fine motor skills (Mische Lawson et al.,
2012), metabolism, nervous system, circulation, and lung functioning
(Maykel et al., 2017).

There are many variations of yoga that have been effective with
academic, social and physical health functioning in preschoolers.
However, Hatha-Yoga has been adapted for use with preschoolers and has been highly successful for physical and mental health
improvements (Ivko, 2015). Hatha-yoga has also been beneficial for
cognitive skills, hyperactivity, attention, and visual-motor coordination (Jarraya et al., 2019).

Particular populations such as preschoolers who come from
families who have immigrated or who are refugees have successfully
used yoga as an intervention to remediate traumatic experiences
and improve school readiness. Syrian caregivers living in Turkey used
yoga and storytelling for these purposes (Goodman & Dent, 2019).

Overall, yoga is a time efficient and economically feasible intervention promoting cognitive, academic, social, and physical health
in preschoolers. It is also a treatment that school personnel find
non-intrusive and easy to implement (Wolff & Stapp, 2019).

Relaxation/Progressive Muscle Relaxation

Progressive Muscle Relaxation (PMR) has successfully been used
with preschool students to promote academic, social/behavioral,
and physical health functioning. Diaphragmatic breathing exercises
in particular, have improved lung functioning as well as enhanced
attention to educational tasks (Kohen & Wynee, 1997). Diaphragmatic
breathing incorporates breath control and focuses on isolating certain
muscle groups to promote deep belly breathing (Prem, 2013). One
study examining an intervention teaching preschool children with
asthma to blow air in a balloon using diaphragmatic breathing noted
significant changes in lung functioning, demonstrating improve-

ments pre and post intervention (Sumartini et al., 2020). Results also found that use of diaphragmatic breathing decreased hyperactivity, increased psychological awareness responses, and lung functioning improved relative to relaxation exercises (Efimenko, 2013).

Further, research examining seven relaxation sessions to 25 preschool aged children with asthma (ages 2-5) and their parents suggested improvement across a variety of measures. Further, data collected before participation, and one year after completion of the program, suggested a statistically significant difference in physician visits and breathing symptom severity scores. In addition, parents reported increased confidence in self-management skills as related to their child's medical condition (Kohen & Wynne, 1997). Although, it is important to mention that research in this area suggests that when working with young children, parents may need support in delivering these interventions at home (Kohen, 2013).

Expressive Arts

Integrating creative arts into the preschool curriculum has been a controversial issue in education (Vars, 2001); however, some research shows it to be successful in help treat preschool students with emotional trauma (Davis, 2010; Ju, 2017) and to support the overall mental health of these youngsters (Beauregard, 2014). A review of 19 different articles corresponding to eight different intervention programs yielded mixed results with regard to the effects of classroom-based creative expression interventions on children's mental health (Beauregard, 2014). Some results indicated that these interventions yielded positive effects with regard to constructs such as hope, coping and resilience, prosocial behaviors, self-esteem, impairment, and emotional and behavioral problems; while other studies indicated there were no effects, suggesting that differences in treatment intervention and fidelity and overall effectiveness are key factors to consider (Beauregard, 2014).

Expressive arts have been used to help preschool children and their families transition back to school after experiencing traumatic natural disasters (Davis, 2010) and to support preschool children with emotional trauma and selective mutism facing life adjustments (Ju, 2017). Both of these studies suggested positive outcomes with regard to preschool children's well-being after intervention. For example, Ju, (2017) measured preschool students' behavior and emotions using the Behavioral and Emotional Rating Scale (BERS) prior to and after immersion in expressive arts therapy and found post-test results indicating an overall improvement in behavioral performance and emotional adaptation, with an almost immediate effect.

While there is some evidence supporting the positive impact of integrating creative arts into the curriculum, the likelihood that the system can be successful without the support of teachers is slim. Teacher support specifically refers to the teachers themselves believing in the benefits of this integration (Öztürk & Erden, 2011). Previous research has found that most preschool teachers' beliefs about art activities were essential to curriculum (Alvino, 2000), but simply finding this important is insufficient for implementation (Baker, 1994; Bresler, 1993; Seefeldt, 1995; Thompson, 1995). In a recent study on teachers' beliefs about arts education and consequential integration with preschool curriculum, the majority of teachers' believed arts was an important part of early childhood education; however, few teachers reported their ability to integrate arts education across content areas, suggesting that training of early childhood educators lacked a focus on integrating creative arts in the curriculum (Öztürk & Erden, 2011).

Physical Activity

Physical activity is known to promote mental and physical well-being in individuals of all ages. It is recommended that physical activities should be implemented for children at a young age to ensure that play becomes a foundation to one component of life-long healthy living (Dwyer et al., 2009). Activities, whether they be sedimentary or physical, in preschoolers play a role in the biomedical outcomes for example weight, bone health and risks associated with cardiovascular disease, as well as psychological outcomes pertaining to mental health (Hinkley et al., 2014). As per the Department of Health and Aging (DOHA), children are expected to undergo at least three hours of physical activity a day once they are able to walk (Hinkley et al., 2014).

Physical activity helps children practice healthy lifestyles, addressing mind body health. It is key to recognize that environment plays a role in the evaluation of the effects of physical activity in the child's quality of mind-body health. A study conducted in 2016 examined the effects of physical activity in an outdoor nature setting or "green space" alongside psychological and physical outcomes (Ward et al., 2016). Results of the study indicated that not only was physical activity positively related to performance in an open environment, but both aspects resulted in greater emotional wellbeing (Ward et al., 2016). This suggests that "green space" is an aspect that, when paired with physical activity, induces greater mental health in children.

Gratitude

In consideration of the history of positive psychology research, gratitude has sparked sizable, and recent, attention amongst those in the general public (Emmons & Shelton, 2002). Yet, according to Emmons and Shelton (2002), the emotion of gratitude has received little research attention in the field. For that which does exist, research examining the effects of practicing gratitude amongst adults shows favorable outcomes for well-being and overall health status (Elosúa, 2015). Adults, for instance, who practiced gratitude more regularly experienced positive emotional feelings, reported more life satisfaction, as well as had decreased emotional experiences of sadness, envy, and worry (Elosúa, 2015). With respect to social behaviors, simply expressing gratitude may increase prosocial behaviors, further increasing a person's feelings of social validation and connection (Grant & Gino, 2010). Although evidence exists examining the relationship between gratitude and physical health for adults and adolescents, studies that exclusively examine the effects of gratitude on preschool students and children are far less frequent. Thus, little is known about the effects of practicing gratitude with younger children based on the current stance of the literature.

In a quest to break the silence on this subject area, Nelson and colleagues (2013) sought to understand exactly how much children understand the concept of gratitude. Previous research suggested that at approximately age seven, children are fully able to conceptualize and grasp the concept, emotion, and feeling of gratitude (Froh et al., 2011). However, Nelson and colleagues (2013) suggest that an understanding of gratitude may occur earlier, around age five. In their study, children ages five and above were able to develop a cursory conceptualization of the feeling of gratitude. Further, when presented with vignettes, children were able to identify both gratitude as a positive emotion, as well as assign positive feelings from that display of gratitude directly related to the benefactor. Nelson (2013) also noted that a student's success with identifying gratitude at age five was best predicted by their emotional knowledge at age three as well as comprehension of others and their emotions at ages three and four. Thus, Nelson's (2013) findings suggest that gratitude may be experienced in children much younger than was once proposed, starting at age five with the ability to identify the emotion as positive and apply those feelings to the benefactor.

Studies exclusively examining gratitude are less common, however studies incorporating gratitude as one component of the intervention showcase the potential array of benefits that may accompany using gratitude to support preschool aged students. For example, in an intervention for preschool students featuring a kindness curriculum intervention, benefits of practicing gratitude were associated with simply participation in the program. Further, those who enrolled in the curriculum exhibited higher social competence, academic achievement, social-emotional skill development, as well as overall physical health when compared to control groups who did not participate in the intervention (Flook et al., 2015).

A two-year study examining mindfulness-based programming for preschool students incorporating lessons on gratitude, results suggested increased executive functioning abilities (working memory and planning/organizing), as well as improved academic performance (vocabulary and reading scores), which emerged during the kindergarten years (Thierry et al., 2016). In sum, cursory evidence suggests the positive impact that incorporating gratitude may have on children's mind body health; however, more research is needed to strictly isolate the effects of gratitude exclusively.

Music

Music education, and exposure to musical instruments, is often part of a young child's school experience. Knowing such, might there be mind body health benefits to engaging in a therapeutic and mindful process of creating and playing music? Although music is somewhat ubiquitous in the classroom of a preschool student, the evidence on the effectiveness of such use is somewhat contradictory and limited. For example, one study assessing preschooler's enrichment of spatial-temporal reasoning found that exposure to musical experiences in preschool helped create "long-term modifications underlying neural circuitry in regions not primarily concerned with music" (Rauscher et al., 1997, p. 7). However, Mehr and colleagues (2013) suggest interpreting such results with caution, particularly as they relate to the cognitive benefits of music with preschool students.

When looking at music from an ecological approach, Klein and Winkelstein (1996), discuss the importance of music in the healing process for children. When working in high intensity health related situations with children, Klein and Winkelstein (1996) report evidence that music can help children cope, withstand pain, and endure difficult tasks, such as physical and occupational therapy. Additional research suggests that music may help preschoolers and toddlers fall asleep faster as compared to a control group not exposed to music during nap time (Field, 1999). Further connections have been noted between using musical objects in play interactions with peers, and that for students who have developmental disabilities, using a musical instrument may help facilitate sustained attention towards a peer playmate (Sussman, 2009). In sum, there is a scarcity of research employing music therapy with preschool aged children. More research needs to be conducted in this area, particularly with preschoolers to determine what is the level of efficacy of music for MBH (Kennelly & Brien-Elliott, 2001).

Bibliotherapy

While traditionally studied within the context of a therapeutic setting, bibliotherapy is a method of communicating and teaching prosocial skills to students and is increasingly implemented in the classroom. Widely applied in schools, bibliotherapy can assist in the development of social and emotional learning growth, as well as enhance problem-solving and solutions, and help with the development of life skills (McCulliss & Chamberlain, 2013). Further, bibliotherapy can readily be adapted in the early education classroom setting. Early educators can utilize bibliotherapy to enhance prosocial skills in young children and to teach preventative methods to cope with hardship as well.

Helping young children develop coping skills is vital in early education. During this time, children are often learning to navigate the social world independent from their primary caregivers. Bibliotherapy can focus on teaching students coping mechanisms, such as taking deep breaths when they are nervous or upset and handling a conflict with a peer. Additionally, bibliotherapy can facilitate social and emotional competence in youth. For example, Kidd and Castano (2013) found reading literary fiction aided in the development of social and emotional competence in youth.

Bibliotherapy is a therapeutic process that is aligned with cognitive-behavioral theory, an evidence-based intervention (Shinohara et al, 2013). Benefits of bibliotherapy vary, and it may be used as a component for an intervention. Examples include treatment for youth with emotional and behavioral needs (Linderman & Kling, 1968), treatment for those with experienced trauma (DeVries et al., 2017), and improved outcomes such as enhancing coping skills for children with a sibling who has a disability (DeVries & Sunden, 2019). As a therapeutic process, it can be used to help children solve problems, cope with those problems, and identify alternative solutions in managing their emotions and behaviors. It can also help children identify and express feelings and thoughts as well as gain insight into their specific situation (Cohen, 1987; DeVries & Sunden, 2019). The bibliotherapeutic process is thought to have four stages: Identification with the character or character's situation, catharsis or emotional cleansing, and development of insight and autonomy and universalization or the stage where the reader feels less secluded or less of an outsider (DeVries et al., 2017; Gregory & Vessey, 2004; McCoy & McKay, 2006).

Components of bibliotherapy that early educators may introduce in their classrooms are multifaceted. Development of self-concept, assistance in problem solving, facilitation of discussion of problems, teaching children that there are often multiple solutions to problems, and finally to letting children know they are not alone in experiencing specific problems are all critical components of implementing bibliotherapy in the classroom (Alex, 1993). Maich and Kean (2004) discuss a four step process to implement bibliotherapy in the classroom, which includes preparation, reading, dialogue, and activity. Preparation includes the careful selection of a book with developmentally appropriate language, reading refers to a teacher led reading reflection, dialogue refers to teacher led discussion in a specific sequence, and activity involves utilizing a hands-on method to enhance expression and creativity (Maich & Kean, 2004).

In sum, bibliotherapy is a method to assist in the development of coping skills as well as social and emotional skills among youth. While bibliotherapy is not a new concept, the idea that it can be utilized as both a preventative fashion as well as a means of treatment is gaining traction in the literature base. Further research is needed in order to analyze the impact of bibliotherapy as a mind body health intervention with preschool populations.

Video Self-Modeling

Video Self-Modeling (VSM) is a social-cognitive intervention where individuals serve as their own models (Dowrick, 1990). The intervention is rooted in social learning theory, which posits that by repeatedly viewing a peer eliciting a specific behavior, an individual will learn to elicit that behavior as well (Bandura et al., 1961). VSM is used to teach desired behaviors that are within the ability of the individual, and that may already be found in their repertoire. To that end, VSM is used to develop, generalize, and maintain goal behaviors. During VSM interventions, individuals watch videos depicting themselves engaging in a behavior that they do not ordinarily display (Dowrick, 1990). VSM allows the individual to act as their own model by using recording and editing procedures to construct short videos in which the individual seems to be exhibiting a desired behavior. When constructing VSM videos, an individual is video recorded in a setting where they typically do not display a desired behavior. Then, video-editing software is used to edit the recording to make it seem as if the individual is fluently engaging in the target behavior within that setting. The intervention is implemented when an individual repeatedly watches their two to three minute VSM video on a schedule that varies in frequency and duration based on the severity of the behavior. VSM draws on the tenets of positive psychology through only using depictions of the person engaging in a desired behavior. That is, VSM videos never show the self-model displaying a behavior that is not preferred or not fluent. By using only positive depictions, VSM is an intervention that allows individuals to learn from the best of their own behavior to promote wellbeing.

Video Self-Modeling can be used to promote numerous behaviors related to positive psychological, social, and physical health outcomes in preschool aged populations. The literature indicates that VSM has been used to successfully increase social initiation behaviors, including appropriate greetings, in samples of typically developing preschool children and among preschoolers with Autism Spectrum Disorder, Downs Syndrome, and Developmental Delays

(Buggey, et al., 2011; Buggey, 2012; Buggey, et al., 2018; Lemmon & Green, 2015). VSM has also been used as an effective intervention to teach preschool aged children social engagement behaviors such as reciprocal play, positive conversational skills, and sustained social interactions (Bellini et al., 2007; Bellini et al., 2016; Lemmon & Green, 2015). Furthermore, the literature has established that VSM has been effective for supporting the gain of spontaneous requesting behaviors among preschoolers with Autism Spectrum Disorder (Wert, 2009; Wert & Neisworth, 2003).

In addition to increasing prosocial behavior, Video Self-Modeling (VSM) can be used to improve behaviors associated with positive academic outcomes in preschool aged populations. Marcus and Wilder (2009) found that VSM was an effective intervention for increasing letter identification skills in a sample of preschool children with Autism Spectrum Disorder. Similarly, VSM was used to teach language skills including age appropriate vocabulary and use of plural morphemes (Whitlow & Buggey, 2004) Additionally, VSM has been shown to increase classroom engagement and on-task behaviors among preschoolers with historically resistant disruptive behaviors (McCoy et al., 2017).

Conclusion

There is no doubt that psychological and educational techniques from within the mind body health framework are beneficial to students in preschool. There are myriad strategies available that are non-intrusive and economically feasible with respect to time and money. . Early intervention is important to the academic, social, behavioral, and physical health development of this age group, arguably more than others, especially so for those at risk. The mind body framework also lends well to cross-disciplinary collaboration and a whole child framework for service delivery. School psychologists and other mental health professionals are well-suited to implement these interventions that are transcendental in terms of interdisciplinary collaboration.

References

Afolayan, J. A. (1992). Documentary perspective of bibliotherapy in education. *Reading Horizons: A Journal of Literacy and Language Arts, 33*(2), 137–148.

Aiex, N. K. (1993) *Bibliotherapy*. In ERIC Clearinghouse on Reading and Communication Skills, B. I. (ED 357333). *ERIC Digest.*

Alvino, F.J. (2000). *Art improves the quality of life: A look at art in early childhood settings* (ED 447936).

Baer, R. A. (2003). Mindfulness training as a clinical intervention: A conceptual and empiricalreview. *Clinical Psychology: Science and Practice, 10*(2), 125–143.

Baker, D. W. (1994). Toward a sensible education: Inquiring into the role of the visual arts inearly childhood education. *Visual Arts Research, 20*(2), 92–104.

Bandura, A., Ross, D., & Ross, S. A. (1961). Transmission of aggression through imitation ofaggressive models. *The Journal of Abnormal and Social Psychology, 63*(3), 575–582.

Beauregard, C. (2014). Effects of classroom-based creative expression programmes onchildren's well-being. *The Arts in Psychotherapy, 41*(3), 269–277.

Bellini, S., Akullian, J., & Hopf, A. (2007). Increasing social engagement in young childrenwith autism spectrum disorders using video self-modeling. *School Psychology Review, 36*(1), 80–90.

Bellini, S., Gardner, L., Hudock, R., & Kashima-Ellingson, Y. (2016). The use of videoself-modeling and peer training to increase social engagement in preschool children on the Autism Spectrum. *School Psychology Forum 10*(2), 207–219.

Berk, L. (2012). *Infants, children, and adolescents* (7th ed.). Pearson.

Bresler, L. (1993). Three orientations to art in the primary grades: Implications for curriculumreform. *Arts Education Policy Review, 94*(6), 29–34.

Buggey, T. (2012). Effectiveness of video self-modeling to promote social initiations by3-year-olds with Autism Spectrum Disorders. *Focus on Autism and Other Developmental Disabilities, 27*(2), 102–110.

Buggey, T., Hoomes, G., Sherberger, M. E., & Williams, S. (2011). Facilitating socialinitiations of preschoolers with autism spectrum disorders using video self-modeling. *Focus on Autism and other Developmental Disabilities, 26*(1), 25–36.

Buggey, T., Crawford, S. C., & Rogers, C. L. (2018). Self-modeling to promote social-initiations with young children with developmental disabilities. *Focus on Autism and other Developmental Disabilities, 33*(2), 11–119.

Campion, J., & Rocco, S. (2009). Minding the mind: The effects and potential of aschool-based meditation programme for mental health promotion. *Advances in School Mental Health Promotion, 2*(1), 47–55.

Cohen, L. J. (1987). Bibliotherapy. *Journal of Psychosocial Nursing and Mental Health Services, 25*(10), 20–24.

Cohen, S. C. L., Harvey, D. J., Shields, R. H., Shields, G. S., Rashedi, R. N., Tancredi, D. J., ... & Schweitzer, J. B. (2018). Effects of yoga on attention, impulsivity, and hyperactivity in preschool-aged children with Attention-Deficit Hyperactivity Disorder symptoms. *Journal of Developmental and Behavioral Pediatrics, 39*(3), 200–209.

Davis, K.M. (2010). Music and the expressive arts with children experiencing trauma. *Journal of Creativity in Mental Health, 5*(2), 125–133.

DeVries, D., Brennan, Z., Lankin, M., Morse, R., Rix, B., & Beck, T. (2017). Healing withbooks: A literature review of bibliotherapy used with children and youth who have experienced trauma. *Therapeutic Recreation Journal, 51*, 48–74.

DeVries, D., & Sunden, S. (2019). Bibliotherapy with children who have a sibling with adisability. *Journal of Poetry Therapy, 32*(3), 135–155.

Dowrick, P.W. (1990). A review of self modeling and related interventions. *Applied and Preventative Psychology, 8*(1), 23–39.

Dwyer, G., Baur, L., Higgs, J., & Hardy, L. (2009). Promoting children's health andwell-being: Broadening the therapy perspective. *Physical & Occupational Therapy in Pediatrics, 29*(1), 27–43.

Efimenko N.N. (2013). Methodological phenomenon of relaxation and tension in themotor rehabilitation of children. *Pedagogìka, Psihologìâ Ta Mediko-bìologìčnì Problemi Fìzičnogo Vihovannâ ì Sportu, 17*(2), 22–27.

Elosúa, M. R. (2015). The influence of gratitude in physical, psychological, and spiritual well-being. *Journal of Spirituality in Mental Health, 17*(2), 110–118.

Emmons, R. A., & Shelton, C. M. (2002). Gratitude and the science of positive psychology. *Handbook of Positive Psychology, 18*, 459–471.

Field, T. (1999). Music enhances sleep in preschool children. *Early Child Development and Care, 150*(1), 65–68.

Flook, L., Goldberg, S. B., Pinger, L., & Davidson, R. J. (2015). Promoting prosocial behaviorand self-regulatory skills in preschool children through a mindfulness-based Kindness Curriculum. *Developmental Psychology, 51*(1), 44–51.

Froh, J. J., Fan, J., Emmons, R. A., Bono, G., Huebner, E. S., & Watkins, P. (2011). Measuringgratitude in youth: Assessing the psychometric properties of adult gratitude scales in children and adolescents. *Psychological Assessment, 23*(2), 311–324.

Froh, J., Sefick, W., & Emmons, R. A. (2008). Counting blessings in early adolescents: An experimental study of gratitude and subjective well-being. *Journal of School Psychology, 46*(2), 213–233.

Goodman, G., & Dent, V. F. (2019). When I became a refugee, this became my refuge: Aproposal for implementing a two-generation intervention using yoga and narrative to promote mental health in Syrian refugee caregivers and school readiness in their preschool children. *Journal of Infant, Child, and Adolescent Psychotherapy, 18*(4), 367–375.

Grant, A. M., & Gino, F. (2010). A little thanks goes a long way: Explaining why gratitudeexpressions motivate prosocial behavior. *Journal of Personality and Social Psychology, 98*(6), 946.

Gregory, K. E., & Vessey, J. A. (2004). Bibliotherapy: A strategy to help students with bullying. *The Journal of School Nursing, 20*(3), 127–133.

Grossman, P., Niemann, L., Schmidt, S., & Walach, H. (2004). Mindfulness-based stressreduction and health benefits: A meta-analysis. *Journal of Psychosomatic Research, 57*(1), 35–43.

Hinkley, T., Teychenne, M., Downing, K. L., Ball, K., Salmon, J., & Hesketh, K. D. (2014).Early childhood physical activity, sedentary behaviors and psychosocial well-being: *A systematic review. Preventive Medicine, 62*, 182–192. https://www.sciencedirect.com/ science/article/pii/S0091743514000723

Hong, P. Y., Hanson, M. D., Lishner, D. A., Kelso, S. L., & Steinert, S. W. (2018). A fieldexperiment examining mindfulness on eating enjoyment and behavior in children. *Mindfulness, 9*(6), 1748–1756.

Huppert, F., & Johnson, D. (2010). A controlled trial of mindfulness training in schools: The importance of practice for an impact on well-being. *The Journal of Positive Psychology, 5*(4), 264–274.

Kohen, D. P. (2013). Teaching children with asthma to help themselves with relaxation/mentalimagery. *Current thinking and research in brief therapy,* 169–192.

Kohen, D., & Wynne, E. (1997). Applying hypnosis in a preschool family asthma educationprogram: Uses of storytelling, imagery, and relaxation. *American Journal of Clinical Hypnosis, 39*(3), 169–181.

Inagaki, K., & Hatano, G. (1993). Young children's understanding of the mind-body distinction. *Child Development, 64*(5), 1534–1549.

Ivko, A., Chusovitina, O.M., & Shvetsova, E.I. (2015). The development of physical qualitiesin children aged 5-6 years old through a range of exercises with elements of hatha yoga. *Вестник Кемеровского государственного университета,* (4-2), 40–45.

Jarraya, S., Wagner, M., Jarraya, M., & Engel, F. A. (2019). 12 weeks of kindergarten-basedyoga practice increases visual attention, visual-motor precision and decreases behavior of inattention and hyperactivity in 5-year-old children. *Frontiers in Psychology, 10,* 1–11.

Ju, C.I. (2014). Effectiveness of teaching in expressive arts therapy-emotional trauma-tizedpreschool children. *Asian Social Science, 10*(12), 195–201.

Kennelly, J., & Brien-Elliott, K. (2001). The role of music therapy in paediatric rehabilitation. *Pediatric Rehabilitation, 4*(3), 137–143.

Kidd, D., & Castano, E. (2013). Reading literary fiction improves theory of mind. *Science, 342,* 377–380.

Kim, K., Wee, S., Gilbert, B., & Choi, J. (2016). Young children's physical and psycho-logicalwell-being through yoga. *Childhood Education, 92*(6), 437–445.

Klein, S. A., & Winkelstein, M. L. (1996). Enhancing pediatric health care with music. *Journal of Pediatric Health Care, 10*(2), 74–81.

Lemmon, K. H. & Green, V. A. (2015). Using video self-modeling and the peer group toIncrease the social skills of a preschool child. *New Zealand Journal of Psychology, (Online) 44*(2), 68–78.

Lim, X., & Qu, L. (2017). The effect of single-session mindfulness training on pre-schoolchildren's attentional control. *Mindfulness, 8*(2), 300–310.

Lindeman, B., & Kling, M. (1968). Bibliotherapy: Definitions, uses and studies. *Journal of School Psychology, 7*(2), 36–41.

Maich, K., & Kean, S. (2004). Read Two Books and Write Me in the Morning! Maich, K. &Kean, S. (2004) Read two books and write me in the morning: Bibliotherapy for social emotional intervention in the inclusive classroom. *TEACHING Exceptional Children Plus, 1*(2), n2. http://escholarship.bc.edu/education/tecplus/vol1/iss2/5

Marcus, A. & Wilder, D.A. (2009). A comparison of peer video modeling and self vid-eomodeling to teach textual responses in children with autism. *Journal of Applied Behavior Analysis, 42*(2), 335–341.

Maykel, C., Ottone-Cross, K.L., Shankar, N.L., Bray, M.A., Byer-Alcorace, G., & Del Campo, M. (2017). Mindful meditation for individuals with asthma and anxiety: Promising results from a multiple baseline study. *Journal of Yoga and Physical Therapy, 7,* 1–10.

McCoy, H., & McKay, C. (2006). Preparing social workers to identify and integrate culturally affirming bibliotherapy into treatment. *Social Work Education, 25*(7), 680–693.

McCoy, D. M., Morrison, J. Q., Barnett, D. W., Kalra, H. D., & Donovan, L. K. (2017). Using iPad tablets for self-modeling with preschoolers: Videos versus photos. *Psychology in the Schools, 54*(8), 821–836.

McCulliss, D., & Chamberlain, D. (2013). Bibliotherapy for youth and adolescents: School-based application and research. *Journal of Poetry Therapy, 26*(1), 13–40.

Mehr, S. A., Schachner, A., Katz, R. C., & Spelke, E. S. (2013). Two randomized trials provide no consistent evidence for nonmusical cognitive benefits of brief preschool music enrichment. *PloS ONE, 8*(12), 1–12.

Mische Lawson, L. A., Cox, J., & Blackwell, A. L. (2012). Yoga as a classroom intervention for preschoolers. *Journal of Occupational Therapy, Schools, & Early Intervention, 5*(2), 126–137.

Nelson, J. A., de Lucca Freitas, L. B., O'Brien, M., Calkins, S. D., Leerkes, E. M., & Marcovitch, S. (2013). Preschool-aged children's understanding of gratitude: Relations with emotion and mental state knowledge. *British Journal of Developmental Psychology, 31*(1), 42–56.

Öztürk, E., & Erden, F. T. (2011). Turkish preschool teachers' beliefs on integrated curriculum: Integration of visual arts with other activities. *Early Child Development and Care, 181*(7), 891–907.

Prem, V., Sahoo, R. C., & Adhikari, P. (2013). Effect of diaphragmatic breathing exercise on quality of life in subjects with asthma: a systematic review. *Physiotherapy Theory and Practice, 29*(4), 271–277.

Rauscher, F., Shaw, G., Levine, L., Wright, E., Dennis, W., & Newcomb, R. (1997). Musictraining causes long-term enhancement of preschool children's spatial–temporal reasoning. *Neurological Research, 19*(1), 2–8.

Razza, R. A., Bergen-Cico, D., & Raymond, K. (2015). Enhancing preschoolers'self-regulation via mindful yoga. *Journal of Child and Family Studies, 24*(2), 372–385.

Seefeldt, C. (1995). Art: A serious work. *Young Children, 50*(3), 39–45.

Shapiro, S. L., Carlson, L. E., Astin, J. A., & Freedman, B. (2006). Mechanisms ofmindfulness. *Journal of Clinical Psychology, 62*(3), 373–386.

Shinohara, K., Honyashiki, M., Imai, H., Hunot, V., Caldwell, D. M., Davies, P., ... & Churchill, R. (2013). Behavioural therapies versus other psychological therapies for depression. *Cochrane Database of Systematic Reviews*. https://www.cochrane.org/CD008696/ DEPRESSN_behavioural-therapies-versus-other-psychological-therapies-for-depression

Sumartini, S., Somantri, B., Suparto, T. A., Andriyani, S., & Salasa, S. (2020). Theeffect of playing blowing balloon therapy to changes in lung function in preschool children (3–5 Years Old) with asthma. In *4th International Conference on Sport Science, Health, and Physical Education (ICSSHPE 2019)* (pp. 238–241). Atlantis Press.

Sussman, J. E. (2009). The effect of music on peer awareness in preschool age children with developmental disabilities. *Journal of Music Therapy, 46*(1), 53–68.

Thierry, K. L., Bryant, H. L., Nobles, S. S., & Norris, K. S. (2016). Two-year impact of amindfulness-based program on preschoolers' self-regulation and academic performance. *Early Education and Development, 27*(6), 805–821.

Thompson, C.M. (1995). Transforming curriculum in the visual arts. In S. Bredekamp & T. Rosegrant (Eds.), *Reaching potentials: Transforming early childhood curriculum and assessment* (pp. 81–98). NAEYC.

Vars, G.F. (2001). Can curriculum integration survive in an era of high-stakes testing? *MiddleSchool Journal, 33*(2), 7–17.

Ward, J. S., Duncan, J. S., Jarden, A., & Stewart, T. (2016). The impact of children'sexposure to greenspace on physical activity, cognitive development, emotional wellbeing, and ability to appraise risk. *Health & Place.* https://www.sciencedirect.com/science/article/pii/S135382921630048X

Wert, B.Y. (2009). A comparison of verbal prompting and video self-modeling on thespontaneous request behaviors of young children with autism spectrum disorders. *Assistive Technology and Autism Spectrum Disorders: Research-Based Practice and Innovation in the Field* [Special Issue]. Assistive Technology Outcomes and Benefits, 5, 70–81.

Wert, B. Y., & Neisworth, J. T. (2003). Effects of video self-modeling on spontaneousrequesting in children with autism. *Journal of Positive Behavior Interventions, 5*(1), 30–34.

Whitlow, C. K. & Buggey, T. (2004). Video self-modelling: An effective intervention for a preschooler with language delays. *Journal of Research in Special Education Needs, 3*(1). https://doi-org.ezproxy.lib.uconn.edu/10.1111/j.1471-3802.2003.00183

Wolff, K., & Stapp, A. (2019). Investigating early childhood teachers' perceptions of a preschool yoga program. *SAGE Open, 9*(1). https://doi.org/10.1177/2158244018821758

Zelazo, P. D., & Lyons, K. E. (2011). Mindfulness training in childhood. *Human Development, 54*(2), 61–65.

Zelazo, P. D., & Lyons, K. E. (2012). The potential benefits of mindfulness training in early childhood: A developmental social cognitive neuroscience perspective. *Child Development Perspectives, 6*(2), 154–160.

Preschoolers and Mind Body Health

Kari A. Sassu

In a report published by the U.S. Department of Education, the former Secretary of Education, Arne Duncan is quoted as having said, "I believe that every single child deserves the opportunity for a strong start in life through high-quality preschool..." (U.S. Department of Education, April 2015). The report goes on to cite research in the fields of neuroscience and education that provide evidence for the critical gains that can be derived by those children who attend preschool programs of high quality. Research evidencing the resultant benefits of early childhood education has long existed and expanded over time, serving as the impetus for much of the legislation addressing the need for high quality early educational programs (see Bracken & Theodore, this issue, for an historical account of legislation related to this effort). Those of us who work in the interest of children recognize the impact of a "strong start," the magnitude and breadth of which cannot be overstated. Children who are the beneficiaries of such develop stronger social-emotional, cognitive, and academic abilities, as well as superior physical health, as compared with those who do not have such opportunities.

When young children enter a preschool setting, they embark on a journey that presents them with opportunities to grow in a multitude of ways and offers promise for their future. As they venture out into a world that extends beyond their immediate families, they are confronted with challenges that, when appropriately structured, set the stage for them to gain a great number of skills across multiple domains. However, it is only through thoughtful, well-informed, multifaceted programming which considers the whole child that we can set children on a course toward their optimal achievement and overall wellbeing.

Early childhood education that addresses students' comprehensive needs must encompass elements that foster healthy physical, cognitive, behavioral, academic, linguistic, and social-emotional development. Articles within this issue have highlighted the connections between various elements of wellbeing, connecting the dots such that we are able to view an image in its entirety. If we can view the child as a whole, with each "dot" of her health as one constituent part of the overall picture, the interrelatedness of all elements of wellbeing and healthy development come clearly into focus.

The mind body health connection has been well established, as has the reciprocal nature of their influence. Mind body health interventions such as those included in this special issue (e.g., mindfulness, muscle relaxation, yoga, etc.) have proven effective in addressing a multitude of physical and mental health challenges in children and adults alike. Not only has scientific inquiry proven these strategies effective with school aged children, adolescents and adults, but there is high social validity for these activities as well (e.g., Keyworth et al., 2014; Luiselli, et al., 2017). Furthermore, we appear to be occupying a space in time wherein the techniques associated with mind body health are gaining momentum in popular culture, with new apps devoted to mindfulness and meditation for children and adults emerging regularly.

Though the research related to the efficacy of mind body health interventions with the preschool population remains limited, that which does exist offers great promise and warrants further exploration. Mind body health interventions for young children are appealing in that there is a relative simplicity of implementation, the required investment (time and/or money) is fairly limited, and the activities often are engaging. Outcomes associated with mind body health interventions such as yoga and progressive muscle relaxation for school-aged children include improvements in physical and mental health, as well as reductions in hyperactivity and inattention (Jarraya et al., 2019). Gains in executive functioning skills such as the ability to reflect on one's behavior and self-monitor, have also been derived from mind body health interventions used with school-aged children (Semenov & Zelazo, 2019; Susman Gertz & Culbert, 2009).

The preschool period is unique in the opportunity it presents for children to reap the greatest benefit from intervention. Early intervention efforts targeting academic, social, behavioral, communication, and other areas of functioning have long been shown to yield the greatest results of any developmental period. If young children can be explicitly taught skills that allow them to self-soothe and relax when young, these skills may prime the way for them to develop more sophisticated strategies that have proven effective and have impacted overall health in older children and adults (e.g., mindfulness, guided relaxation, etc.).

If we are to capitalize on this critical window of opportunity presented in the preschool years, it will require that we effectively address the complex and intricately connected elements of children's development during this stage. Housed in their small beings are many complex and interrelated changes occurring simultaneously. The best scenario for optimal outcomes when investing in a holistic approach, is that professionals representing various disciplines serve together, in a collaborative and multidisciplinary fashion, focused on the whole child. Our collaborative efforts should be focused on creating connections that allow for increased opportunities to maximize and sustain overall wellbeing, in all its faceted and nuanced ways, beginning in early childhood, and continuing throughout the lifespan. Though some factors related to a child's development cannot be mediated by preschool education, there are many that can (e.g., nutrition, physical exercise, social skill building, cognitive flexibility, etc.). Mind body health interventions hold the promise of equipping young children with skills that will serve them well in the daily activities of their youth and allow them to build healthy habits that will remain with them throughout their lifetime.

References

Bracken, B. A., & Theodore, L. A. (2020). Promoting health and wellness in young children: Preschool assessment. *Perspectives on Early Childhood Education, 5*(1), 143–173.

Jarraya, S., Wagner, M., Jarraya, M., & Engel, F. A. (2019). Twelve weeks of kinder-garten-based yoga practice increases visual attention, visual-motor precision and decreases behavior of inattention and hyperactivity in 5-year-old children. *Frontiers in Psychology, 10,* 1–11.

Keyworth, C., Knopp, J., Roughley, K., Dickens, C., Bold, S., & Coventry, P. (2014, April). A mixed-methods pilot study of the acceptability and effectiveness of a brief meditation and mindfulness intervention for people with diabetes and coronary heart disease. *Behavioral Medicine, 40* (2), 53–64, https://doi.org/10.108 0/08964289.2013.834865

Luiselli, J. K., Worthen, D., Carbonell, L. & Queen, A. H. (2017). Social validity assessment of mindfulness education and practices among high school students. *Journal of Applied School Psychology, 33*(2), 12 –135, https://doi.org10.1080/1537 7903.2016.1264531

Semenov, A. D., & Zelazo, P. D. (2019). Mindful Family Routines and the Cultivation of Executive Function Skills in Childhood. *Human Development, 63,* 112–131. https://doi.org10.1159/000503822

Susman Gertz, D. & Culbert, T. (2009). Pediatric self-regulation. In Carey, W. B., Coleman, W. L., Crocker, A. C., Elias, E. R., & Feldman, H. M., (Eds.), *Developmental Behavioral Pediatrics* (pp. 911–922). Elsevier.

U.S. Department of Education (2015, April). *A matter of equity: Preschool in America.* https://files.eric.ed.gov/fulltext/ED555741.pdf

List of Contributers

Vincent C. Alfonso, PhD, is Interim Dean of the Ferkauf Graduate School of Psychology at Yeshiva University. Prior to this position, he was Professor in and Dean of the School of Education at Gonzaga University in Spokane, Washington and Professor in and Associate Dean of the Graduate School of Education, Fordham University, New York City.

Sai Aravala is a graduate of the University of Connecticut who majored in molecular cell biology. Her research interest is in mind-body health.

Aarti P. Bellara, PhD, is an Assistant Professor in the Research Methods, Measurement, and Evaluation Program in the Department of Educational Psychology at the Neag School of Education.

Zeynep Biringen, PhD, completed her doctorate in Developmental Psychology at the University of California, Berkeley, in 1987 and a (research) MacArthur Postdoctoral Fellowship at the University of Colorado School of Medicine's Dept of Psychiatry, 1987-1991. She transitioned to clinical work for a few years, completing a respecial-ization in Clinical Psychology at the University of Colorado, Boulder and an APA-accredited child clinical internship at the Albert Einstein School of Medicine (Montefiore Hospital) in the Bronx in 1993. After active clinical work with young children and families at the Boulder Mental Health Center and licensure in 1996, she transitioned back to research. She has been on the faculty of Colorado State University since 1996 and is a Professor of Human Development & Family Studies. She works in the research areas of emotional availability, attachment, and mindfulness, both in terms of basic science ques-tions as well as prevention/intervention studies.

Naomi R. Boucher is a second year Masters student in the Clinical Mental Health Counseling program at Ball State University. They currently work as a therapist in training with a focus on helping clients and families recovering from trauma and substance use. Once they complete their degree in July 2020, they will go on to be a fulltime therapist for a domestic violence shelter in Marion, IN.

Bruce A. Bracken, PhD, obtained his Bachelor of Science degree from the College of Charleston and Master's and Doctoral degrees from the University of Georgia. He is currently a Professor at The College of William & Mary. Bruce received the "Senior Scientist" award from the American Psychological Association (Division 16) in 2009 and the 2012 "Lifetime Achievement Award" from the University of Georgia for his contributions to preschool assessment, psychoeducational assessment, and psychometric applications to social justice.

Adeline Bray is a graduate of the University of Connecticut, December 2019. Her research interests are inthe area of physical health and wellness.

Melissa Bray, PhD, is a Professor and the Director of the School Psychology program within the Neag School of Education at the University of Connecticut. Her research interests are in the area of interventions for communication disorders mainly stuttering, classroom disruptive behavior, and physical health and wellness, especially asthma and cancer.

Mary Decker, PhD, is currently an instructional designer for the University of Missouri. Her research interests focus on Universal Design for Learning and making learning accessible and meaningful for all students.

Johanna deLeyer-Tiarks is a doctoral candidate at the University of Connecticut. Her research interests include self-modeling, mind-body health, and virtual reality interventions to support positive academic, behavioral, and social-emotional outcomes.

Jessica Dirsmith, PhD, NCSP, is a Pennsylvania and nationally certified school psychologist and a licensed psychologist and teaches at Duquense University. Dr. Dirsmith focuses on disseminating systems-level efforts that are efficient, effective, and evidence-based in order to improve prevention, intervention, and identification practices in schools.

Joseph R. Engler, PhD, is an Associate Professor and Director of School Psychology at Gonzaga University in Spokane, Washington. Prior to this appointment, he was the Director of School Psychology at Minot State University in Minot, North Dakota.

Tara Hofkens, PhD, is a Research Assistant Professor at the Curry School of Education and Human Development. Her research program examines how stress influences children's engagement, learning, and development in school, with an emphasis on developing interventions to improve equity and excellence in K-12 education.

Jayanthi (Jay) Kandiah, PhD, is a Professor of Nutrition and Dietetics in the Department of Nutrition and Health Science (NHS) at Ball State University (BSU). She is also the Associate Dean for the College of Health and Interim Department Chair of NHS at BSU. As a registered dietitian nutritionist (RDN) and a nutrition researcher she has published many refereed articles and has presented at national/international conferences. Dr. Kandiah has held several leadership positions in her profession and has been the recipient of many accolades. Dr. Jay's areas of nutrition research include clinical, preventive, and alternative health with varied populations. She completed her Pediatric Nutrition Fellowship at Indiana University School of Medicine. An area of her passion in pediatrics is working with children with special needs, including those with Autism Spectrum Disorder.

Cheryl Maykel, PhD, is an Assistant Professor in Counseling and School Psychology at Rivier University. She is a nationally certified school psychologist with state certification in New Hampshire. Her current research interests are in the areas of mind-body health, physical activity, and classroom disruptive behavior.

Constance McIntosh, PhD, is an Associate Professor in the School of Nursing in the College of Health at Ball State University. She earned her doctoral degree in special education with a cognate in nursing. Her line of research combines her knowledge of nursing and special education while focusing on the role of the nurse in identifying, evaluating and treating children with special needs including Autism Spectrum Disorder (ASD). She serves as the primary camp nurse at a camp for children with ASD. Dr. McIntosh is well published and had conducted numerous national presentations. Dr. McIntosh served on the Indiana State Board of Nursing for eight years with three years as president. She is active member of numerous national and international nursing organizations, holding various leadership roles. She has co-authored two books.

Tutrang Nguyen, PhD, is an Institute of Education Sciences Postdoctoral Fellow at the School of Education and Human Development at the University of Virginia. Her research focuses on early childhood education programs and policies.

Robert C. Pianta, PhD, is Dean of the Curry School of Education and Human Development, Novartis Professor of Education and Professor of Psychology, and Founding Director of the Center for Advanced Study of Teaching and Learning (CASTL). Dr. Pianta's research and policy interests focus on the role of teacher-student relationships and interactions in student success; he has led research and development on measurement tools and interventions that help teachers interact with students more effectively and that are used widely in the United States and around the world.

Cory D. Ray is a second-year graduate student in Gonzaga University's Education Specialist in School Psychology program. Prior to that, he spent eleven years as a general education classroom teacher in both Washington and Nevada.

Jessica S. Reinhardt, PhD, NCSP is an Associate Professor of Practice in the Psychological Studies in Education Department at Temple University. Her professional interests include: graduate training, multicultural counseling in schools, and assessment of neurodevelopmental disorders.

Erik A. Ruzek, PhD, is a Senior Research Scientist at NWEA. His research examines the connections between students' school experiences and their motivation, engagement, and learning.

Kari Sassu, PhD, NCSP, is the Director of Strategic Initiatives for the Center of Excellence on Autism Spectrum Disorders at Southern Connecticut State University. She concurrently serves as a professor in the Counseling and School Psychology department at SCSU. Dr. Sassu is a licensed psychologist, a Nationally Certified School Psychologist (NCSP), and holds certifications as both a school psychologist and a school administrator in the state of Connecticut.

Melissa Stormont, PhD, is a Professor in the Department of Special Education at the University of Missouri. She has written extensively in the areas of early childhood and prevention science. She is and has been involved in numerous federal and local grants to support the use of evidence-based social, emotional, and mental health assessments and practices for children. Currently she is the Co-Director of the Boone County Early Childhood Coalition.

Lea A. Theodore, PhD, is Professor and Coordinator of the Doctoral Program in School Psychology at Adelphi University. Her career focus has been on promoting science, practice, and policy surrounding the development of effective and efficient intervention strategies to improve student academic and behavioral functioning. Dr. Theodore is active in Div. 16 of the American Psychologica Association (APA), serving myriad positions. She extended her contributions to APA in nationally elected positions, including President of Div. 16, VP-Professional Affairs and VP-Membership. She was recently appointed to serve on the Committee on Division/APA Relations (CODAPAR) and also elected to serve as a Division 16 Council Representative. She also served as Associate Editor for APA's School Psychology Quarterly. Dr. Theodore was the recipient of the Jean A. Baker Mid-Career Service Award from Division 16 of the APA in 2019. Dr. Theodore has provided psychoeducational services in private practice and consulted with public and private schools, hospitals, publishing companies, and behavioral health centers. As an advocate for mental health services for children and families, she has lobbied legislators on Capitol Hill several times.

Adrian E. Tovar, PhD, is currently a bilingual school psychologist for the Mount Vernon City School District in New York. He recently received his doctorate degree in School Psychology from St. John's University in Queens, New York. He is Mexican-American and originally from California.

Virginia E. Vitiello, PhD, is a Research Assistant Professor at the University of Virginia's CASTL research center. She studies early childhood education, school readiness, and early elementary school experiences of children from low-income families, with an emphasis on social-emotional development and self-regulation.

Jenna M. White is a third-year graduate student in Gonzaga University's Education Specialist in School Psychology program. She is completing her school psychology internship at Medical Lake School District in Medical Lake, Washington.

Jessica V. Whittaker, PhD, is a Research Associate Professor at the Center for Advanced Study of Teaching and Learning at the University of Virginia. Her primary research interests lie in examining the association between early teacher-child interactions and children's academic and social-emotional outcomes.

Emily Winter is nationally certified school psychologist and a doctoral student at the University of Connecticut. Her research interests include body image, student athletes, and mind-body health.

Hannah E. Wurster, PhD, is an infant mental health clinician and researcher. She received her master's degree in Marriage and Family Therapy from and Ph.D. in Applied Developmental Science, both from Colorado State University. Following this, she completed a postdoctoral fellowship in the One Health Institute at Colorado

State University. Her clinical work focuses on supporting young children and their families recover from traumat c experiences. Her research areas are attachment, emotional availability, intergenerational trauma, and community-engaged research.

Zheng Zhou, PhD, is a Professor in the Psychology Department at St. John's University in New York. Her research interests include children's mathematical reasoning, basic relational concepts acquisition, and school adjustment.

Perspectives on
Early Childhood Psychology and Education

PECPE publishes twice a year, in the fall and spring. These two issues on specific focuses are typically guest-edited and can also include a few general articles.

Editorial Policy and Submission Guidelines

Perspectives on Early Childhood Psychology and Education focuses on publishing original contributions from a broad range of psychological and educational perspectives relevant to infants, young children (to age 8 years), families, and caregivers. Manuscripts incorporating evidence-based research, theory, and practice within clinical, community, developmental, neurological, and school psychology perspectives are considered. In addition, the journal accepts test and book reviews, literature reviews, program descriptions and evaluations, clinical studies, and other professional materials of interest to psychologists and educators working with young children. Proposals for special focus topics may be made to the Editor.

Format: Manuscripts should be original work not currently submitted for publication to other journals. Authors must follow the guidelines of the *Publication Manual of the American Psychological Association* (Sixth Edition). Manuscripts may not exceed 35 double-spaced pages in length, including the cover page, abstract, references, tables, and figures.

Submission: Submit an electronic copy of the manuscript for editorial review. Avoid including any identifying author information in the text. Selection of manuscripts is based on blind peer review. Include a cover page with the following information: the title of article, author(s) full name(s), title(s), institution or professional affiliations, and mailing and email address of primary author. The cover page will not be sent to reviewers.

Selection Criteria:

- Importance of topic in early childhood psycho ogy and education
- Theory and research related to content
- Contribution to professional practice in early childhood psychology and education
- Clear and concise writing

Submit manuscripts to the Editor electronically at the following email address: PECPE@bsu.edu.

CALL FOR PAPERS

We are seeking a special focus and general manuscripts for the next issues of *PECPE*. If you are interested in submitting a topic and being the guest editor, please send a brief (approximately 250 words) proposal to Dr. David McIntosh, Editor-elect, *PECPE*: PECPE@bsu.edu.

Manuscripts should be original work not currently submitted for publication to other journals. Authors must follow the guidelines of the *Publication Manual of the American Psychological Association* (Sixth Edition). Manuscripts may not exceed 35 double-spaced pages in length, including the cover page, abstract, references, tables, and figures. Avoid including any identifying author information in the text. Selection of manuscripts is based on blind peer review. Include a cover page with the following information: the title of article, author(s) full name(s), title(s), institution or professional affiliations, and mailing and email address of primary author. The cover page will not be sent to reviewers.

Volume 5, Issue 1 of
Perspectives on Early Childhood Psychology and Education
was published in Spring 2020
by Pace University Press

Cover and Interior Design by Sara Yager
Cover and Interior Layout by Delaney Anderson
The journal was typeset in Minion and Myriad
and printed by Lightning Source

Pace University Press

Director: Manuela Soares
Associate Director: Stephanie Hsu
Design Consultant: Joseph Caserto

Graduate Assistants: Delaney Anderson and Francesca Leparik
Graduate Student Aide: Shani Starinsky

www.ingramcontent.com/pod-product-compliance
Lightning Source LLC
Chambersburg PA
CBHW061006280326
41935CB00009B/848